YOU MUST READ

YOU MUST READ

Books That Have Shaped Our Lives

with contributions from

*Joel R. Beeke, Alistair Begg, Jerry Bridges,
Mark Dever, J. Ligon Duncan, R. Albert Mohler, Jr.,
John MacArthur, Stuart Olyott, R. C. Sproul,
Derek W. H. Thomas, Geoffrey Thomas*

and many others

THE BANNER OF TRUTH TRUST

THE BANNER OF TRUTH TRUST
3 Murrayfield Road, Edinburgh EH12 6EL, U.K.
P.O. Box 621, Carlisle, PA 17013, U.S.A.

ISBN:
Cloth-bound: 978 1 84871 565 3
Paperback: 978 1 84871 566 0
Epub: 978 1 84871 567 7
Kindle: 978 1 84871 568 4

Typeset in 11/13 pt Adobe Garamond Pro at
The Banner of Truth Trust, Edinburgh

Printed in the U.S.A. by
Versa Press, Inc.,
East Peoria, IL

To

IAIN AND JEAN MURRAY

With the affection and appreciation

of grateful friends

Contents

Introduction

You Must Read is an ambiguous title. As Christians 'we are what we read'. God's word is the instrument by which the Holy Spirit renews our minds and transforms our lives. The same is true, to a lesser extent, of Christian literature. The biographies of Christians whose lives have left a permanent mark on the church often disclose the influence of a particular book, or books, they themselves have read. So, *You Must Read* is a perennial maxim. You really must read!

But we also use these words when we are enthusiastic about a good book. We instinctively ask our friends, 'Have you read …?' And if the answer is 'no' we tend to say 'Oh, *you must read* …'

But where do you begin? There are so many books from which to choose. Many of us want to ask, 'Can somebody please tell me what books I should read?' *You Must Read* provides some answers.

There is in fact a three-dimensional story behind these pages.

For some time we have thought of inviting a number of friends to contribute to a book about books—in which each of them would write a chapter on a book that had been a significant help to them in their Christian lives. We all enjoy listening to, or reading about, what has shaped Christians we know, especially if they have had an influence on us. Our hopes have now become a reality in *You Must Read*. We are deeply grateful to each of the contributors for making it possible.

A number of these friends are household names to many Christians; others will be new names to some. They come from a variety of geographical locations, churches, and spheres of ministry. But they are united with us in our common allegiance to the authority of Scripture, the supremacy of Christ, and the pursuit of the glory of God. We hope that you will not only find their personal stories enjoyable and their discussions instructive, but also, as you come to the end of many of these chapters, that you will find yourself saying '*I must read* …'

You will, however, soon notice a second dimension in *You Must Read*, as you progress from one chapter to another. All of the books chosen by our contributors currently have the same publisher!

They did not all originally have the same publisher. Indeed the majority did not. Many are old classics, once forgotten. Their original publication dates range over the past five centuries. But in the last half century or so they have been republished and are now repeating the impact they had on their first readers.

What is the statistical probability of thirty-five contributors from several different countries being asked to write on a book that has influenced them, and all choosing books from the same publisher? If the publishers invite them to choose a book from their own catalogue, then it is one hundred per cent probable!

This is the case here. But the motivation for this volume is not financial profit (the publishers are a not-for-profit organisation, in British terminology a *Trust* regulated by the U.K.'s Charity Commissioners). Nor are the authors (or publishers) suggesting that these are the *only* books you must read. The project has come together in this way only because we have known something about the books that have influenced our contributors, and all of us are eager that others will discover what we have already been privileged to discover.

Our contributors share a particular burden for younger men and women to read these books. Many of them, you will notice, encountered the book they recommend when they were young, even teenagers.

Often the deepest influences on our lives lie hidden from sight. Younger Christians (and especially younger ministers) sometimes want to imitate the fruit they see in those they admire, without either knowing, or drawing on, the spiritual nutrients that lie in the soil of the lives or ministries they respect. These pages are one way in which contributors can stress to us that if we are to grow tall we need deep roots, and say to us 'To understand my life, and how I think and serve, you need to read what I have read.'

The third dimension embedded in *You Must Read* is one you have probably noticed, but perhaps without realizing its full significance.

These pages are dedicated to Iain and Jean Murray, whose vision, dedication, ministry, and encouragement has undergirded the publication of every volume (without exception) selected in *You Must Read*. Humanly speaking, without their joint service of our Lord it is unlikely that many of these books would have been published in our lifetimes, and also improbable that other publishers would have caught their vision and published similar books. Their ministry has been wonderfully supported by family and friends, of course. But together they have borne the burden and the heat of the day, through encouragements and discouragements, enthusiastic support, and sometimes opposition.

All of us who have contributed to these pages owe Iain and Jean a debt of gratitude and affection. Our joint feeling has always been that Iain in particular would not want a traditional *festschrift* to celebrate their service. In any case such a volume would have required contributors to write in an historical-theological vein. Doing so for the biographer of D. Martyn Lloyd-Jones, Jonathan Edwards, John Murray, A. W. Pink, John MacArthur, Archibald G. Brown, with numerous other historical and biographical pieces, would have made too many friends doubtful that their work would survive his mental red pen as he perused their offerings! So our joint gift is affectionately offered to them in this form—echoing the Murrays' own life burden.

The dedication of *You Must Read* is perhaps especially appropriate since this year of its first publication marks the sixtieth anniversary of Iain and Jean Murray's marriage, as well as the sixtieth anniversary of Iain's being set apart for the ministry of the gospel, and also, remarkably, the sixtieth anniversary of *The Banner of Truth* magazine which he founded. We hope that these pages will encourage many to discover the riches of Christian literature which over these six decades the Murrays have helped to recover for our own generation and for any generations that are still to come.

Edward Donnelly
Sinclair Ferguson
Ian Hamilton
Mark Johnston
Fred Raynsford
Tom Richwine

Trustees of The Banner of Truth Trust
Edinburgh, March 2015

I

The Forgotten Spurgeon

Iain H. Murray

R. Albert Mohler, Jr.

JUST about every survey of contemporary evangelicalism reveals the enormous popularity of Charles Haddon Spurgeon. This is especially important when seen over against the fact that in the early decades of the twentieth century, Spurgeon was largely a forgotten figure in the United States and a neglected figure in Great Britain. Spurgeon was seen at that time as a relic of a bygone Victorian age and a paragon of an evangelicalism thought to have passed into oblivion.

And yet, by the last third of the twentieth century a renaissance of interest in Spurgeon had taken place. Spurgeon's voluminous works had never gone totally out of print. As one of the most prolific writers in the history of the English language, Spurgeon enjoyed the prestige of being constantly in print from his adolescence until the present day. But a remarkable and very important aspect of this renaissance of interest in Charles Spurgeon must be noted: it was a very truncated and reduced understanding of the man and his message.

The early phase of this renaissance of interest in Charles Spurgeon had to do mostly with his devotional writings. This is important in itself as evidence of the continuing vitality of Charles Spurgeon's ministry. His devotional works, especially his various meditations on the Psalms, regained their place at the centre of evangelical devotional life. And yet, the real man had been at least partly co-opted by sentimentality at the expense of the theological substance and deep conviction of his ministry.

Most specifically, it was Charles Spurgeon's theology that was either neglected or rejected. Spurgeon's confessional and convictional evangelicalism, deeply rooted in reformed orthodoxy and in a confrontational biblical theology, had been replaced by a plastic Spurgeon who was largely an invention of a superficial and sentimental age. Furthermore, the greatest cost of this reduction was the loss of Spurgeon's passion for the gospel of the Lord Jesus Christ—a gospel he preached in all of its glory, wonder, and power.

Now, in the early decades of the twenty-first century, it is clear that a very different renaissance of interest in Charles Spurgeon has taken place. This time, it is found most especially in a generation of evangelicals who look to Spurgeon as an exemplar of the pastoral ministry, as a mentor in robust conviction and theology, and as an example of how to manage theological controversy—even at the expense of personal prestige.

This new and far more comprehensive recovery of Charles Spurgeon was largely made possible by the work of Iain H. Murray and the Banner of Truth Trust. The Trust's vigorous publication of Spurgeon's works, including many of his most controversial works, has opened up a stream of doctrinal and theological health for many evangelicals who have been desperately seeking just such an example in the trying context of our own times.

A central contribution to this renaissance of interest in Spurgeon must be directly traced to Iain Murray's own *The Forgotten Spurgeon*. First published in 1966, it exploded on the playground of the evangelicals, awakening at least a portion of them to the *real* Charles Spurgeon—the man and his message. The Spurgeon evangelicals had forgotten was the Spurgeon that was now rediscovered. As Murray wrote, 'The only way to deal with Spurgeon's theology is to accept it or forget it: the latter is what I believe has largely happened in the twentieth century. And Spurgeon without his theology is about as distorted as the cheap China figures of Spurgeon which were offered for sale by charlatans more than a century ago.'[1]

That kind of bracing prose is exactly what got the attention of that generation of evangelicals and an ever broader readership of young evangelicals, hungry for just the kind of theological and pastoral example that the real Charles Spurgeon represents.

---

[1] *The Forgotten Spurgeon* (Edinburgh: Banner of Truth Trust, 2009), p. 5.

In *The Forgotten Spurgeon* Murray presents Spurgeon in terms of the theological context of his age and the theological controversies of his life. As he makes clear, Spurgeon never sought controversy. On the other hand, he never ran from it. He presents modern-day evangelicals with a singularly important model of conducting theological controversy.

To many modern evangelicals this statement may come as a double surprise. Some will see the portrait of Spurgeon that appears in *The Forgotten Spurgeon* as a surprise since the only Spurgeon they have known is the very kind of 'cheap China figure' that Murray referenced. But the second surprise to many evangelicals will be to learn that Charles Spurgeon is an example even as his foes considered him vanquished and many of his own friends considered the end of his ministry a tragedy.

In that sense, the very fact that *The Forgotten Spurgeon* was written in 1966 is incontrovertible evidence that Spurgeon was not vanquished and that his ministry did not end in tragedy. In a very real sense, *The Forgotten Spurgeon* represents an important vindication of Spurgeon's ministry and message.

The three controversies presented in *The Forgotten Spurgeon* help us to understand, not only the chronological sequence of Spurgeon's ministry but also the development of Spurgeon as a convictional pastor and pastoral theologian.

The Forgotten Spurgeon offers modern readers the opportunity to understand a Spurgeon formerly lost in the mists of history. It describes the young Spurgeon, 'The picture which emerged was not that of a jovial pulpit phenomenon upon whom men lavished their praise but rather of a youth whose arrival amidst the soothing and sleepy religious life of London was about as unwelcome as the Russian cannons which were then thundering in the far-off Crimea.' As Murray continues, 'The facts come as somewhat of a jolt to us, for we have more or less become accustomed to look upon Spurgeon as a benign grandfather of modern evangelicalism.'[1]

To be fair, Murray does present Spurgeon as capable of great joy and even of being described as 'grandfatherly' in relation to today's evangelicals. Nevertheless, his book offered the most important corrective to the Spurgeon who had been tragically separated from

[1] *Ibid.*, p. 47.

his conviction, his confessionalism, his courage, and from the controversies of his own times.

In one of the most ground-breaking sections of the book, Murray reminds us of Spurgeon's early battle to define a biblical Calvinism over against the twin dangers of Hyper-Calvinism and Arminianism. Spurgeon never wavered from biblical Calvinism nor did he ever minimize human responsibility. The Arminianism he fought was Arminianism as it is classically defined—and Spurgeon understood classical Arminianism to be a false gospel that demanded refutation, confrontation, and anathema. On the other hand, he also understood the danger of Hyper-Calvinism, and he was bold to identify it too as a great enemy of the gospel of Jesus Christ.

The pastoral aspect of *The Forgotten Spurgeon's* presentation of Charles Spurgeon also becomes evident in the acknowledgment that Spurgeon himself believed that he was most likely thoroughly Arminian at the time he was converted. Nevertheless, he was drawn into a full understanding of the gospel—an understanding that led him to oppose Arminianism resolutely. With characteristic care Murray writes: 'Let it be noted that the point in dispute between the biblical teaching and Arminianism is not whether man's will is active in *conversion*; on this there can be no question; the issue concerns how that activity originated.'[1]

In explaining Calvinism's biblical understanding of the gospel call to sinners to trust Christ for salvation, Murray summarizes: 'Arminians say that sinners are commanded, therefore they must be able; Hyper-Calvinists say they are not able, therefore they cannot be commanded. But Scripture and Calvinism sets forth *both* man's inability and his duty, and both truths are a necessary part of evangelicalism—the former reveals the sinner's need of a help which only God can give, and the latter, which is expressed in the exhortations, promises and invitations of Scripture, shows them the place in which his peace and safety lies, namely, the person of the Son of God.'[2]

Furthermore, 'Spurgeon saw Arminianism to be a departure from the purity of New Testament evangelism and, in asserting religious superficiality to be one of its attendant consequences, he recognized

[1] *Ibid.*, pp. 89-90.
[2] *Ibid.*, pp. 106.

what has become so characteristic of modern evangelicalism. It was not so much the advent of musical accompaniments and inquiry rooms that alarmed him, though he was troubled by these things and had no time for them, but rather the disappearing emphasis on the necessity of the Spirit's work and the streamlining of conversion into a speedy business.'[1]

But Spurgeon's confrontations with Arminianism and Hyper-Calvinism set the stage for the most cataclysmic controversy of his life and ministry—the Down-Grade Controversy. In a brilliant historical survey, Iain Murray takes us through Spurgeon's conflicts with the Evangelical Alliance and the Baptist Union of Great Britain and Ireland. In both cases, he reveals Spurgeon's abiding conviction that any compromise upon the inspiration, infallibility, and inerrancy of Scripture will lead to disaster, and his correlated conviction that the rejection of a confessional responsibility on the part of either the Evangelical Alliance or the Baptist Union would likewise lead to disaster. In short order, Spurgeon was proved to be right on both accounts. Nevertheless, Spurgeon's foes believed that they had bested Spurgeon in the controversy and that they held the upper hand. *The Forgotten Spurgeon* settles the historical score, not in order to gain an advantage in partisan argument, but to retrieve from a forgotten history the most vital lessons for contemporary evangelicalism.

Looking back, it is haunting to recognize just how similar the issues of central debate in the Down-Grade Controversy and the issues of debate in contemporary evangelicalism must be seen to be. The similarities are not only haunting, they are absolutely shocking to many contemporary evangelicals. Then, as now, the central issue is the authority and inspiration of Scripture. Then, as now, the secondary debate is over the necessity of a confession of faith. Then, as now, the battle lines are drawn between those who will affirm the unconditional authority and the total truthfulness of Scripture, and those who try to find some *via media* between the Bible's own revelation of its nature and authority and the demands of an increasingly secularized society. Then, as now, the cry comes that any requirement for confessional integrity is a violation of human conscience that also reflects a lack of confidence in Christ's church.

[1] *Ibid.*, p. 112.

Spurgeon's main argument in the Down-Grade Controversy, that the acceptance of higher-critical views of Scripture would be disastrous for the Evangelical Alliance and for the Baptist Union, was proved to be correct in very short order. But what we also discover is the broken-heartedness of Charles Spurgeon as he watched both the Evangelical Alliance and the Baptist Union destroy themselves through theological confusion and cowardice. The Baptist Union's abdication of its own ability to discipline its members led Spurgeon to declare: 'Every Union, unless it is a mere fiction, must be based upon certain principles. How can we unite except upon some great common truths?'[1]

By the end of his ministry, Spurgeon had been forced by conscience to resign from the Evangelical Alliance and then, in one of the most tragic chapters of modern church history, the Baptist Union censured him—the greatest preacher of the age—for the crime of defending the Baptist Union's own originating convictions.

In lucid prose Iain Murray sets out the central lessons of the Down-Grade Controversy. He makes very clear that 'an unwillingness to define precisely any doctrinal issue, a readiness to reduce what constitutes the content of orthodox Christianity to a minimum, and a "charity" which made men unwilling to question the standing of any denomination in the sight of God so long as it *professed* the "Evangelical Faith"' was itself a recipe for disaster. Furthermore, as Murray makes evident, the Down-Grade Controversy revealed that British Nonconformity was no longer ruled by the Scriptures, and that the Baptist Union was now being led by those who argued for an outright accommodation of truth with error.

I must end this reflection on a very personal note. In 1993, I was elected President of The Southern Baptist Theological Seminary in Louisville, Kentucky, U.S.A. That institution was, in itself, a classic example of the very Down-Grade that Spurgeon had described. As a matter of fact, Spurgeon was the object of ridicule and condescension whenever he was mentioned on that campus during the time that I was a student in earlier years. And yet, when I was elected President over twenty years ago now, it was with a mandate to bring the institution back to confessional fidelity, to an unembarrassed and

---

[1] *Ibid.*, p. 163.

unhesitant affirmation of the faith 'once for all delivered to the saints', and to the theological foundation upon which it had been set—a theological foundation that was in complete agreement with the comprehensive theological system and preaching of Charles H. Spurgeon. Indeed, the founder of The Southern Baptist Theological Seminary, James Petigru Boyce, was himself a great admirer of the famous London preacher, as was his colleague on the founding faculty, John A. Broadus (considered by many to be the 'Spurgeon of the United States').

I simply cannot calculate the importance to me of the example of Charles Spurgeon as I undertook the task of bringing reformation and theological correction to a great and historic theological institution. Furthermore, the recovery of The Southern Baptist Theological Seminary came within the larger context of what has become known as the 'Conservative Resurgence' within the Southern Baptist Convention. This was a massive movement, largely driven by faithful lay people within the denomination, that led to the ousting of an accommodationist denominational leadership, and the election of solidly evangelical pastors and leaders to denominational offices. In fact, virtually every one of these men was driven by Spurgeon's example.

The reason for this should be abundantly clear: the downgrade in the Southern Baptist Convention during the last half of the twentieth century mirrored precisely the downgrade of the Baptist Union of Great Britain in the previous century. The difference was this: our sovereign Lord allowed the recovery of the Southern Baptist Convention in a way that has never occurred in the Baptist Union of Great Britain. And so, in one of the strangest displays of divine providence, the Spurgeon who was rejected in Great Britain became, a full century later, the great inspiration for the theological recovery of a great Baptist denomination an ocean away.

In my study, clearly within my view, is a bust of Charles Spurgeon and a collection of his works. The books are consulted very frequently and those volumes are to me as treasured friends. In my official office of the seminary hangs one of the first and most important original oil portraits of Charles Spurgeon—a portrait that had been given to the seminary shortly after Spurgeon's death, and had never been displayed publicly until it was placed in the most prominent place within my office.

Even as a teenage boy, I grew to love Charles Spurgeon because I found him to be a trustworthy guide to my understanding of Scripture and an inspirational mentor in matters of Christian devotion. But the example of Spurgeon that served as my constant inspiration during the fiercest days of conflict and turmoil in the great battle on the campus of The Southern Baptist Theological Seminary and on the other side of that battle until this very day, is the Spurgeon that I met in Iain Murray's *The Forgotten Spurgeon*. This is the Spurgeon that has been my constant companion, counsellor, and friend throughout the last twenty years and more I have served in this office. This is the Spurgeon for which I owe so much to Iain Murray and his most important book.

In the years since, I have given away countless copies of *The Forgotten Spurgeon* and it is my great honour to share this word of personal testimony about the importance of Charles Spurgeon and the importance of this book. I have come to know its author during these years, and to see that his heart is as pastoral as his pen, and his life as exemplary as his writings. I am unspeakably thankful for *The Forgotten Spurgeon*. An army of young convictional ministers, committed to the very convictions that were defended and preached by Charles Spurgeon, is now being sent out into the world from many important evangelical centres, including The Southern Baptist Theological Seminary. The Spurgeon who was rejected at the end of the nineteenth century is an example to countless very young ministers at the beginning of the twenty-first century. Thanks largely to *The Forgotten Spurgeon*, he is forgotten no more.

2

The Works of John Bunyan

Faith Cook

A YOUNG woman stood under the dim light of a flickering street lamp waiting for a bus to take her back to her lodgings. The year was 1958 and in her hand she held a book with a grey-green cover—newly published. The print was small, the light poor, but it hardly seemed to matter. I had reached page 32 of *The Select Works of Jonathan Edwards*, volume 1. My attention was riveted. As I read of the occasion when Edwards rode into the woods to pray and 'had a view that for me was extraordinary of the Son of God … and of his wonderful, great, full, pure and sweet grace and love, and meek and gentle condescension', I was aware that I was on holy ground. I too was being changed. Here was a dimension of spiritual experience that was new to me—one that I longed to know.

My twenty-first birthday was approaching. All I now wanted was to own more books from this new publisher. Soon I was the proud possessor of such titles as *The Holy Spirit* by George Smeaton, Thomas Watson's *Body of Divinity*, *Select Sermons of George Whitefield*, and others.[1] Since then many more titles have had a profound influence on my life, not least the *Letters of Samuel Rutherford*. But perhaps, above all, pride of place must go to the three massive volumes of *The Works of John Bunyan*, edited by George Offor and republished in 1991 from the 1854 edition.

Most are familiar with Bunyan's classic, *The Pilgrim's Progress*, many of us from childhood days; the fierce spiritual struggle narrated in his autobiography *Grace Abounding to the Chief of Sinners* is also well known. Fewer have read Bunyan's more complex allegory, *The Holy*

[1] All published by the Banner of Truth Trust.

War, depicting the Christian life as a battle. Even fewer know that John Bunyan wrote more than fifty other titles, many being semi-autobiographical—treasure troves of profound teaching and delight. In volumes 1 and 2 of Bunyan's *Works* George Offor included his experimental and doctrinal pieces, mainly extensions of his preached messages, together with a number of controversial pieces on some of the burning issues of the day. Meanwhile in volume 3 we find Bunyan's allegorical works, together with various meditations and poems.

Born on the outskirts of Elstow, near Bedford, in November 1628 and dying in 1688, Bunyan's sixty-year life spanned one of the most turbulent periods of English history when the Civil War ripped the country apart, pitting Parliament against its king, Charles I. A wild and godless youth, whose language was appalling, Bunyan married at the age of twenty. His young and poverty-stricken wife brought little with her into the marriage apart from two religious books, but these started John off on his long and abortive attempts to reform himself until he reckoned that he 'pleased God as well as any man in England'.

Not until he first overheard the women of the Independent Meeting in Bedford speaking of their spiritual experiences as they sat together on a doorstep, did Bunyan become truly concerned about his own spiritual state:

> Their talk was about a new birth, the work of God on their hearts
> … also of how God had visited their souls with his love in the Lord
> Jesus, and with what words and promises they had been refreshed,
> comforted, and supported against the temptations of the devil.

This shook Bunyan. Never had he heard of such a thing as the 'new birth' and it set him urgently longing to know true spiritual life. Those who write on Bunyan are uncertain about when he was actually converted—not surprising since even he was unsure about it—but most likely it was shortly after this, for he records, 'The Bible became precious to me in those days', a statement that strongly suggests a renewed mind. The next three years were ones of distressing and ceaseless Satanic onslaught on John Bunyan's young faith before he gained a measure of true assurance.

In 1655, now twenty-seven years of age, Bunyan joined the Bedford Meeting whose pastor, John Gifford, had patiently counselled him through the years of darkness and doubt. Quickly his fellow members recognised John's outstanding gifts both as an exhorter and as a preacher. From the very first, his scorching, convicting words sprang straight from his own experience: 'I preached what I felt, what I smartingly did feel', he confessed, 'even that under which my poor soul did groan and tremble to astonishment.'

With Oliver Cromwell's death in 1658 and Charles II established on the throne in 1660, such preaching quickly aroused the antagonism of local magistrates and clerics alike. In November 1660 Bunyan was arrested, brought to trial and imprisoned for lay preaching and for refusing to worship at a local parish church. From the age of thirty-two until he was forty-four, he languished in Bedford Jail, rat-infested, crowded, stinking, and cold, having to leave his wife and his four small children without support.

All this took place two years before the cruel *Act of Uniformity* of 1662 was passed, when two thousand other ministers and teachers were evicted from their livings for conscience's sake. Yet these very circumstances have given us today the priceless heritage of Bunyan's writings, enriching and encouraging generations of the Lord's people. Yet it was not easy:

> I found myself a man, and compassed with infirmities; the parting with my wife and poor children hath oft been to me in this place as the pulling the flesh from my bones, and that not only because I am somewhat too fond of those great mercies, but also because I should have often brought to my mind the many hardships, miseries and wants that my poor family was like to meet with, should I be taken from them.

But in spite of his suffering John Bunyan gives us a key to his endurance—a most vital key for our day:

> I was made to see that if ever I would suffer rightly I must first pass a sentence of death upon everything that can properly be called a thing of this life, even to reckon myself, my wife, my children, my health, my enjoyments, and all as dead to me and myself as dead to them.

On its own this would seem a somewhat negative concept, but Bunyan hastily adds his secret of endurance, for instead of these human comforts he was learning '*to live upon God that is invisible*'.

And the reward was great, for as Bunyan discovered through his twelve long years of imprisonment,

> He [God] can make those things that in themselves are most fearful and terrible to behold, the most pleasant, delightful and desirable things. He can make a gaol more beautiful than a palace ... He can so sweeten our sufferings with the honey of his word ... and [make it] so easy by the spreading of his feathers over us that we shall not be able to say that in all the world a more comfortable position can be found.

Another secret of Bunyan's endurance during those grim years was his communion with God in prayer. A first book written from prison was on this subject. *A Discourse Touching Prayer* has been attractively republished by the Banner of Truth Trust in the Puritan Paperbacks series under the simpler title of *Prayer*. Perhaps one of the finest definitions of prayer ever penned comes from these pages.[1] However, Bunyan had already begun his writing four years before he was imprisoned. After one or two controversial pieces, he had embarked on a major work, a masterly treatise on a subject which has occupied the minds and pens of some of our best theologians ever since—the relationship between law and grace: a work he entitled *The Doctrine of Law and Grace Unfolded*. Stemming from his own deep conflicts on this very subject, the work reflects the influence and help he had received from Martin Luther's writings.

In our own day when Christians have teetered between a legalism that leads to a constant sense of guilt and a frequent careless disregard for the law of God, Bunyan's teaching provides a balance and a source of rich pastoral challenge and encouragement. In it he exults in the liberating power of grace under the New Covenant. Although the law of God remains a rule of life for the believer, it has lost its power to condemn. He points to Christ, standing at God's right hand as the Mediator of that New Covenant, who turns aside all the fearful accusations of the law, sin, and the devil for his people:

> Here thou mayst through faith look the very devil in the face, and rejoice, saying O Satan! I have a precious Jesus, a soul-comforting Jesus, a sin-pardoning Jesus. Here thou mayst hear the biggest thunder

[1] *A Discourse Touching Prayer*, *Works*, vol. 1 (Edinburgh: Banner of Truth Trust, 1991), p. 623.

crack that the law can give and yet not be daunted. Here thou mayst say, O law! thou mayst roar against sin, but thou canst not reach me; thou mayst curse and condemn, but not my soul, for I have a righteous Jesus, a holy Jesus, a soul-saving Jesus ... and he hath delivered me from thy threats, from thy curses, from thy condemnations; I am out of thy reach, out of thy bounds ... I am brought into another covenant ... even through the blood of Jesus.[1]

Perhaps among the most encouraging and liberating words I have ever read come from this remarkable treatise and lie at the very heart of our gospel—the invincible power of the blood of Christ to cleanse the conscience:

Again, when I have been loaden with sin, and pestered with several temptations, and in a very sad manner ... I have found that when tears would not do, prayers would not do, repentings and all other things could not reach my heart, O then! one touch, one drop, one shining of the virtue of the blood ... hath in very blessed manner delivered me, that it hath made me to marvel. O! it has come with such life, such power, with such irresistible and marvellous glory, that ... it quenches all the fiery darts and all the flames of hell fire, that are begotten by the charges of the law, Satan and doubtful remembrances of my sinful life.[2]

Such words remind us that at the sight of the cross in *The Pilgrim's Progress* Christian's burden rolled away and he gave 'three leaps for joy and went on [his way] singing'.

Not long ago I enquired of a university graduate whether he had read *The Pilgrim's Progress*. To my surprise he had neither read the book nor heard of the author and was astonished to learn that Bunyan's book has been second only to the Bible in its worldwide sales. Certainly, *The Pilgrim's Progress* is a spiritual classic in every sense, but few know that as Bunyan was sitting in his dingy prison he had started writing another book. He had been freed for six brief months during 1666, but now he was back in prison with little hope of release. Perhaps he was tempted to despair. Perseverance in the Christian race was all-important. So he wrote in block capitals: THEY

---

[1] *Doctrine of Law and Grace Unfolded*, vol. 1, p. 563.
[2] *Ibid.*, p. 550.

THAT WILL HAVE HEAVEN MUST RUN FOR IT. These words (based on 1 Cor. 9:24, 'So run that ye may obtain') were to be the theme of a short work which he would call *The Heavenly Footman*.

I started reading this work when on my own one Saturday evening some years ago. My spiritual life had dropped into a lethargic state, and as I read I became truly frightened. Unless I was 'running for heaven', Bunyan warned, I could lose out at the end of the race. Satan is doing all he can to hinder us. 'If I win, I win all, if I lose, I lose all, SO RUN!',[1] Bunyan seemed to shout from the pages. But he was not unmindful of human frailty and could say with pastoral tenderness, 'When thou hast run thyself down weary, then the Lord Jesus will take thee up and carry thee. Is that not enough to make any poor soul begin his race?'[2]

Suddenly Bunyan put aside this work he was writing, for ideas began teeming into his brain about the Christian life as a pilgrimage. He tells us quaintly:

> And thus it was: I writing of the way
> and race of saints in this our gospel day
> fell suddenly into an allegory
> about their journey and the way to glory.[3]

And so *The Pilgrim's Progress* was born, and only later did Bunyan complete *The Heavenly Footman*.

Above all, John Bunyan was a pastor and a preacher. One who heard him when he was freed to preach at last could say that his words made his hearers feel 'as if an angel had touched their souls with a coal of holy fire from the altar'. Perhaps the most beautiful examples of Bunyan's preaching are found in *Come and Welcome to Jesus Christ* and *The Jerusalem Sinner Saved*—the latter published in 1688, the year of his death. The Banner of Truth Trust has made both these sermons available as separate paperbacks. The evangelical pathos of the preacher as he urges the guilty, broken, and despairing to come to Christ is a much-needed emphasis in our own day:

[1] *The Heavenly Footman*, *Works*, vol. 2 (Edinburgh: Banner of Truth Trust, 1991), p. 386.

[2] *Ibid.*, p. 391.

[3] *The Pilgrim's Progress*, 'Author's Apology', *Works*, vol. 3 (Edinburgh: Banner of Truth Trust, 1991), p. 85.

What ground now is here for despair? If thou sayest, The number and burden of my sins, I answer, Nay: that is rather a ground for faith; because such an one, above all others, is invited by Christ to come to him, yea, promised rest and forgiveness if they come … What! Despair of bread in a land that is full of corn! Despair of mercy when our God is full of mercy![1]

'Coming sinner,' Bunyan urges in *Come and Welcome to Jesus Christ*, 'Christ inviteth thee to dine and sup with him. He inviteth thee to a banquet of wine and his banner over thee shall be love.'[2]

All Bunyan's experimental writings sprang from his own deep realisation of God's great mercy and love to him—a sinner. Perhaps it was never better expressed than in words found in his sermon entitled *The Saints' Knowledge of Christ's Love*, published as *All Loves Excelling* in a separate paperback edition by the Trust:

Why should anything have my heart but God, but Christ? He loves me, he loves me with love that passeth knowledge. He loves me, and he shall have me: he loves me and I will love him: his love stripped him of all for my sake. Lord, let my love strip me of all for thy sake.[3]

We have great cause for thankfulness to the Banner of Truth Trust for making these priceless works from the past available to pastors and their congregations in our own day.

---

[1] *The Jerusalem Sinner Saved, Works*, vol. 1, p. 91.
[2] *Come and Welcome to Jesus Christ, Works*, vol. 1, p. 281.
[3] *The Saints' Knowledge of Christ's Love, Works*, vol. 2, p. 39.

3

Today's Gospel: Authentic or Synthetic?

Walter J. Chantry

Thomas E. Richwine

FROM the opening words of the Bible, God reveals himself as the sovereign creator, sustainer, and ruler of all. This world manifests the glory of his eternal power, wisdom, and goodness (*e.g.* Rom. 1:19-20). Evangelicals around the world readily acknowledge these general truths. But many evangelicals struggle specifically with the nature of God's sovereignty in salvation. Is God as sovereign in salvation as he is in nature? If so, then what—if any—is the role of the human will in salvation? Does God's election apply to our salvation or only to the roles in which we serve him in his kingdom? The answers to these questions will have an obvious impact on the character of our evangelism.

In the late 1960s, Walt Chantry, then a young Baptist minister in Carlisle, Pennsylvania, was burdened to see a restoration in the churches of the biblical emphasis on God's sovereign graciousness in evangelism and in the teaching that was given on conversion. In 1970, seven years after graduating from Westminster Seminary in Philadelphia, his first book, *Today's Gospel: Authentic or Synthetic?* was published. Since then it has been reprinted sixteen times; its impact has been felt all over the world.

Today's Gospel is based on Mark's account of Jesus' well-known interaction with the rich young ruler (Mark 10:17-29; see also Matt. 19:16-28 and Luke 18:18-30). It carefully examines the dynamic interplay between Jesus and the young man and draws out a series of principles for contemporary Christians to apply as we endeavour to fulfil the Great Commission (Matt. 28:19-20). The entire book is itself an exhortation to Christians to pattern both their theology of salvation and their practice of evangelism after the Master.

In particular Walt Chantry addresses the vital questions 'What's wrong with evangelism today?' and 'How should we witness?' Six lively chapters unfold deep biblical truths including God's character, the relationship between the law and the gospel, repentance, faith in Christ, and dependence on God. The burden?

> Look closely then at the Master Evangelist of all ages. Listen to his message, observe his motives, and note his methods. Then reflect on your own ministry. In the young man of 30 A.D. you will see the faces of young men of 1970. To reach them, you must say what our Lord said. To please God you must labour as Christ laboured. Cast off the shackles of evangelical traditions! Refuse to pay for outward unity with the coins of fundamental truth. Learn to follow the Christ of the Scriptures in evangelism. Lay hold of the authentic gospel and discard the synthetic.[1]

What accounts for the vast appeal of *Today's Gospel* for more than forty years, across denominational and geographic boundaries, to young Christians, and to mature ministers? Why have nearly 300,000 copies found their way into the hands of eager readers—many of whom are reading English as a second language?

Several answers might be given, but readers of *Today's Gospel* often give one of two.

First, Chantry's writing is simultaneously powerful, loving, faithful to Scripture, compelling, without personal bias, accessible, and challenging. He is pastoral in approach and drives his points to the hearts of readers. He urges obedience to God's word over mere understanding.

Second, he addresses real spiritual needs; teaching, exhorting, correcting, training, and encouraging his readers to conform their lives to God's will.

I have a personal reason for deeply appreciating the importance and value of *Today's Gospel*. As a young college student in 1972, I was

[1] W. J. Chantry, *Today's Gospel: Authentic or Synthetic?* (Edinburgh: Banner of Truth Trust, 2013), p. 9.

invited to a youth group meeting sponsored by Grace Baptist Church where Walt Chantry served as pastor. My only interest in the event was a young woman with whom I wanted to spend some time. I thought I was a Christian. After all, I had been baptized as an infant, and catechized and confirmed in a Lutheran church. I felt no need to hear the message that I would later hear that summer's day. Spending an afternoon at the lake with a beautiful girl was my sole motivation for accepting the invitation.

The afternoon unfolded largely as I had planned. The young lady was as captivating as I had hoped, the weather was beautiful, food plentiful, and the scheduled activities were fun. Sitting through a short Bible message certainly wouldn't spoil an otherwise perfect day, would it? After all, like the rich young ruler of Mark 10, I had an interest in eternal life and an expectation that I was headed in that direction. While I might not have been able to say about the Ten Commandments, 'all these I have kept since I was a boy' (Mark 10:20), I certainly did not see myself as a sinner who needed a Saviour.

God, of course, had other plans, as I was to discover.

I had never heard a minister speak the way Walt Chantry did. He read several verses from Paul's First Letter to the Corinthians and dealt with them in a manner to which I was certainly not accustomed, with an obvious conviction that what he had read was nothing less than the very words of God. They were true, trustworthy, and had power to change our hearts. This was not my typical religious experience. No, this minister was very different, but I did not—at the time— know why.

At one level I understood that the message was relevant and demanded something from me. I had the same reaction that Jesus' hearers had at the conclusion of the Sermon on the Mount; this man 'taught as one who had authority' (Matt. 7:29).

It took two more years of listening sporadically to his sermons before my heart was broken and I bowed to Christ in faith. But this first exposure showed me the heart of the man who would become my pastor for nearly twenty years and a close friend for more than twice that long. (To complete the story, three years after this initial gathering God gave me my greatest earthly blessing; that young woman became my wife.)

Most readers do not have this personal dimension to their reading of *Today's Gospel*. Yet they 'see' and 'feel' the same heart for the lost, commitment to biblical truth, and powerful heart-searching exegesis as they read. And this in a large measure helps to explain the universal appeal of this small book.

But a pastor's heart, powerful exegesis, and clear communication alone cannot account for the usefulness of *Today's Gospel*. More importantly, its message has resonated with so many readers because of the way it addresses common weaknesses that were present in churches in the 1970s. Sadly these same problems are present, perhaps even exacerbated, in many of our churches today. One in particular stands out: the relationship between God's moral law and the gospel.

Confusion about preaching both the law and the gospel is not confined to recent times. Since the Reformation Christians have struggled to express the biblical relationship between the law and the gospel. Thus some four hundred years ago Robert Bolton, the seventeenth-century English Puritan and noted preacher, wrote:

> A man must feel himself in misery, before he will go about to find a remedy; be sick before he will seek a physician; be in prison before he will seek a pardon. A sinner must be weary of his former wicked ways before he will ever have recourse to Jesus Christ for refreshing. He must be sensible of his spiritual poverty, beggary, and slavery under the devil, before he thirst kindly for heavenly righteousness, and willingly take up Christ's sweet and easy yoke. He must be cast down, confounded, condemned, a castaway, and lost in himself, before he will look about of a Saviour.[1]

In the following century Jonathan Edwards also dealt with the importance of the moral law in the preaching of the gospel. He witnessed at first hand a loss of power in gospel preaching when well-meaning ministers neglected the law in order to make Christ's message palatable to sinners. In his study of Edwards' teaching Iain Murray explains:

> The primary means of so dealing with the conscience is the law of God, 'for by the law is the knowledge of sin' (Rom. 3:20). The law, rightly

---

[1] Robert Bolton (1572–1631), *Instructions for a Right Comforting Afflicted Consciences* (1640), p. 175.

preached, does not simply bring sin into focus by the proclamation of broken commandments, it places man before the divine holiness of which those commandments are an expression. It faces men with the majesty of God and it shows them why they have a reason to fear God. Its function is 'that every mouth may be stopped and all the world may become guilty before God' (Rom. 3:19). The characteristic of a revival is that a profound consciousness of sin and need is profound in many persons at the same time by an awareness of God.[1]

In 1962, just a few years before Chantry submitted his manuscript, Dr Martyn Lloyd-Jones addressed this same subject pointedly:

So we will never appreciate grace until we have understood the teaching of the law and have seen ourselves under the law. Those who dismiss the law will never know much about grace. Part of our trouble is that we have dismissed the law. And because we have done that, we have never realized our true need. We are too healthy. We talk too glibly about 'loving the Lord'…

Do not dismiss what was given through Moses. You will never know much about grace if you do. To dismiss the law shows a complete misunderstanding of it. The trouble with us is that we have been healed too quickly, too lightly; we are in too much of a hurry. We want relief and we want peace. No, No! The trouble with us is that we have substituted believism for faith; we have rushed to grace before the law has done its work upon us. We are impatient with the law. We want Christ presented positively. We want to come immediately to the gospel. We do not want introductions. And because we do not want introductions, we have no gospel, finally. No, No! We must be clear about this: there is only one way to know and to appreciate the grace of God in Jesus Christ, and that is to know the depth of iniquity that is brought out by the law given through Moses.[2]

Using Jesus' encounter with the rich young ruler, Walt Chantry also presses his readers to believe that

[1] Iain H. Murray, *Jonathan Edwards: A New Biography* (Edinburgh: Banner of Truth Trust, 1987), pp. 129-30.
[2] D. M. Lloyd-Jones, *Born of God* (Edinburgh: Banner of Truth Trust, 2011), pp. 41-2.

God's law is an essential ingredient of gospel preaching. The absence of God's holy law from modern preaching is perhaps as responsible as any other factor for evangelistic impotence of our churches and missions.[1]

Explaining the Bible's definition of sin he writes:

The word 'sin' makes no sense apart from God's righteous law. How could the young ruler understand his sinfulness if he completely misunderstood God's law? How can today's sinners, who are totally ignorant of God's holy law and its demands upon them, look at themselves as condemned sinners? The idea of sin is strange because God's law is foreign to their minds.[2]

If a fundamental misunderstanding of God's moral law produced a defective definition of sin and ineffective evangelism in the 1960s and 1970s—as Lloyd-Jones and Chantry asserted—then it is certainly true today. When God blesses churches and nations with reformation and revival he does it with clear, faithful Bible preaching. We must, therefore, strive to evangelize as our Saviour did—lovingly, truthfully, and clearly, but never by diminishing the role of the moral law. Chantry insists:

Our Saviour used the law as a primary tool of evangelism. He knew that preaching the Ten Commandments was the only way to teach a sinner his guilt and thereby stir within him a desire for God's grace.[3]

Today's Gospel shows how Jesus brings the spiritual nature of the tenth commandment to bear on the human heart:

Christ was using God's word, 'Thou shalt not covet', as a knife to lance the festering sore of greed in the man's soul. The sin was invisible to the human eye. It did not show its colours on the surface of the ruler's behaviour. But in all its filth and ugliness, covetousness ruled in his soul. Like a dart, the law of God pierced the conscience of this youth for the first time.[4]

[1] *Today's Gospel*, p. 36.
[2] *Ibid.*, p. 37.
[3] *Ibid.*, p. 39.
[4] *Ibid.*, p. 44.

It is just such preaching today that will show men and women their violations of the tenth commandment, as well as the other nine.

Today God's moral law is nearly erased from public consciousness. Therefore,

It is imperative that preachers of today learn how to declare the spiritual law of God; for, until we learn how to wound consciences, we shall have no wounds to bind with gospel bandages.[1]

The relationship between law and gospel is but one example of the relevance of *Today's Gospel.* Among the other important themes it addresses are repentance, faith in Christ, and Christian assurance. In fact the book is a contemporary *multum in parvo*—much in little; certainly a 'must read' for every young preacher of the gospel—and more seasoned ones too. For the truth is that *Today's Gospel* is as much a message for the twenty-first century as it was for the closing decades of the twentieth.

[1] *Ibid.*, p. 45.

4

The Reformed Pastor

Richard Baxter

Edward Donnelly

I BEGAN reading Banner of Truth books in late 1964, having
been converted a few months earlier. Five years later, I attended
my first Leicester Ministers' Conference[1] as a young pastor and
heard two Murrays—Professor John Murray thrilling me through his
teaching and Iain Murray encouraging me with his interest and affection, developing into a lifelong friendship. About eight years after
this he invited me to give my first conference address. What a panic
beforehand! But I had been reading and enjoying Richard Baxter's *The
Reformed Pastor* and so decided to try a review and commendation
of it. This book has been a constant blessing for me ever since—
re-reading it every few years and always finding it directing, challenging and encouraging.

Why Baxter? John Newton, writing a century after him, put it this
way: 'Some of Mr Baxter's sentiments in divinity are rather cloudy
... But, by what I have read of him, where he is quiet, and not ruffled
by controversy, he appears to me, notwithstanding some mistakes,
to have been one of the greatest men of his age.' He is particularly
valuable for several present needs.

In the providence of God we are seeing a renewed interest in
reformed truth, the doctrines of grace. But there is a danger that a
man, in the first flush of enthusiasm for what he has discovered, may,
in his very efforts to be thoroughly reformed, become a caricature of

[1] A conference held almost annually since 1962 at the University of Leicester in
England.

that which he admires. It is precisely here that Baxter can help us, for where he is strong, some today are weak. Three characteristics of his preaching speak beneficially to our current situation.

1. Baxter's preaching was characterized by clear, memorable instruction.

He believed that a preacher should reason with his hearers. 'We should be furnished with all kinds of evidence so that we may come as with a torrent upon their understandings, and with our reasonings and expostulations to pour shame upon their vain objections, and bear down all before us, that they may be forced to yield to the power of truth.' He was always concerned to clear up possible misunderstandings, giving explanations for what he was saying. His sermons had a logical structure—first the 'opening' of the text, then the explanation of difficulties, followed by 'uses' and an appeal.

The truths he preached were the fundamentals. 'Throughout the whole course of our ministry, we must insist chiefly upon the greatest, most certain and most necessary truths, and be more seldom and sparing upon the rest ... Many other things are desirable to be known, but some must be known, or else our people are undone for ever. A preacher must be oft upon the same things, because the matters of necessity are few.' This is, however, very different from preaching which traces a superficial path through a few well-trodden passages and despises anything else as 'not the gospel'. Baxter covered all of Scripture, dealing deeply and arguing closely. He set forth these fundamentals in all the fulness of their interrelationship and application. But he believed that preaching should meet people's greatest needs and that the 'matters of necessity' should be at the forefront.

These were taught in simple language, for since the purpose of the preacher was to teach, he must speak so as to be understood. In those days of sermon-tasters he was criticized for the plainness of his speech and had to combat the pride of his heart, as it urged him to a more ornate style: 'God commandeth us to be as plain as we can, that we may inform the ignorant ... but pride stands by and contradicteth all, and produceth its toys and trifles ... It persuadeth us to paint the window that it may dim the light.'

This surely challenges us. We may aim at giving reasoned expositions of truth, but do we seek to answer possible difficulties, marshal arguments to convince minds—or have we been made lazy by uncritical approval? Are we so afraid of being labelled 'fundamentalists' that we spend most of our time in the lesser-known corners of Scripture? It is possible for a man to win quite a reputation as the manager of a delicatessen for reformed gourmets, producing theological rarities which are unobtainable elsewhere—while many of his hungry flock look up and are not fed. It is a mistake so to concentrate on 'what is desirable to be known' that we neglect 'what must be known'. Do our people really understand the central truths concerning God's covenants, Christ's person and work, sin, regeneration, repentance and faith? Until the foundations of their faith are firmly established, we do well to lay less emphasis upon the superstructure.

Do we preach in simple language? No doubt we try to avoid over-academic expressions, and it is true that many of the mighty words of Scripture must never be omitted from our vocabulary, but expounded and incorporated into the thinking and speech of our hearers; but do we make the effort needed to avoid thought-benumbing clichés, in order to present the truth in a fresh, contemporary garb? Baxter calls us to a preaching ministry in which the fundamentals of the faith are explained with attractiveness and clarity.

2. Baxter's preaching was characterized by a passionate evangelistic appeal.

The great reality which moulded his ministry was the fact that we must all appear before the judgment seat of Christ. Extreme bodily weakness increased his awareness that there was but a step between him and death, which he referred to as his 'neighbour'. Every duty was to be carried out, every sermon preached, in the light of the great day. 'I daily know and think of that approaching hour', he says.

This awareness of eternity made Baxter an emotional preacher. 'If you want to know the art of pleading', said Spurgeon, 'read Baxter.' Yet his emotion was not undisciplined, but fuelled by his comprehension of truth. 'Light first, then heat' was his motto—first the exposition of the truth, then the words of piercing appeal springing from it. At the close of *A Call to the Unconverted* he appeals to his hearers with such tenderness that we can almost see tears upon his cheeks: 'My heart is troubled to think how I shall leave you, lest I should leave you as I found you, till you awake in hell ... I am as hearty a beggar with you this day, for the saving of your own souls as I would be for my own supply, if I were forced to come begging to your doors. And therefore if you would hear me then, hear me now. If you would pity me then, be entreated now to pity yourselves ...'

The focus of his preaching was an urgent invitation to receive Christ. Baxter preached for a verdict, seeking to 'drive sinners to a stand and make them see ... that they must unavoidably be either converted or condemned'. His words at the close of 'Making Light of Christ and Salvation' are powerful and pointed: 'When God hath shaken those careless souls out of their bodies, and you must answer for all your sins in your own name, Oh then what would you give for a saviour! ... You that cannot make light of a little sickness, or of want, or of natural death, no, not of a toothache, but groan as if you were undone; how will you then make light of the fury of the Lord, which will burn against the contemners of his grace? ... What say you? Do you mean to set as light by Christ and salvation as hitherto you have done and to be the same men after all this? I hope not.' The sharp edge was always present—a choice had to be made, an offer of mercy accepted or rejected.

Yet this is far removed from shallow decisionism. The Arminian preacher may be afraid of what the mind can say to the heart after the meeting has finished, and so he may try to compel a decision from the will before second thoughts lead some people from Christ. Not only was Baxter not afraid of second thoughts, he was counting on them, hoping that his hearers would reflect deeply upon what had been preached. So we find him planting time-bombs in their minds, applications which would continue to speak after his voice had fallen silent. 'I cannot now follow you to your several habitations to apply this word to your particular necessities, but oh that I might make every man's conscience a preacher to himself ... ever with you! That the next time you go prayerless to bed, or about your business, conscience might cry out, Dost thou set no more by Christ and thy salvation? ... That the next time you are ready to rush upon known sin ... conscience might cry out, Is Christ and salvation no more worth, than to cast them away, or venture them to thy lusts? ... That when you are next spending the Lord's day in idleness or vain sports, conscience might tell you what you are doing.' He takes each facet of life and enlists it, so that the sinner may be hemmed in by an environment in which every part declares the claims of God.

Whether fairly or not, reformed preachers have in many quarters a reputation for being restrained and impersonal in their delivery. It may be a reaction against the excesses of the age, against sound without sense. But has it become overreaction? Understanding the misery of human depravity and the wonder of sovereign grace, we should be most deeply moved when such truth grips us. Has the development of our heads so shrivelled our hearts as to render us suspicious of genuine emotion? The 'five points' can be treated as a theological minefield through which the preacher tiptoes, so afraid of blowing himself up on the horns of a careless expression that he ceases to long for the conversion of his hearers. But our preaching is a travesty if it lacks an earnest pleading with men to receive an all-sufficient Christ, freely offered to all who hear. It is precisely because grace is sovereign and free that we can urge it passionately—because the redemption purchased by Christ is complete and certain that we can commend it so glowingly—because God has chosen some out of his mere good pleasure that we can preach confidently. If we are to stand in the line of biblical, reformed preachers, we will take note of this element in Baxter's preaching.

3. Baxter's preaching was followed by systematic pastoral counselling.

He made no division, today often common, between preaching and pastoral work, for he understood what Paul meant when he reminded the Ephesians that he had taught them 'publicly and from house to house'. The task is one—the same truth communicated to the same people for the same end—the glory of God through their salvation or condemnation. Perhaps this is where Baxter may prove most serviceable to ministers of today—in the forging of a strong link between pulpit and pastorate.

He expected conversions to result from preaching, advising his brother ministers, 'If you long not to see the conversion and edification of your hearers, and do not preach and study in hope, you are not likely to see much success.' The preacher must be filled with grief if his people do not respond. 'I know that a faithful minister may have comfort when he lacks success ... but then, he that longeth not for the success of his labours can have none of this comfort, because he was not a faithful labourer ... What if God will accept a physician though the patient die? He must, notwithstanding that, work in compassion, and long for a better issue and be sorry if he miss it.'

This longing for results drove him to the homes of his people and to the work of catechizing. Had they embraced the gospel offer of mercy? Did the seed sown need further cultivation? Were there weeds to be removed from the soil? These questions could be answered only in personal conversation. At first, he shrank from the work: 'Many of us have a foolish bashfulness, which makes us backward to begin with them, and to speak plainly to them'—but, as he gained experience, this pastoral counselling became 'the most comfortable work, except public preaching, that ever I yet did set my hand to'.

It was his earnestness as a preacher which made him such a diligent pastor. His home visitation was a means of expanding and further applying what had been said in the pulpit, finding that people would not take his preaching seriously unless it was enforced by close personal dealing. In a classic passage from *The Reformed Pastor* he says: 'They will give you leave to preach against their sins, and to talk as much as you will for godliness in the pulpit, if you will but let them alone afterwards, and be friendly and merry with them when you have done ... For they take the pulpit to be a stage; a place where preachers must show themselves and play their parts ... and what you say they regard not, if you show them not, by saying it personally to their faces, that you were in good earnest and did indeed mean them.'

His pastoral work not only enforced his past preaching but helped him preach more pointedly and relevantly. 'It will furnish you with useful matter for your sermons, to talk an hour with an ignorant or obstinate sinner; as much as an hour's study will do, for you will learn what you have need to insist on and what objections of theirs to repel.' He got to know his people—their personalities, problems, temptations, way of life—and was thus enabled to preach sermons tailored to their peculiar needs. In order to be a true preacher, a man must be a true pastor. We may recognize the centrality of preaching, but do we ever use this as an excuse for pastoral indifference? Does the fact of having preached publicly against men's sins absolve us from the responsibility of confronting them in their homes concerning those same sins? We are called to be diligent students in the word, to be much in the secret place. But our study may become a convenient refuge from reality and we may all too easily salve our consciences over an unpaid visit by reading yet another book. Many of us have discovered, to our shame, that the courage with which we have preached can evaporate during the walk to the door of the meeting-house. Having thundered boldly against sin, we may have found ourselves trying to conciliate, with an especially warm smile or handshake, those very individuals whose consciences we were seeking to wound, to prefer almost that God should be angry with them than that they should be angry with us.

Personal counselling can be no substitute for the preached word, but, as a means of enforcing and applying that word to the individual conscience, it fulfils a unique function. It will also serve to make us better preachers. As we go from house to house, occasional mists of our study may be blown away and we will return to prepare sermons which are rooted in the life and language of the people.

This then is Richard Baxter of Kidderminster. A preacher who laboured to make plain the truth of God, who spoke from a burning heart as he pleaded with his people to close with Christ. A pastor who knew his sheep by name, speaking to them personally about the great concerns of their souls. He is not merely an historical curiosity, but a challenge and a stimulus.

I have been blessed by *The Reformed Pastor* for many years and would encourage you to read it from time to time. In his *Dying Thoughts*, Baxter lays bare the preacher's heart:

> My Lord, I have nothing to do in this world, but to seek and serve thee; I have nothing to do with a heart and its affections but to breathe after thee; I have nothing to do with my tongue and pen, but to speak to thee, and for thee, and to publish thy glory and thy will.

5

What Is an Evangelical?

D. Martyn Lloyd-Jones

Alistair Begg

FOR the past twenty years it has been our pattern, as elders at Parkside Church, Cleveland, Ohio, to read through a book together. The objective is to grow in our understanding of Christian doctrine and to become increasingly united in heart and mind. The privilege and responsibility of choosing which book to read, falls to me. When we started this practice it seemed wise to begin with a small book, and it was partly for this reason that I chose *What Is an Evangelical?* by D. Martyn Lloyd-Jones.

The primary reason for deciding to read this title with my elders was because, in a theological climate of increasing vagueness and confusion, it is important that we are clear and convinced about what it means for us to affirm evangelical convictions. Instead of just assuming that we were all on the same page in these matters, we decided to ensure that we were, and this brief book proved to be just what we needed to meet that objective.

I have a vivid recollection of the occasion when my fellow elders were introduced to the book. Having read the book and benefited from it immensely, I was very keen to see how they would receive it. I placed a copy on the table at each man's place and before the book was even opened there was a strong reaction at first. This was on account of the photograph of 'the Doctor' on the front cover. The picture of Martyn Lloyd-Jones could hardly be described as warm or welcoming, and the elders, most of whom had never seen Lloyd-Jones, had some fun at the expense of the rather dour and tight-lipped expression on the preacher's face. 'So, is this what an evangelical looks like?' they asked! They learned quickly that the serious demeanour was on account of his high view of preaching, a view which to a man they now share.

It makes sense that the front cover pictures the author in his pulpit because the content of this book is primarily taken from three addresses he gave to the International Fellowship of Evangelical Students (IFES) conference in Austria in 1971. The back cover provides an apt summary of Martyn Lloyd-Jones' motivation in delivering these addresses: 'Dr. D. Martyn Lloyd-Jones became deeply concerned with what he believed to be subtle but real shifts in commitment to the biblical gospel.'

He based these addresses on the opening verses of the Letter of Jude, believing that the early 1970s were not dissimilar to the times in which Jude found himself. Lloyd-Jones was in a unique position to make these observations since he had been at the formation of the IFES in the 1940s and he had been engaged long enough in Christian ministry to detect the subtle shifts. The history of the church reveals a tendency to deviate from the truth and to make what may appear to be only minor changes; but over time those minor changes will prove to be of major significance. Beginning with the emergence of the Ephesian wolves (*Acts* 20), Lloyd-Jones shows how this process of degeneration can be seen for example in the conflict in the Missouri Synod of the Lutheran Church, the Christian Reformed Church in Grand Rapids, Michigan, and the Free University in the Netherlands. 'It is no use assuming that because a thing has started correctly it is going to continue to be correct. There is a process at work, because of sin and evil, which tends to produce not only change but even degeneration.'

As a result of this tendency there is a constant need for definition, and in these addresses the focus is not on the Christian in general, but on the *evangelical* Christian. Arriving at such a definition involves ruling certain things out and declaring others in. Lloyd-Jones puts his cards squarely on the table when he declares, 'We believe that ultimately the evangelical faith is the only true expression in doctrine of the Christian faith itself.'

There is a challenge to be faced in defining the evangelical position as distinct from the Christian in general. How do we determine the boundaries? What is to be considered a secondary matter about which equally convinced evangelical Christians may disagree, and what is to be regarded as central and non-negotiable? The author's personal view comes later, but first he addresses two main dangers. On the one hand, the danger of being too tight or rigid and detailed in definition about issues that are not essential to salvation. This schismatic tendency was seen in Corinth, among people who were in agreement about the centralities of the faith but who were divided and separated from one another over allegiance to their favourite preacher or over the matter of food offered to idols.

Going back to the reading of this book with my elders: I should tell you that they were highly amused by the author's observation that when it came to this danger of being too rigid and schismatic, 'The country that illustrates this point more clearly perhaps than any other is Scotland.' His illustration of the Burghers and the Anti-Burghers, culminating as it does with a minister's wife's declaration, 'You may still be my husband but you are no longer my minister', is not to be missed.[1]

The second danger is the exact opposite of the first. Lloyd-Jones saw it as the greater danger at the time. It is the danger of 'being so broad, so wide and so loose' that we leave ourselves with no definitions at all. Lloyd-Jones saw this ecumenical tendency not simply on the horizon, but present in an alarming fashion in places where one might not have expected it to appear. There is nothing cavalier about Lloyd-Jones' approach. He was convinced of the call to unity, as his sermon on John 17 aptly illustrates, but he was unwilling to countenance a unity at the expense of the central truths of the gospel. Like George Whitefield before him, he believed in 'evangelical unity'. It was therefore at some personal expense that he pointed to the dangers of the approach of the Billy Graham campaigns in shaking people's convictions as to what exactly it means to be evangelical. His concern was equally for the gospel in pointing out that C. S. Lewis 'was never an evangelical and said so quite plainly himself'.

And how bold of him to make his point by saying of Malcolm Muggeridge, who subsequently joined the Roman Catholic Church,

---

[1] Alistair Begg is a native of Scotland.—Ed.

Having read his last book, which is called *Jesus Rediscovered*, I would not hesitate to say that Malcolm Muggeridge is not a Christian at all. He does not believe in the virgin birth, he does not believe in the miracles as facts, he does not believe in the atonement, he does not believe in the literal physical resurrection, he does not believe in the person of the Holy Spirit, he does not believe in prayer.

It is important to keep in mind that his starting point was the call of Jude in his day to 'contend for the faith that was once for all delivered to the saints'. In today's politically correct environment we may find ourselves unsettled and convicted by Martyn Lloyd-Jones' willingness to 'take a stand'. To simply critique liberalism does not qualify one as evangelical. Karl Barth, Lloyd-Jones said, was a critic of liberalism but that did not mean he was a man of evangelical convictions; in fact he never was.

Lloyd-Jones was not contentious. He was not in the business of making enemies. So why, if he was concerned for unity, would he take the approach he did? Let him answer for himself.

Our real reason for definition and contending for this faith, is that we believe it to be vital to the preservation of the true gospel … We are not concerned merely to be polemical; our intent is a very practical one. We are concerned for the souls of men and women. We are here to spread the good news of salvation and to win people out of darkness and into light. That is why we should be so careful about the truth and always contend for it.

Those of us who had the privilege of listening to Lloyd-Jones preach can testify to this passion. He was, he said, an evangelist. He was deeply concerned about the *preservation* of the gospel because it was vital for the *proclamation* of the gospel. If you have never read his *Evangelistic Sermons* preached at Aberavon, let me commend them to you.[1]

In his preaching, Lloyd-Jones was constantly emphasizing the need for a person to think properly. It is therefore quite striking that in his second address to the IFES conference, he gives considerable space to the 'distrust of reason'. One of his guiding principles was this:

[1] D. Martyn Lloyd-Jones, *Evangelistic Sermons at Aberavon* (Edinburgh: Banner of Truth Trust, 1993).

while others may think philosophically, the evangelical must think biblically. He must start with the Bible, for it is his sole authority. Nothing should be added to it and nothing subtracted from it, and the evangelical Christian confines himself and submits himself completely to its teaching.

Once again if you ever heard Lloyd-Jones preach from the second half of 1 Corinthians 1, you will still hear a faint (maybe not so faint) echo of his voice as you read, 'Where is the one who is wise? Where is the scribe? Where is the debater of this age? Has not God made foolish the wisdom of the world?'

Throughout church history a failure to recognize the danger in this area has led to confusion and to a loss of gospel conviction. Lloyd-Jones shows from church history that when men trust to reason and to earthly philosophy, they inevitably go astray. In one of the more provocative statements of the book, he says, 'Let me state it still more bluntly by putting it to you like this, that the true evangelical is not only distrustful of reason, but he is also distrustful of scholarship.'

This, he says, does not mean being anti-intellectual or becoming obscurantist, but it means keeping reason and scholarship in their place as 'servants and not masters'. He saw the place of reason as determining *how* we think and not in telling us *what* to think. We should not be afraid of scholarship, but we should be fearful of the quest for intellectual respectability, which results in submission to philosophy and reason. The deadest periods in the history of the church have been when that approach was predominant. Lloyd-Jones refers to this as evangelicalism's inferiority complex.

It is now forty-four years since these addresses were given and twenty-three years since the publication of this book. It is impossible to miss just how prophetic Lloyd-Jones' observations proved to be. Consider how the quest for academic acceptance on the part of supposed evangelicals plays out in the contemporary theological issues facing the church.

What is the evangelical perspective on the Genesis narratives? Can you imagine that Martyn Lloyd-Jones would regard any man as a true evangelical who flirts with the denial of the historical Adam? Yet it is within the context of current evangelicalism that the debate occurs. The battle is between 'the wisdom of God' and the 'wisdom of man'. A. W. Pink in his *Gleanings in Genesis* has a purple passage regarding this matter: scientists must

> bring their declaration into accord with the teaching of Genesis 1, if they are to receive the respect of the children of God. The faith of the Christian [we might say evangelical Christian] rests not in the wisdom of man, nor does it need any buttressing from scientific *savants*. The faith of the Christian rests upon the impregnable rock of Holy Scripture and we need nothing more.[1]

The evangelical inferiority complex looks to bring Genesis 1 into accord with scientific philosophy, and the impact on evangelical faith is devastating.

Or consider the denial of the exclusivity of Christ. What is at stake? The truthfulness of Jesus, the impetus to world mission and therefore the salvation of the lost and the integrity of the gospel. The evangelical rejects for the gospel's sake, and on the basis of Scripture, the pluralism that declares all religions to be the same; the universalism which declares that all will eventually be saved; and the inclusivism which affirms that the Holy Spirit will apply the work of Christ apart from conscious faith in Christ.

What is to be said about the hot-button issue of homosexuality and the church? How are the principles laid out in this book to apply to this theological issue? At the heart of the argument is the same battle about the reliability and finality of the biblical record. The suggestion that the Bible is outmoded and completely out of touch with popular views of tolerance has an increasing hold within the framework of Christianity. Once again Lloyd-Jones' book is a help in this particular battle.

And what of the issue of social justice and the gospel? There is arguably no area in which Christians have put the cart before the horse to such an extent and at such a cost for the gospel. When I am with college students I like to provide this quote from George Smeaton and then listen as they react to it: 'To convert one sinner from his way, is an event of greater importance, than the deliverance of a whole kingdom from temporal evil.' The contemporary emphasis on good deeds is in danger of merely duplicating the 'social gospel'

[1] A. W. Pink, *Gleanings in Genesis* (Chicago: Moody Press, 1922), p. 11.

of an earlier era, which was the product of a loss of confidence in the gospel. The good deeds that were foreordained for us to do are not substitutes for gospel proclamation.

> We must go on to assent that man is spiritually dead, and that he is totally incapable of any spiritual good, 'dead in trespasses and sins', not merely slightly defective—and that it is not true to say that he has it in him, if he only applies himself, to believe in God and to arrive at God. We must assert, as the scriptures do, that man is totally dead, that the advances in science make no difference whatsoever to the fact that all men are 'by nature the children of wrath even as others' (Eph. 2:3), that 'all have sinned and come short of the glory of God' (Rom. 3:23).

The concluding section of the book deals with matters that are very important and worthy of discussion and debate, but should be, Lloyd-Jones suggests, regarded as 'non-essential' because they are not essential to salvation. This section has proved to be very influential and immensely helpful in forming our thinking as a church leadership.

In passing let me say that I find it quite ironic that some who profess to be in the lineage of Martyn Lloyd-Jones do not share his perspective on these issues. This helps me to understand something of the distinction between what I would regard as the best of British evangelicalism and the expression of American fundamentalism. This is not a plea for theological vagueness but rather a willingness to maintain fellowship in the gospel with someone who does not share the same perspective on, for example,

- Election and predestination
- Subjects and mode of baptism
- The question of church polity
- Views of the millennium (not one of them can be proved)
- The baptism of the Spirit and spiritual gifts

That is quite a list and it is a forceful reminder of the danger of schism and the true basis of fellowship in the gospel. We had a good illustration of this a few years ago when the speakers at our Basics Conference at Parkside were Eric Alexander, Dick Lucas, and Derek Prime: a Presbyterian, an Anglican, and a Free Church man. In the Q & A session, the message came across loud and clear: these men had more in common with each other than they had with their denominational framework. Why was that? Because they are 'gospel men'. They are *evangelicals* first and foremost. May their tribe increase!

6

The Valley of Vision

Arthur Bennett

Mark G. Johnston

PRAYER is, without doubt, one of the greatest blessings God gives in salvation. It lets us know that, not only does he speak to us through his word, but also that we can speak to him—and he will listen.

This is no small thing. Even though we so easily take prayer for granted, we should never lose sight of the privilege it entails. The God from whom we are estranged invites us to commune with him —to open our hearts and express the deepest thoughts, desires and longings of our souls—and he will commune with us.

Yet it is the sheer scale of what that privilege means that makes us realise how much we need to grow in how we pray. It is not just that our praying can so easily become jaded—slipping, as Jesus warns, into the kind of 'babbling' and 'many words' that masquerade for prayer but go unheard by the Father—but that it simply doesn't progress. Just as it would be strange if the level of our conversation with our parents as adults was no different from what it was like when we were teenagers, so too in the way we 'converse' with God as we pray.

It is an age-old problem. Jesus' disciples were deeply conscious of it (perhaps because they had heard Jesus praying), so they asked him, 'Lord, teach us to pray' (Luke 11:1). It cannot have been that they were complete novices when it came to prayer, but rather that they realised how much they still had to learn in the art of engaging with God in this way.

The very request the disciples make of Christ and the way he responds should be a double encouragement to anyone and everyone who wants to develop a life of prayer. On the one hand, it reminds us that there is no shame in admitting that our praying is never what it could or ought to be. On the other hand, it shows us that it is Jesus' greatest pleasure to bring us into a richer, deeper experience of this dimension of our relationship with God.

He does this in two very obvious ways. The first is by giving us his Holy Spirit as 'the Spirit of sonship by whom we cry out, "*Abba*, Father"' (Rom. 8:15). The second is by giving us the Lord's Prayer. Both are important to an understanding of what is involved in prayer.

The only way a person can begin to truly pray—that is, to pray in a way that genuinely engages with God—is when God himself gives both the right and the ability to do so. By nature we have no right to speak to God because our sin has alienated us from him and barred us from his presence. So, even though many people who are not Christians 'pray' it is to gods made in the human imagination and not to the God who makes himself known in Scripture. However, when someone has been given new life by God's Spirit and come to faith in God's Son, one of the very first blessings they are given is 'the right to be called the children of God' (John 1:12-13). From that moment they are brought into an unimaginably close and intimate relationship with God as their heavenly Father, Jesus as their elder brother and the Holy Spirit as the Spirit of sonship.

Only when we grasp this aspect of what it means to pray do we then begin to appreciate more fully what Jesus is teaching his followers through the Lord's Prayer. The fact that we have this prayer recorded in two slightly different versions (Matt. 6:9-13; Luke 11:2-4) indicates that at its most basic level it is meant to be seen as a pattern for all prayer: 'This, then, is *how* you should pray ...' (Matt. 6:9). Its opening words, 'Our Father in heaven', immediately remind us of the closeness of our relationship with God through Christ. The rest of the prayer provides a template for the balance, priorities, and flow of the kind of prayer that unfolds within that relationship.

At the same time Christ taught this prayer to his disciples as a prayer that they and the church at large could use as a set prayer: 'When you pray, *say* ...' (Luke 11:2). In that sense it was intended to be the family prayer of the people of God through the ages. It is a prayer that is bound up with our unique identity as God's children and it unites all Christians everywhere, regardless of language, culture, or even their location in history. And as such, although it is a prayer that is ever old, it is also ever new and fresh and never fails to evoke a deep sense of just how rich our relationship with God really is.

The value of written prayers

Clearly there is something quite unique about the Lord's Prayer—not least because it is 'the Lord's' and was given to his church in its infancy as a special gift—but at the same time it is part of a wider heritage that is often missed. This was not the only prayer God gave to his people. The Old Testament is full of recorded prayers. Indeed there is an entire book in the Hebrew Bible that is an anthology of 150 prayers: many, if not all, of which could be sung as well as said. And we have numerous prayers that were offered by New Testament believers that have not only been given a place in God's revealed word, but have also been regularly 'borrowed' by Christians down through the ages for both private devotion and public worship.

When the disciples asked Jesus to teach them to pray, it was not as though they were starting from scratch. They were beginning to realise that his coming as God's promised Messiah had raised the business of praying to a new level in God's great plan of redemption. The Lord's Prayer shows us the great high-water mark of the goal of that redemption.

What is interesting is the fact that this prayer not only becomes the benchmark for the other prayers found in the New Testament—which reflect its balance, priorities and flow—but it does the same for many of the prayers that have found their way into the shared tradition of the church.

Why is this significant? Because it can be tempting to be suspicious of prayers that have been written down, especially for those who place a high premium on praying 'out of the moment'. There is, without doubt, a vital place for praying in our own words, out of our immediate circumstances in life, as an expression of the genuineness of our relationship with God. In our communications with others we would think it strange to constantly have to reach for a prepared script to guide us in what we want to say. But, just as there are times when in addressing others we can be helped by having a prepared statement to hand, so too when we approach God in prayer.

This is especially true in public worship when the person leading in prayer during the service does so, not as if engaging in some private act of devotion to God; but as a public person, acting for, with, and on behalf of a gathered congregation of fellow worshippers. The members of the congregation are not to be spectators or passive auditors, but active participants in words offered in their stead, which speak for them, and to which they can say a hearty 'Amen!' So it is important for the one leading the congregation in prayer to think through the prayer beforehand—even to the point of writing it out in full.

Public prayer may also be offered as the whole congregation says the words of the prayer together. As noted already, the Lord's Prayer is the most universal of such prayers, but there is a rich heritage of other written prayers that could be used corporately. One of the best-known examples of this is *The Book of Common Prayer* compiled under the influence of Thomas Cranmer for use in the Church of England, but it is by no means the only one.

The Puritans (who first emerged within the Church of England, united by their desire to see it reformed more fully) recognised the value of giving careful thought to what we pray as well as to how our prayers are offered. Their prayers were arguably the most influential component of their piety and many of those prayers have survived in written form.

One of the most surprising features of the resurgence of interest in the Puritans that began during the second half of the twentieth century was the wide range of Christians who gravitated towards their republished prayers. When Arthur Bennett, a canon of St Albans Cathedral, put together an anthology of Puritan prayers and devotions under the title *The Valley of Vision* in 1975,[1] it almost immediately struck a chord with Christians from many different ecclesiastical backgrounds. Indeed, the ongoing popularity of this collection should give us pause for thought as to the way in which

[1] Arthur Bennett, ed., *The Valley of Vision: A Collection of Puritan Prayers and Devotions* (Edinburgh: Banner of Truth Trust, 1975). Originally published in paperback *The Valley of Vision* is also available in a leather-bound gift edition (2002).

these prayers—some of which were written down almost four hundred years ago—still resonate with so many people today.

Enjoying God for who he is

No small part of the appeal of these prayers lies in their ability to savour God for who he is *in himself*. They express the worshipper's delight in God, not primarily because of what he does or gives, but for his own sake. This comes out in the prayers collated in Bennett's anthology not merely in the fact that many of them are specifically focused on relishing God in all his glory, but in the way that they all express a rich awareness of who God is and what he is like, regardless of the particular needs which are expressed in the prayers.

The only reason this may come as a surprise to many of us is because we are so accustomed to hearing prayers that are dominated by a sense of our own need rather than by a sense of the greatness of the God to whom we pray for the meeting of those needs. If the Lord's Prayer is the archetypal model prayer, then its opening words and its underlying consciousness of the God to whom it is addressed says it all in terms of this crucial element of our praying.

We love God and delight in him, not primarily because of what we receive from him, but for all that he is in himself. Only when we 'lose ourselves' in him do we begin to truly find ourselves and experience the kind of life he intended us to have.

Such an awareness brings us into the realm where prayer becomes a rich expression of communion with God. Even though he is beyond all human thought, and his ways are past finding out, as we reflect on what he has made known of himself in his word and through his Son, we are able to engage with him in a thoughtful and meaningful way. More than that, we begin to appreciate the extraordinary privilege of knowing this God in Christ, not from a distance, but up close and personal as his children.

John Stott has noted that one of the greatest longings in the human heart is for transcendence: the realisation that there is something, or rather, someone, who is greater and more glorious than ourselves. The church has often sold the world short in this realm by presenting a God who is too small and who lacks weight and substance. But that is not the God we meet in the Bible, nor is it the God of whom the Puritans, and countless others like them, were conscious as they prayed. The heartbeat of prayer is energised by a deep awareness of the God before whom we bow in prayer.

The horizons of our praying

It follows that if our view of God is too small then the prayers we offer will be small and limited as a consequence. Even within the limits of the Lord's Prayer, which in so many ways seems short and simple, there is a height, depth, and breadth that should take our breath away. It takes us from the heights of the Holy Father who is in heaven to the terrible depths of the evil that lurks all around us on earth. It talks about our simple need of 'bread', but also about God's glorious provision of a kingdom. There is nothing too small and insignificant, or too great and seemingly unattainable, that falls outside the scope of our praying.

We see something of that scope in the prayer-psalms of the Old Testament: they manage to cover an extraordinary array of issues that take their authors through the entire spectrum of human emotions. It is for that reason the Psalms not only speak *to us* in what they reveal of God and teach about his purpose, but they also speak *for us* as we struggle to find words to express ourselves before God in similar life situations.

That same scope and variety has been reflected in the recorded prayers of God's people throughout the ages. We see them eloquently expressed in the prayers and collects for the common man that lay at the heart of the older liturgy of the Church of England, prayers that traverse the needs of the nation and the world while at the same time plumbing the depths of the human heart. We see them too in the rich variety of the Puritan prayers assembled and arranged by Canon Bennett in *The Valley of Vision*.

From prayers of worship and adoration to prayers of penitence and confession, prayers for the daily needs of life to prayers for the church and those who serve in it—there is hardly a circumstance of life which is not addressed somewhere in this anthology—a feature that enhances its usefulness as an aid to personal prayer.

Robert Murray M'Cheyne, a young minister whose own life and ministry was shaped by the Puritans in so many ways, once observed,

'What a man is on his knees before God, that he is, and nothing more.' Our prayer life is a telling barometer of the health of our relationship with God. But we should also remember that we never kneel alone before God in prayer. Not only has God given us the resources of heaven in his Son and by his Spirit to enable us to come to him and find words by which we can express ourselves to him, he has also given us the resources of his family. We have the encouragement and example of brothers and sisters in the faith— from the past as well as the present—who are role models in prayer. *The Valley of Vision* introduces us to some of them and allows us to benefit from their spiritual legacy.

7

Jonathan Edwards: A New Biography

Iain H. Murray

Sharon James

WHEN Iain H. Murray's *Jonathan Edwards: A New Biography* was published in 1987, it was the first full-length biography of Jonathan Edwards (1703–58) to have been published for nearly fifty years.[1] In contrast to many previous biographers who had not shared Edwards' faith, Murray wrote with the conviction that he was not dealing merely with the historical account of an eighteenth-century church leader, but that he was describing the living reality of God's presence and activity.[2] While drawing on the primary sources, and always aiming for truth and accuracy, he hoped that this 'popular' level biography[3] would inspire many readers to explore the writings of Jonathan Edwards for themselves. He was also humble enough to look forward to future contributions on the same subject: 'One day, we trust, a definitive and theologically dependable Life of Edwards will yet be written.'[4]

The biography begins by setting the scene, and then outlines Edwards' life. Converted at the age of seventeen, and having studied at Yale College, in 1726 Edwards was called to assist his grandfather

---

[1] Iain H. Murray, *Jonathan Edwards: A New Biography* (Edinburgh: Banner of Truth Trust, 1987).

[2] *Ibid.*, 'On Understanding Edwards', pp. xix-xxxi.

[3] *Ibid.*, p. xxx.

[4] George Marsden, *Jonathan Edwards* (Yale University Press, 2003), is a longer work, drawing on previously unused sources, and extremely useful in filling out the historical context. It is complementary to Murray's work. At a popular level Murray's biography remains more accessible.

at the Congregational Church, Northampton, Massachusetts. The following year, he married Sarah Pierrepont, an exceptionally godly young woman aged seventeen.

In 1729 on his grandfather's death, Edwards succeeded him as sole minister. He would see remarkable spiritual awakening in 1737, and then again between 1739 and 1741. At this time revival was experienced in communities throughout New England, leading to fierce controversy. In 1750, the church at Northampton dismissed Edwards from the ministry.[1] Eventually he and his family relocated to a remote frontier settlement called Stockbridge, where he pastored a small number of British colonists, as well as two more sizeable communities of Mohican and Mohawk Indians. In 1757, Edwards' son-in-law (the President of Princeton College), died, and Edwards accepted an invitation to succeed him. Shortly after arriving in Princeton, he died from a smallpox vaccination.

Edwards left a vast corpus of writing, both published and unpublished.[2] This biography includes helpful discussion of all Edwards' major works. Each is placed within the context of Edwards' own life and ministry, as well as within the historical context. An appendix outlines all Edwards' published writings.

I will mention just three of the themes of Murray's biography which I have found helpful.

1. Enjoying the beauty of the triune God

When my husband Bill and I left our church at Geneva Road, Darlington in 1988 to embark on three years of theological training in Toronto, the church gave us a goodbye gift: Murray's recently published biography of Jonathan Edwards. There could have been no better gift, and, in subsequent years, this biography is one I have

[1] The presenting issue was disagreement over who was qualified to partake at the Lord's Table; Edwards' predecessor had allowed those to participate who had made no personal profession of faith; Edwards wished to end this practice.

[2] In 1974, the Banner of Truth published a two-volume set of the entire *Works of Jonathan Edwards* available at that point (1,897 pages); this is still available. The entire corpus of Edwards' works, including previously unpublished works, is now available online through the Jonathan Edwards Center at Yale University website. The Works of Jonathan Edwards project at Yale has been bringing out scholarly editions of Edwards based on fresh transcriptions of his manuscripts since the 1950s.

returned to many times.[1] For while Jonathan Edwards is remembered for his powerful intellect, the heartbeat of his life and ministry was the necessity of holy affections. 'Knowing God' is not just about intellectual understanding. It is about our heart.

In 1972, the first Carey Family Conference was held in Sussex, England, where Pastor Wayne Mack from the U.S.A. preached two unforgettable messages on hell and heaven. He commended a new booklet, on sale for just 13 new pence (or 2 shillings and sixpence). As a young teenager I could afford that! And so I read *Heaven: A World of Love* by Edwards, a powerful sermon on 1 Corinthians 13:8-10.[2] Edwards began:

> God is the fountain of love, as the sun is the fountain of light. And therefore the glorious presence of God in heaven, fills heaven with love, as the sun, placed in the midst of the visible heavens in a clear day, fills the world with light. The apostle tells us that 'God is love'; and therefore, seeing he is an infinite being, it follows that he is an infinite fountain of love. Seeing he is an all-sufficient being, it follows that he is a full and overflowing, and inexhaustible fountain of love. And in that he is an unchangeable and eternal being, he is an unchangeable and eternal fountain of love.[3]

The power of this sermon lay in Edwards' vision of the beauty of the triune God, a vision that gripped me as a young teenager as I read his words. And Murray's biography of Edwards wonderfully evokes the excitement the young Edwards experienced as he increasingly glimpsed the infinite beauty of God.

The popular caricature of Edwards as merely a 'hell-fire preacher' could not be more wrong. Edwards' commitment to God was the

---

[1] I have read and enjoyed Marsden's biography twice. But, for spiritual encouragement, I have returned to Murray's biography more times than I can remember. And on returning, I have never failed to find inspiration—not least because the author succeeds so beautifully in pointing beyond Jonathan Edwards to the triune God Edwards loved and served.

[2] Jonathan Edwards, *Heaven: A World of Love* (London: Banner of Truth Trust, 1970). The sermon was part of Edwards' sermon series on 1 Corinthians 13, also published by the Trust under the title *Charity and Its Fruits*. It has since been reprinted separately in the Pocket Puritans series (Edinburgh: Banner of Truth Trust, 2008).

[3] *Heaven: A World of Love* (Edinburgh: Banner of Truth Trust, 2008), pp. 14-15.

commitment of a lover transfixed with the beauty of the beloved. The infinite, eternal, triune God is the source of all true beauty, and the one who himself is infinitely beautiful.

2. The reality of revival

By the spring of 1735 Jonathan Edwards reported that he was seeing thirty conversions a week. Three hundred people were converted in a six-month period. Excitement in the town was intense. The Edwards found their home crowded with people wanting spiritual advice. Northampton was not the only town affected: similar scenes were taking place in towns throughout New England.

The revival caused bitter division among the ministers of New England. Around a third of them dismissed it as merely human emotion and mass hysteria. Jonathan Edwards was realistic enough to understand this reaction. He agreed that a dramatic 'conversion experience' meant precisely nothing unless it was followed by a lifetime of obedience. It could be worse than useless, because the excitement of the 'experience' could lead individuals to believe that they were infallible. 'Revival' could overflow into fanaticism. Heightened excitement could lead people into actions that were misguided, while they claimed it was the guidance of the Holy Spirit. Uneducated people were thrilled by the notion that God would speak directly to them, and make claims that were ineffably silly. Newly converted individuals denounced mature leaders as lacking the Spirit. Yet the presence of the false did not negate the presence of the true.

To defend the reality of true revival, Jonathan Edwards wrote an analysis entitled the *Distinguishing Marks of a Work of the Spirit of God*. He also set out a description of the revival of religion at Northampton in 1735 in his *Narrative of Surprising Conversions*, as well as a detailed description of the revival of 1740–42 which was originally set out in a letter to a fellow minister in Boston.[1]

When Edwards set out to analyse the unusual scenes that had resulted from this phenomenon called 'revival' he had a case study

---

[1] My father, Erroll Hulse, who worked with Iain Murray at the Banner of Truth Trust in the early 1960s, recalls that when the Trust reprinted these works in 1965, they had a powerful spiritual impact on the staff at the Banner offices then in London.

beside him. His own wife had an extraordinary experience. Indeed, when he returned from a preaching engagement early in 1742, the whole town was wondering whether she would even survive until his return. She had been prostrated physically with religious ecstasy; she had been so taken up with a sensation of the love of God that she had leaped for joy, had sometimes been unable to stop talking, and at other times rendered speechless.

Edwards did not rush to conclusions. He was willing to face the possibility that this could be due to nervous instability. He asked Sarah to sit down and describe every detail. She gave him a precise account of her spiritual experience which had lasted for seventeen days from January 19th to February 4th, 1742. It was, concluded her husband, the most intense, pure, unmixed and well-regulated of any he had seen. He went on to explain that the long-term effect in Sarah's life was remarkable. She was now entirely resigned to God. She had given over to God the choice of life or death, for herself and her loved ones. She let God choose comfort or pain. Jonathan Edwards, of all people, would know if this was just a passing phase. It was not. He could testify to her continual peace, cheerfulness and joy in the following months and years.

The reality of Sarah's 'resignation of all to God' would be tested all too soon. While carried away with a sense of the love of God, she had visualised some 'worst-case scenarios'. What if the townsfolk turned on her and she was thrown out into the wilderness in the midst of winter? What if her husband turned against her? What if she had to die for Christ? She felt that:

> The whole world, with all its enjoyments and all its troubles seemed to be nothing: My God was my all, my only portion. No possible suffering seemed to be worth regarding: all persecutions and torments a mere nothing.[1]

Murray's biography vividly describes the challenges presented to the family in the years following Edwards' dismissal from the church in Northampton. They had to face war, slander, intrigue, bereavement, poverty, and a move to an isolated and dangerous frontier settlement.

[1] The account of Sarah's testimony is included in full in Sereno E. Dwight, 'Memoirs of Jonathan Edwards', in vol. 1 of the *The Works of Jonathan Edwards* (Edinburgh: Banner of Truth Trust, 1974), pp. lxii-lxx.

Their serenity and poise in the face of trials demonstrated that the powerful sense of God's presence during revival had not been mere passing emotion.

During the last thirty years, I have often drawn encouragement from the example of Jonathan and Sarah Edwards during those difficult times. They proved that when every earthly prop was removed, nothing could separate them from the love of God (Rom. 8:39).

3. The call for prayer for revival

In 1747, Edwards wrote an appeal for concerted prayer for God to bring blessing to the nations by means of revivals, entitled:

> An Humble Attempt to Promote Explicit Agreement and Visible Union of God's People in Extraordinary Prayer for the Revival of Religion and the Advancement of Christ's Kingdom on Earth, Pursuant to Scripture Promises and Prophecies concerning the Last Time.[1]

Edwards was responding to the call issued by a number of Scottish ministers for a concerted effort among the churches to pray together for revival. He wished to support this effort with a work which laid out scriptural encouragements, as well as answers to objections. He began with an exposition of Zechariah 8:20-23, which depicts people from many nations gathering for prayer:

> And the inhabitants of one city shall go to another, saying, 'Let us go speedily to pray before the LORD, and to seek the LORD of hosts: I will go also. Yea, many people and strong nations shall come to see the LORD of hosts in Jerusalem and to pray before the LORD.

---

[1] Christian Focus has reprinted *An Humble Attempt* (*A Call to United, Extraordinary Prayer*, [Fearn, Ross-shire: Christian Focus, 2004], with a foreword by David Bryant). The foreword traces the impact of the *Humble Attempt* in the years since its original publication. After the Banner of Truth Trust had reprinted the *Works of Jonathan Edwards* in 1974, including the *Humble Attempt* (vol. 2, pp. 278-312), Glynn Williams (then Pastor of Tinshill Baptist Church in Leeds) and Erroll Hulse attempted to initiate a regular concert of prayer for revival among fellow ministers. There was little enthusiasm. But when they relaunched the appeal in 2012, there was a positive response, and regular united meetings for revival are continuing in the Yorkshire area and beyond.

Edwards anticipated that if God poured out a spirit of prayer, this would in turn be used in the fulfilment of his purposes. The *Humble Attempt* needs to be read alongside *The History of Redemption*, Edwards' survey of God's purpose for the history of the world. From passages such as Psalm 110 he argued:

> It is natural and reasonable to suppose, that the whole world should finally be given to Christ as one whose right it is to reign ... Such being the state of things in this future promised glorious day of the church's prosperity, surely it is worth praying for.[1]

The Northamptonshire Association of Baptists in England responded to this call with a monthly prayer meeting for revival, and then, in 1795, the directors of the newly formed London Missionary Society urged that the first Monday of every month be set aside for concerted prayer for world mission. Prayer meetings multiplied, and many believe that prayers were answered in the Second Evangelical Revival (sometimes referred to in Britain as 'the Forgotten Revival') as well as in the great nineteenth-century Protestant missionary movement. While the spread of the gospel throughout the world might have seemed an impossible dream in Edwards' own day, many would regard the prayers stirred up by his appeal as being one factor in the tremendous expansion of the church into every continent.

Now nearly thirty years old, Iain Murray's biography of Edwards can no longer be described as 'a new biography'. But it still speaks powerfully into our contemporary situation. In the light of the claims of the charismatic movement, Edwards' analysis of what is genuine and what is counterfeit in spiritual awakening is still of vital importance. The overwhelmingly subjective focus of contemporary evangelicalism means that Edwards' insistence on God-centred religion is more timely than ever.

And I will no doubt be returning to this book again, as I have so often in the past, when I want to be pointed afresh to the beauty of the triune God, when I need to be reminded of the truth that nothing can separate us from the love of God, and when I need to be revived in my own prayers for God's kingdom to come and his will to be done throughout the whole earth.

[1] Jonathan Edwards, *A Call to United, Extraordinary Prayer* (Fearn, Ross-shire: Christian Focus, 2004), pp. 70, 88.

8

The Calvinistic Methodist Fathers of Wales

John Morgan Jones and William Morgan

Geoffrey Thomas

I BEGAN my only ministry in 1965 in Aberystwyth, and it was probably at that time that I noticed John Aaron, a fourteen-year-old schoolboy, wiry, medium height, intelligent, spectacled, looking rather like the young Daniel Radcliffe, the actor who played the character Harry Potter, especially in the opening instalment of that film series. I might have noticed him because with his four siblings and parents he was attending the Welsh Baptist Chapel, Bethel, diagonally across the road from the church where I am the minister. In Bethel in the late 1860s our mother church had decided to plant an English language meeting place, Alfred Place English Baptist Church, in what was then a 100% Welsh-speaking small town. The railway was advancing to Aberystwyth and would soon be complete. English holiday visitors were expected to be arriving by the trainload. The character of the town was changing. The first university college of Wales was about to open in a fine building at the southern end of the promenade. In fact in 1965 John Aaron's father, Dr Richard Ithamar Aaron, was the professor of philosophy at the university. His father before him, William Aaron, had once chuckled to Dr Martyn Lloyd-Jones, 'I did not want him to have any ordinary name and so I slipped in that middle name Ithamar.' Dr Lloyd-Jones said to me, 'As if having a distinctive surname like Aaron was not enough! Richard Aaron's father was quite a character.' In the Bible Ithamar was one of the sons of Aaron the high priest.

Professor Richard Aaron was a fine gracious man, beloved by his students, a man of great integrity. He was an authority on John Locke and British epistemology. When Eryl Davies, the future principal of the Welsh Evangelical School of Theology, was finding some intellectual difficulties with the Christian faith during his years at Aberystwyth university he went to Professor Aaron and was helped by him.

In 1969 John Aaron went south to Swansea to study physics at the university, and while he was there he met some Christians in the college cross-country club. They were also living in the hall of residence with him and they invited him to the Christian Union. Thus John met historical Christianity. For example, he heard teaching on the second coming of Christ, and such a future event surprised him much. He had attended church in Aberystwyth for eighteen years and had never heard a mention of the glorious return of the Son of God. Sometime during the middle of his first year at university John became a Christian. He was soon attending what is now Ebenezer Baptist Church, Swansea, and profited from the preaching of Dr Leighton James. He was a student at the university in Swansea for seven years, getting his PhD and then his school-teacher's certificate in his final year.

Soon he was married and his fluency in his first language, Welsh, enabled him to understand some of the more valuable nineteenth-century books on Christianity in the Welsh language, such as the enormous biography of *John Jones of Talsarn* and also the two volumes of the history of the Calvinistic Methodist Fathers of Wales. One weekend Maurice Roberts, then editor of the *Banner of Truth* magazine, was preaching in Swansea and he encouraged John by reading a chapter on the life of John Evans of Bala that Dr Aaron had translated. It was soon published in the magazine! Then Iain Murray counselled him to go ahead with a translation of the central chapters in the biography of John Jones which dealt with the atonement controversy amongst the Calvinistic Methodists. This was published by the Banner of Truth in 2002, *The Atonement Controversy*. Then John sent to Iain Murray four typical chapters of the history of the *Calvinistic Methodist Fathers of Wales*. 'Get on with it', was Iain's response. 'How much of it?' asked John, and he was encouraged to translate all the 1,500 pages in two volumes as in the original. He had at that time translated about 300 pages, and so this became John's vocation in the next years, retiring from his school teaching for three years to give himself wholly to this task.[1] The two volumes were finally published in the year 2008.

The volumes consist of biographies of the leading men who preached throughout Wales in the eighteenth century. Most attention, about 300 pages, is given to Howell Harris in the first volume, along with nine other men. Then in the second volume the biographies of twenty men are recorded, and how their lives intertwined. The most attention is paid to Thomas Charles (about 100 pages) and then the same length is devoted to John Elias. This is an extraordinary accomplishment, first by John Morgan Jones who wrote much of the first volume and the entirety of the second volume, and then by John Aaron for his painstaking translation. Why should these volumes be prized? John Aaron suggests some reasons:[2]

1. In the Scriptures God's people are called upon often to remember, study and learn from God's glorious actions in the past. The Calvinistic Methodist revival in Wales is one of the most remarkable examples in church history of what the prophet Isaiah described as a nation being born at once, Zion travailing and bringing forth her children. This should be essential reading for Christians.

2. The experiences related by the men and women caught up in these periods of refreshing from the right hand of the Lord provide unique lessons for people today. Their experiences were in essence the same as those of every believer in every age, yet in intensity they far surpassed that which is generally the case today. To read their words in journals, diaries and letters is to be particularly struck by their continued awareness of the ministry of the Holy Spirit in his church.

The response of the young Dr Martyn Lloyd-Jones to this book is worth quoting: 'For sheer stimulus and enjoyment there were no

[1] Iain Murray was quite indispensable in reading his translations. For example, he would question a sentence or two in *The Atonement Controversy*; 'This sounds odd. Are you sure that this is right?' John would go back to the Welsh and would discover that he had mistranslated it. Some of the uncertainties of Owen Thomas, the author of the biography of *John Jones of Talsarn*, were also revealed.

[2] John Morgan Jones and William Morgan, tr. John Aaron, *The Calvinistic Methodist Fathers of Wales* (Edinburgh: Banner of Truth Trust, 2008), vol. I, pp. viii-x.

volumes which he prized more highly than *Y Tadau Methodistaidd* which relate the lives of the fathers of Welsh Calvinistic Methodism. They were constantly in his hands in the early years.'[1]

3. Though the mind of the modern Welshman has been determinedly secularized and he cannot find any relevance in the spiritual experiences of people of past centuries, other peoples in the world, in China, Korea, Africa and South America, would recognize these phenomena and understand the work of God the Holy Spirit. They may not have the length of history of spiritual revivals and visitations. They cannot look back to the eighteenth century and be overwhelmed with the fact of God changing their land, but the detailed description of the progress of a national work of God in Wales can truly help them in understanding what has happened in their lands in the past century.

4. Might not the reminder of what is possible for the people of God at any time and in any country provoke in us that necessary spiritual jealousy that results in prevailing prayer? 'I have set watchmen on your walls, O Jerusalem, who shall never hold their peace day or night. You who make mention of the LORD, do not keep silent, and give him no rest till he establishes and till he makes Jerusalem a praise in the earth' (Isa. 62:6-7).

There is also the all-round ministry of these men with their separate strengths: for example, the spiritual worship and praise seen in the marvellous hymns of William Williams, Pantycelyn; the commitment to exegetical preaching in a lifelong ministry exercised in one place evident in Daniel Rowland, Llangeitho; the soul-analysis and the record of God's dealings found in the scores of diaries kept by Howell Harris; the awakening ministry of a preacher like John Elias; the commitment to reformed orthodoxy manifest in the ministry of Thomas Charles and his *Bible Dictionary*, and his influence in the ultimate formulation of the 1823 Confession of Faith accepted unanimously by the denomination nine years after his death.

One of the delights of these two volumes is their sheer readability. They are page-turners, unconsciously humorous at times, vivid and breathtaking in the account of conversions, the growth of the

[1] Iain H. Murray, *D. Martyn Lloyd-Jones: The First Forty Years* (Edinburgh: Banner of Truth Trust, 1982), p. 156.

churches, and the size of the gatherings. There is scarcely a page which does not have an illustration which a preacher cannot but use the very next Sunday. The blank pages at the end should be full of pencil marks noting page numbers with a brief index heading. There are simply too many things worth noting to keep in one's mind without such assistance. There was a time when my wife and I had a volume each in bed and then we would read aloud to one another portions that struck us!

These two volumes are the Hebrews 11 of the greatest age of growth and blessing in the Welsh church since the apostolic period. For example, two men went to the island of Anglesey, the Baptist Christmas Evans and the Calvinistic Methodist John Elias, and on that island through their ministries they planted over forty churches and the whole life of Anglesey was changed for the best. The people were happier, family life was stronger, education was transformed and a spirit of love for one's neighbours pervaded every part. There was a happy peace on the first day of the week as the islanders said, 'We do not live for our farms and secular vocations, but for the God who made us and has blessed us through our lives especially by his grace in salvation. Our chief end is to glorify and enjoy him.'

These fascinating books introduce us to the true giants of the Welsh pulpit. They ministered in a period that was not blighted by the pulpiteering and personality cults that sprang up in the latter half of the nineteenth century and afflicted and virtually destroyed preaching (with some notable exceptions). To enter into the lives of these godly men is to breathe purer air, and it stirs up within us a longing to know more of the divine blessing they experienced in such great abundance, though not without many heartaches and trials.

9

Expository Thoughts on the Gospels

J. C. Ryle

———

Derek W. H. Thomas

I FIRST encountered J. C. Ryle's *Expository Thoughts on the Gospels* forty years ago, in 1974, in a seven-volume edition published that year by James Clarke & Co. Ltd.[1] Having been told that 'ministers need books, and especially commentaries' (and I had made the decision that I would proceed immediately to seminary following the completion of my undergraduate degree), I began to acquire as many books as I could. And, so I was told, there is no one quite like the godly Bishop Ryle on the Gospels.

And so it has proved to be ever since. I doubt, for example, that I have ever preached on a Gospel passage without consulting what Ryle had to say about it. Of course, there are far more detailed commentaries with insights into nuances of the passage that Ryle does not even attempt to examine. For that is not Ryle's purpose. What he gives are expository *thoughts*, crystallized nuggets of pastoral and spiritual insight designed to help pilgrims on their journey through this world and to the next.

These seven volumes were not intended for ministers as such; rather, they were written with family devotions in mind—brief exposition and pointed application to help Christian families gathered for daily

———

[1] J. C. Ryle's *Expository Thoughts on the Gospels* were first published in seven volumes between 1856 and 1873. The Banner of Truth Trust first reprinted these in paperback format in 1986. A completely new, retypeset, cloth-bound edition was published by the Trust in 2012, and a new ebook version in 2015.

prayer in their own homes. Ministers might also make use of them as aids in pastoral visitation.

I bought these volumes initially as *commentaries*, to add to what would become, as I write, part of a collection of hundreds of commentaries on individual books of the Bible (in addition to commentaries on the entire Bible). Some are dear friends without which my understanding of Scripture would be greatly impaired—Hodge and Murray on *Romans*, Plumer and Kidner on the *Psalms*, Owen on *Hebrews*, Leighton on *1 & 2 Peter*, to name just a few. They are friends that have helped me in the study as I have reflected on the meaning of a passage of Scripture.

There are also commentaries that are, well, just plain dull to read—like watching paint dry. It would be unthinkable to simply read them. They are, of course, necessary. Deeply technical on matters of language, context, genre and background, they are for consultation *only*. But they almost always appear bereft of pastoral and spiritual insight.

Ryle's *Expository Thoughts*, on the other hand, are non-technical and rigorously pastoral. Interestingly, in separate prefatory comments to each Gospel, Ryle insists that his readers know that he has read somewhere between fifty and eighty commentaries in his preparations (and he lists the authors). *Mark* was published first (1856), followed by *Matthew* (1858), both in single volumes. *Luke* appeared in the same year as *Matthew*, but in two volumes. *John* appeared in three volumes, stretching over a period of eight years (1865, 1869, 1873). In addition to the commentary, Ryle also provides 'Notes', set in a smaller type-face, thus encouraging the less inclined to pass them by. In *John*, the last to be written, these 'Notes' are considerably lengthier and occasionally contain remarks concerning the Greek text or a particular commentator.

At no point do the volumes detract from their main ambition—to state 'as briefly as possible the main scope and purpose of the passage under consideration'.[1] Nor does Ryle intend to comment on every verse. As Ryle explains, his aim is to be 'plain and pointed, and to choose what an old divine calls "picked and packed" words'.[2]

---

[1] *Expository Thoughts on the Gospels: Matthew* (Edinburgh: Banner of Truth Trust, 2012), p. v.

[2] *Ibid.*

It is precisely here, at the level of pastoral insight and skilled application, that Ryle, like Thomas Watson, or Matthew Henry, is in his element. In many ways he excels the best of such commentators in what might be summarized along three lines of thought: simplicity, focus, and direction.

First, his no-nonsense, to-the-point manner, employing relatively simple, everyday words whilst at the same time conveying truths and ideas of the very deepest sort, could be (and often is) interpreted as ineptitude on Ryle's part. These volumes have, therefore, been dismissed as unsophisticated and naïve. 'Lampooning Bishop Ryle as a ham-fisted, Bible-punching caveman, a heavy-handed primitive, a bull in a china shop, and a faded old clown', writes J. I. Packer, 'has been popular sport among non-evangelicals from Ryle's day to our own. But I see him as a single-minded Christian communicator of profound biblical, theological, and pastoral wisdom, a man and minister of giant personal stature and electric force of utterance that sympathetic readers still feel ("unction" was the old name for it)...'[1] Second, on every page (yes, *every* page!), Ryle's sense of direction (his focus, if you will) is clear. For it is the gospel, one that is the focus of Scripture itself, that is before his mind every time he comments. As he makes clear in *Knots Untied*, a book I purchased at the same time as Ryle's *Expository Thoughts* (in addition to two more volumes by Ryle, *Practical Religion* and *Holiness*), interpreters of the Bible must keep before them four 'distinctive principles':

(i) the absolute supremacy of Scripture,

(ii) the sinfulness and corruption of all mankind,

(iii) the work and office of our Lord Jesus Christ, and

(iv) the inward work of the Holy Spirit in the heart of man.[2]

The focus is doggedly persistent: 'We say that life eternal is to know Christ, believe in Christ, abide in Christ, have daily communion with Christ, by simple personal faith, and that everything in religion is useful so far as it helps forward that life of faith, but no further.'[3] Third, Ryle's direction in these volumes is the *holiness of the believer*

---

[1] J. I. Packer, *Faithfulness and Holiness* (Wheaton, IL: Crossway, 2002), p. 11.

[2] J. C. Ryle, *Knots Untied* (London: Thynne, 1898, 10th ed.), pp. 2-7.

[3] *Ibid.*, p. 4.

in all of life. The 'true grace of God', Ryle writes, 'is a thing that will always make itself manifest in the conduct, behaviour, tastes, ways, choices and habits of him who has it. It is not a *dormant* thing.'[1] Commenting on the Sermon on the Mount and Jesus' reference to salt and light, Ryle writes: 'It will never do to idle through life, thinking and living like others, if we mean to be owned by Christ as his people. Have we grace? Then it must be *seen*.—Have we the Spirit? Then there must be *fruit*.—Have we any saving religion? Then there must be a difference of habits, tastes, and turn of mind, between us and those who think only of the world. It is perfectly clear that true Christianity is something more than being baptized and going to church. "Salt" and "light" evidently imply *peculiarity* both of heart and life, of faith and practice. We must dare to be singular and unlike the world, if we mean to be saved.'[2]

John Charles Ryle, born in 1816, the son of a Macclesfield silk manufacturer and banker who went bankrupt in 1841, became, in 1880, at the age of sixty-four, the first bishop of the city and diocese of Liverpool, serving in this capacity until his death at the age of eighty-four. Educated at Eton and Christ Church, Oxford, Ryle left university determined to become a politician, an ambition denied him by his father's bankruptcy. Bishop Ryle's life is truly a 'riches to rags' story, one which shaped the contours of his approach to the Christian life thereafter. Converted in 1837 (Ryle was twenty-one), following his massively successful university education, Ryle, as the eldest son, managed the compulsory sale of his family's 1,000-acre property, an experience that almost undid him. Four years later, in 1841, he entered the ministry, initially as a curate in a parish in Exbury, Hampshire, in the New Forest, a position from which he would resign (for health reasons) after five months. In 1843, he was preferred to the rectory of St Thomas, Winchester, and the following year to Helmingham, Suffolk. In 1861 he resigned it for the vicarage of Stradbroke in the same county. In 1869, he was made rural dean of Hoxne, and in 1872 honorary canon of Norwich.

In April 16, 1880, having been offered the Deanery of Salisbury, Ryle was summoned to meet the Prime Minister, Benjamin Disraeli,

[1] *Ibid.*, p. 6.
[2] *Matthew*, p. 30, commenting on Matt. 5:13-20.

in London where he was offered the bishopric of Liverpool. He would occupy the post for the next twenty years until his death.

Ryle married three times but his first two wives died young. The first marriage was on 29 October 1845, to Matilda Charlotte Louisa, the second, in March 1850, to Jessy, daughter of John Walker, and the third, on 24 October 1861, was to Henrietta. He had a daughter by his first wife, and three sons by his second wife.

What can you expect upon turning to J. C. Ryle's *Expository Thoughts on the Gospels*? Confining ourselves to one or two brief quotations from each of the seven volumes, thoughts like these:

On the ease of forsaking Christ

How many, under the influence of excited feelings, have promised that they would never be ashamed of Christ! They have come away from the communion table, or the striking sermon, or the Christian meeting, full of zeal and love, and ready to say to all who caution them against backsliding, 'Is thy servant a dog, that he should do this thing?' And yet in a few days these feelings have cooled down and passed away: a trial has come and they have fallen before it. They have forsaken Christ![1]

On viewing Christ in the Old Testament

We know from our Lord's own words in another place, that the Old Testament Scriptures 'testify of Christ' (John 5:39). They were intended to teach men about Christ, by types, and figures, and prophecy, till he himself should appear on earth. We should always keep this in mind, in reading the Old Testament, but never so much as in reading the Psalms. Christ is undoubtedly to be found in every part of the Law and the Prophets, but nowhere is he to be found, as in the Book of Psalms. His experience and sufferings at his first coming, are the subjects of many a passage in that wonderful part of God's word. It is a true saying that we should look for Christ quite as much as David, in reading the Psalms.[2]

[1] *Matthew*, pp. 296-7, commenting on Matt. 26:47-56.
[2] *Expository Thoughts on the Gospels: Mark* (Edinburgh: Banner of Truth Trust, 2012), p. 210, commenting on Mark 12:35-44.

And again, to the disciples on the Emmaus Road,

> Christ was the substance of every Old Testament sacrifice, ordained in
> the Law of Moses. Christ was the true Deliverer and King, of whom
> all the judges and deliverers in Jewish history were types. Christ was
> the coming Prophet greater than Moses, whose glorious advent filled
> the pages of the prophets. Christ was the true seed of the woman who
> was to bruise the serpent's head,—the true seed in whom all nations
> were to be blessed,—the true Shiloh to whom the people were to be
> gathered,—the true scapegoat,—the true brazen serpent,—the true
> High Priest of whom every descendant of Aaron was a figure. These
> things, or something like them, we need not doubt, were some of the
> things our Lord expounded to them on the way to Emmaus.[1]

On the Lord's Supper

> ... he that comes without faith has no right to expect a blessing.
> Empty he comes to the ordinance and empty he will go away.
>   The less mystery and obscurity we attach to the Lord's supper, the
> better will it be for our souls. We should reject with abhorrence the
> unscriptural notion that there is any oblation or sacrifice in it,—that
> the substance of the bread and wine is at all changed,—or that the
> mere formal act of receiving the sacrament can do any good to the
> soul. We should cling firmly to the great principle laid down at its
> institution, that it is eminently a *commemorative* ordinance, and that
> the reception of it without faith and a thankful remembrance of the
> sacrifice can do us no good.[2]

On being ashamed of Christ

> The wickedness of being ashamed of Christ is very great. It is a proof
> of unbelief. It shows that we care more for the praise of man whom
> we can see, than that of God whom we cannot see.—It is a proof of
> ingratitude. It shows that we fear confessing him before man who was
> not ashamed to die for us upon the cross. Wretched indeed are they

[1] *Expository Thoughts on the Gospels: Luke* (Edinburgh: Banner of Truth, 2012),
vol. 2, p. 373, commenting on Luke 24:13-35.
[2] *Luke*, vol. 2, pp. 295-296, commenting on Luke 22:14-23.

who give way to this sin. Here, in this world, they are always miserable. A bad conscience robs them of peace. In the world to come they can look for no comfort. In the day of judgment they must expect to be disowned by Christ to all eternity, if they will not confess Christ for a few years upon earth.[1]

On the sinfulness of sin and the need for a Redeemer

Would we know ... the exceeding sinfulness of sin? Let us often read these first five verses of St John's Gospel. Let us mark what kind of being the Redeemer of mankind must needs be, in order to provide eternal redemption for sinners. If no one less than the Eternal God, the Creator and Preserver of all things, could take away the sin of the world, sin must be a far more abominable thing in the sight of God than most men suppose. The right measure of sin's sinfulness is the dignity of him who came into the world to save sinners. If Christ is so great, then sin must indeed be sinful![2]

On the death of Christ

We must never suppose for a moment that our Lord had no power to prevent his sufferings, and that he was delivered up to his enemies and crucified because he could not help it. Nothing could be further from the truth than such an idea ... The plain truth is, that our Lord submitted to death of his own free will, because he knew that his death was the only way of making atonement for man's sins. He poured out his soul unto death with all the desire of his heart, because he had determined to pay our debt to God, and redeem us from hell. For the joy set before him he willingly endured the cross, and laid down his life, in order that we, through his death, might have eternal life. His death was ... the death of a triumphant conqueror, who knows that even in dying he wins for himself and his people a kingdom and a crown of glory.[3]

---

[1] *Luke*, vol. 1, p. 238, commenting on Luke 9:23-27.
[2] *Expository Thoughts on the Gospels: John* (Edinburgh: Banner of Truth Trust, 2012) vol. 1, p. 3, commenting on John 1:1-5.
[3] *John*, vol. 2, p. 140, commenting on John 10:10-18.

YOU MUST READ

On abiding in Christ

To abide in Christ means to keep up a habit of constant close communion with him,—to be always leaning on him, resting on him, pouring out our hearts to him, and using him as our Fountain of life and strength, as our chief Companion and best Friend.—To have his words abiding in us, is to keep his sayings and precepts continually before our memories and minds, and to make them the guide of our actions, and the rule of our daily conduct and behaviour.[1]

[1] *John*, vol. 3, p. 78, commenting on John 15:7-11.

10

The Autobiography of C. H. Spurgeon:
Vol. 1: The Early Years; Vol. 2: The Full Harvest

Jonathan Watson

IN AN attic of 45 Sunningdale Park, Bangor, Northern Ireland, an old cardboard box lay undisturbed for about fifteen years. Then, in about 1980, a young Christian lad discovered it when rummaging through the loft looking for something else. Curiosity got the better of him; temporarily halting his search, he sat down and lifted up the lid of the box. Inside lay a few strange items. There was a large black leather-bound Bible, written, it seemed, by a man called Scofield! Sitting next to this massive tome were a few other old and well-worn books, considerably smaller in size. The author of these bore a name the young lad wasn't quite sure how to pronounce—it certainly wasn't a name commonly found among the good people of Ulster: 'Charles Haddon Spurgeon'. The books were *All of Grace*, and *John Ploughman's Talk, or Plain Talk for Plain People.*

Through the friendly cautions of a much older and wiser Christian, the *Scofield Bible* was soon put back in the box and returned to the roof-space, never to see the light of day again. But *All of Grace* and *John Ploughman's Talk* were kept to hand, read, and re-read often. In fact they became the first books in my new Christian library. The pencil markings they bear on their thick, yellowed pages, made in my grandfather's hand, only further endear these precious volumes to me. They remind me not only of the vital godliness of my grandfather, but also of the value Spurgeon's writings have had to at least three generations of Christians since the great preacher's death in 1892.

These books were my first introduction to the writings of C. H. Spurgeon, and I have to confess that he has since become my favourite author. Over the years since I made the exciting discovery of the two Spurgeon titles mentioned above, I have bought all sixty-three volumes of Spurgeon's sermons and many of his other books. Among them, the choicest are the abridged two-volume edition of his autobiography, *The Early Years* and *The Full Harvest*.[1] I love to read Spurgeon because I find such help and encouragement from his life and his writings.

But just in case you have not heard of Spurgeon before or know little about him, let me give you a brief outline of his life.

A summary of his fifty-seven years

Charles Haddon Spurgeon was born on June 19, 1834 in Kelvedon, Essex. He was the eldest of seventeen children born to John and Eliza Spurgeon. When he was just eighteen months old he was taken to live with his grandparents at their home in the village of Stambourne. There he lived until about the age of seven or eight. This arrangement may have been the result of poverty in his parents home, or because of his mother's health; we cannot be sure of the reason, but the fact is that his grandparents had the greater share in his early education, certainly in those formative years of his childhood. Then he went back to join his parents, who by this time had moved to Colchester. Both his grandfather and father were ministers of the gospel in Congregational or Independent chapels. Spurgeon went to school in Colchester, then for a year to a school in Maidstone. He was by then fourteen and already seemed to know as much as his teacher, so at the age of fifteen he went to Newmarket to be a tutor in a school there. A year later, in 1850, he took up another position as a teacher's assistant in a Cambridge school, and remained there until 1853.

Converted at fifteen and baptised not long before his sixteenth birthday in 1850, he preached his first sermon in 1851. Not long after in the same year, he became the part-time pastor of the small Baptist church at Waterbeach, a few mile outside Cambridge. Three years later he was invited to preach in London. He was only nineteen

[1] C. H. Spurgeon, *The Early Years* (London: Banner of Truth Trust, 1963) and *The Full Harvest* (Edinburgh: Banner of Truth Trust, 1973) have been reprinted often.

and a completely unknown figure when his voice was first heard in London at New Park Street Chapel, Southwark on December 19, 1853. The congregation soon called him to be their pastor and in that congregation (which moved to the newly built Metropolitan Tabernacle in 1861) Spurgeon remained until his death on January 31, 1892. So he served for almost forty years in London. He died in the South of France, in the Riviera town of Mentone, near the Italian border, his health utterly broken, at the age of fifty-seven.

That is but a brief summary of his life—brought up in East Anglia, 'the Galilee of England' as he used to call it; surrounded by a great deal of Puritan and Nonconformist influence, with godly parents and grandparents; preaching in London from 1854 to 1891; his last sermon at the Metropolitan Tabernacle delivered on June 7, 1891, and then dying the following January.

Let me now share with you some of the ways in which Spurgeon's writings, particularly his autobiography, encourage me.

His devotion to Christ

Spurgeon's devotion to Christ encourages me to love the Lord. At the age of fifteen and just a few weeks after his conversion he could write: 'I feel now as if I could give up everything for Christ and then I know that it would be nothing in comparison to his love.' From the time of his conversion Spurgeon's life was to be one long exposition of Paul's words to the Philippians, 'For me to live is Christ'—obedience to Christ, consecration to Christ: his time, his talents and all that he was, he happily gave to the Lord Jesus from that moment on.

And how did he fare? Did he live to regret his life of devotion to the Saviour? Judge for yourself—these were his last words in the Metropolitan Tabernacle, spoken on 7 June 1891:

If you wear the livery of Christ, you will find him so meek and lowly of heart that you will find rest unto your souls. He is the most magnanimous of captains. There never was his like among the choicest of princes. He is always to be found in the thickest part of the battle. When the wind blows cold he always takes the bleak side of the hill. The heaviest end of the cross lies ever on his shoulders. If he bids us carry a burden, he carries it also. If there is anything that is gracious, generous, kind, and tender, yea, lavish and superabundant in love, you always find it in him. His service is life, peace, joy. Oh, that you would enter on it at once! God help you to enlist under the banner of JESUS CHRIST!

His commitment to Scripture

Spurgeon's commitment to the Bible as the inspired, inerrant and infallible word of God encourages me to treasure the Holy Scriptures above all else. His ministry, from the early 1850s to the 1890s, coincided with a period of widespread departure from the Protestant view of the Bible as the inspired word of God. The battle between the old and the new divinity became particularly fierce in the 1880s, the last decade of Spurgeon's life. But throughout his life and ministry Spurgeon remained faithful and true to Scripture. 'The Bible is not God', he once said, 'but it is God's voice, and I do not hear it without awe.' He held to the inerrancy and infallibility of the Bible. 'We will not have it that God, in his Holy Book makes mistakes about matters of history, or of science, any more than he does upon the great truths of salvation. If the Lord be God, he must be infallible; and if he can be described as in error in the little respects of human history and science, he cannot be trusted in the greater matters.'

Spurgeon was no professional clergyman who merely read the Bible in order to preach it to others. His personal commitment to Scripture is best summed up in these words: 'Oh, to have the word of Christ always dwelling inside of us;—in the memory, never forgotten; in the heart, always loved; in the understanding, really grasped; with all the powers and passions of the mind fully submitted to its control!'

His grasp of the doctrines of grace

Spurgeon's understanding of the doctrines of grace encourages me to avoid the pitfalls of Hyper-Calvinism on the one hand and Arminianism on the other. What a debt we all owe to Iain Murray for *The Forgotten Spurgeon* and *Spurgeon vs. Hyper-Calvinism*—books which show us so clearly from Spurgeon's own writings and sermons the relation of the doctrines of grace to the rest of Scripture teaching! Reading Spurgeon on the grace of God in the gospel always leads to worship and praise, and you will want to respond by exclaiming: 'What a great God! What a great Saviour! What a great salvation!

Praise God from whom all blessings flow!' I will never forget the time I discovered and first read his sermon about the Syro-Phoenician woman coming to Christ ('How to Meet the Doctrine of Election', *Metropolitan Tabernacle Pulpit*, vol. 30, #1797). What a warm, passionate, and winsome way Spurgeon had of preaching the grace of God in the gospel! He offered Christ most freely to lost sinners, and yet in a way that did no violence to the perfect harmony of the whole counsel of God as revealed in Scripture.

His dependence on the Holy Spirit

Spurgeon's dependence on the Holy Spirit, as manifested in his strong emphasis on prayer, encourages me. His example and teaching remind me that orthodoxy is never enough. We need the Spirit's presence and power—and those who feel this need to pray continually for divine help just as Spurgeon himself did.

That emphasis struck me forcibly as I read through in one sitting the little Banner of Truth paperback volume entitled *The Letters of C. H. Spurgeon*. Time and again the great man confessed his utter reliance upon the Holy Spirit. Take just one example of this dependence—the letter he sent to the members of the Pastors' College Association inviting them to attend the conference of 1891:

> College Conference again! O that the Lord would be in our midst this year in the fulness of his grace and power, and may we each one know it. Come up to the feast if you can, and bring HIM with you, for our one great longing is to meet the KING himself. Being of one heart and soul, as I trust we are, we come together with one accord and wait for the one Spirit. HE will be the subject of our thoughts and prayers, and the object of our praises, and we shall need his sacred aid that by his light we may see himself. I implore you to join with me in special private pleadings with God for a remarkable blessing. We cannot ask too much …

His pursuit of holiness

Spurgeon's lifelong pursuit of holiness encourages me to do the same. Hebrews 13:7 tells us to 'Remember your leaders, those who spoke to you the word of God. Consider the outcome of their way of life, and imitate their faith.' What a wonderful, yet heart-searching and stimulating book is Spurgeon's *Lectures to My Students*. Who can read chapters like 'The Minister's Self-Watch', or 'The Minister's Private Prayer' without being humbled and emptied of self and pride—and yet at the same time thoroughly stirred up to pursue holiness of life and character?

> It will be in vain for me to stock my library, or organize societies, or project schemes, if I neglect the culture of myself; for books, and agencies and systems are only remotely the instruments of my high calling; my own spirit, soul, and body, are my nearest machinery for sacred service; my spiritual faculties and my inner life are my battle axe and weapons of war.

His compassion for the lost

Spurgeon's compassion for lost souls encourages me to keep before my mind the great goal of the Christian's life:

> Go on to win other souls. It is the only thing worth living for. God is much glorified by conversions, and therefore this should be the great object of life.

His compassion for the lost and his great God-centred longing to win them for Christ is perhaps no more clearly seen than in a letter Spurgeon wrote to a young boy called Arthur Layzell. Arnold Dallimore was shown this highly prized letter by Arthur's son, George Layzell of Ontario, Canada.

> My Dear Arthur Layzell,
> I was a little while ago at a meeting for prayer where a large number of ministers were gathered together. The subject of the prayer was 'our children'. It soon brought tears to my eyes to hear those good fathers pleading with God for their sons and daughters. As they went on entreating the Lord to save their families my heart seemed ready to burst with strong desire that it might be so. Then I thought, I will write to these dear sons and daughters, to remind them of their parents' prayers.

But Spurgeon did much more than simply tell the children of their fathers' prayers. In this letter to young Arthur Layzell the great preacher of the Victorian era tenderly yet persuasively pleaded with the young lad to be saved:

You need what father and mother seek for you and you need it now. Why not seek it at once? I heard a father pray, 'Lord, save our children, and save them young.' It is never too soon to be safe; never too soon to be happy; never too soon to be holy. Jesus loves to receive the very young ones … I pray you think of heaven and hell, for in one of those two places you will live forever. Meet me in heaven. Meet me at the mercy seat. Run upstairs and pray to the great Father, through Jesus Christ.

Yours very lovingly,
C. H. Spurgeon

Dallimore adds a few interesting details to this letter: 'Although sick, tired, and very busy, Spurgeon took time to write to a boy—one whom he had never met and of whom he had learned through the prayers of his parents.'[1]

'He that winneth souls is wise' was one of Spurgeon's often-quoted Scripture references. Oh that all who read these pages might have the same sincere compassion for the lost and perishing as resided in the tender heart of C. H. Spurgeon!

[1] Arnold Dallimore, *Spurgeon, A Biography* (Edinburgh: Banner of Truth Trust, 2014) pp. 228-30.

II

Exposition of the Epistle to the Romans

Robert Haldane

Maurice Roberts

ALDANE'S great commentary on *Exposition of the Epistle to the Romans*,[1] has played an important part in my life.

It is often said that a man is known by his friends. It might as truly be said also that a man is known by his books. What we read shapes our whole outlook on life. If we are correct in thinking that the mind is the primary faculty of the soul then it must follow that our character, outlook and worldview must be the natural results of our lifetime of reading. I must pay tribute to the above-mentioned book. It is representative of a large number of Christian books which have shaped my theology and my attitude to God, to truth and to devotion.

Allow me to be autobiographical for a while so as to explain what I have just said about the importance and influence of books. I was converted to Christ in 1957 while studying classics at one of the colleges of Durham University. Up to that date my reading had not been in the Bible. My one ambition was to become a teacher. Somehow I had from an early age been fond of books. While still a teenager I had taken the bus from my home-town of Sale, in Cheshire, to Manchester, where I had discovered a second-hand book-maker existed. It is hard to say why one loves dusty old books! But some of us seem to be born with that instinct. In those days a teenage boy had only half-a-crown or so to spend each week. But my option was to spend it on one or two old books from the Manchester

---

[1] *Exposition of the Epistle to the Romans* (London: Banner of Truth Trust, 1958).

open-air market. The result was that as time went on I had a small but growing collection of old and yet treasured writers: well-known novelists of Victorian days, and poets like Milton, Wordsworth and Scott. Noticing that my little book collection had no Bible I purchased a small-print Authorised Version, which had in it the *Book of Common Prayer* as well!

This is where I was at when, as an undergraduate, I was brought to faith in Christ as a young person of eighteen. Under God I owe my conversion to another student, who kindly and yet faithfully witnessed to me and led me to a good meeting of the Christian Union. By grace I was saved, and, again, by God's marvellous grace, I lived to see my dear sister saved and also our dear parents, now in glory.

When grace changes our heart it also alters our reading habits too. The old collection was removed and another class of books now began to enter the home which reflected the importance of knowing Christ as Saviour. These early Christian books were evangelical and helpful to a young convert. But there was much still to learn. Let me say briefly how I met the doctrines of Calvinism. The experience is related to Haldane on Romans.

I was a converted believer for about three years before I saw the importance of Reformed theology. A fellow Christian in the university Christian Union had for some time been reading the sermons of Dr Martyn Lloyd-Jones. One day he asked me the question: 'For whom did Christ die?' 'For all men', was my answer. 'Then why are not all saved?' he replied. The force of this logic changed my life!

I now bought Calvin's *Institutes*, recently republished in 1957 by James Clarke of London. The price on this priceless work at that date was about twenty-five shillings, and I scrupled to spend so much in case it was 'bad stewardship'!

I was moving towards the doctrines of grace. Another very important event for me about this time was listening to Iain Murray preach to our Christian Union members at a pre-term conference, held, I think, in the Lake District. I had never before heard such excellent exposition of the word of God. I was now launched on the journey to an understanding of the grand reformed faith, albeit as yet a very raw beginner.

How then did Haldane cross my path? It was in the home of the dear friend mentioned above who had asked me, 'For whom did Christ die?' He had a complete set of the recently published American edition of Robert Haldane on Romans. I was very ignorant about biblical commentaries at the time. But I took down, as I remember, one of the green-backed slender volumes of this commentary and I read Haldane's expository thoughts—I think they were based on a verse in Romans 7. I felt the comments were solid, helpful and wise.

The Banner of Truth Trust edition had come out in 1958, with an interesting foreword by Dr Lloyd-Jones. I am grateful to God that in his kind providence I came to possess and to prize this *Exposition of Romans*. It has both love and life; and it always treats the Bible as the inerrant and infallible word of God.

Robert Haldane's life is very interesting and deserves to be well known. His dates were 1764–1842. His family was wealthy, and he lived on his estate at Airthrey near Stirling in Scotland. He had, before his conversion, been sympathetic towards the politics of the French Revolution. But he was converted through the influence of David Bogue, minister in Gossport, and for the rest of his life he laboured to spread the gospel at home and abroad.

He laid out many thousands of pounds in support of the Society for Propagating the Gospel at Home. This worthy society prepared men for the ministry, printed Bibles and published religious tracts. Robert, together with his younger brother, James Alexander Haldane (1768–1851), did a great deal to promote the gospel in Scotland. Crowds would gather to listen to the 'Haldane preachers', in a day when Scottish church life had become sadly all too dead in the national church, because of the Moderatism of that time.

In 1816, when he was about fifty years of age, Robert Haldane went to Switzerland and to Geneva. Here, in God's providence, he met some students who were preparing for the ministry. They had no proper understanding of God's word and, indeed, appear to have been entirely unconverted. But Robert Haldane invited them to the rooms where he was staying at Geneva, and in this way he expounded to them the Epistle to the Romans.

As Dr Lloyd-Jones puts it in his foreword: 'One by one they were converted, and their conversion led to a true Revival of religion, not only in Switzerland, but also in France.' Among the young men who were in this way converted to faith in Christ were J. H. Merle d'Aubigné, Fredéric Monod and César Malan.

The *Exposition of the Epistle to the Romans* was published by Robert Haldane at the request of the men named above who had been so much blessed through hearing his exploits in his rooms in Geneva. This fact needs to be borne in mind. Haldane's commentary is not just valuable as a faithful exposition of Paul's great Epistle to the Romans. It is a book full of gospel light, love, and life. The teaching here had kindled the fires of true religious awakening and revival in Europe. Men's lives had been transformed by the truths of Holy Scripture.

It is important to know these background facts relating to the publication of this *Exposition of Romans*. It is a reminder to us that our own beloved land of Britain very much needs to be awakened and revived. Our own generation of churchgoers needs to feel again the *power* of the grand old truths which God has revealed in his word.

To state the matter like that is to stir up important questions in our own minds. What was it in the Epistle to the Romans which led to a religious revival on the continent in Haldane's day? Could the same truths, under God's blessing, be the means of a much-needed revival in our own day? These are questions which lead us to look again at the Epistle to the Romans itself.

The first point of excellence in Haldane's exposition of Romans is stated in the very first verse of his preface: 'All scripture is given by inspiration of God.' Here is where every expositor of God's holy word ought to start. He goes on to say: 'In the New Testament, the Epistle to the Romans is entitled to peculiar regard. It is the only part of Scripture which contains a detailed and systematic exhibition of the doctrines of Christianity ... More especially, the glorious doctrine of justification by faith is clearly unfolded and exhibited in the strongest light.'

Those who love truth must hate error. This is very clearly seen all through this excellent *Exposition of Romans*. Haldane, to protect his readers from theological error, faithfully and tirelessly warns against the teachers of German Neology (theological Liberalism). All through the book he conscientiously exposes the dangerous mistakes of Professor Moses Stuart of America (1780–1852), of Professor

Friedrich August Tholuck (1799–1877) of Germany, and of Dr James Macknight (1721–1800), a Scottish minister, who wrote what Haldane describes as a 'well-known heterodox commentary'! In so combating the evil of false teaching Robert Haldane was not indulging in unkind criticism but following in the steps of his great Master, the Lord Jesus Christ, who affirmed the truth but also exposed the falsehood of the Pharisees.

The systematic way in which Paul opens up the entire subject of man's salvation is very faithfully reflected in this admirable *Exposition*: the universal sinfulness of all mankind, justification by faith alone without works, the inability of the moral law to save men, the union of all believers with Christ in a state of grace, and the comforts enjoyed by the true believer in this life in spite of his many sufferings.

What does Haldane make of the 'righteousness of God' (Rom. 1:17)? It is God's marvellous solution to man's greatest problem: 'God has provided for him a righteousness—the complete fulfilment of the law in all its threatenings and all its precepts—by which, being placed to his account through faith, he is acquitted from guilt, freed from condemnation, and entitled to the reward of eternal life.'[1] How Luther would have jumped for joy if he had had this *Exposition* in his early days as a monk and before he saw the true meaning of 'the righteousness of God' in the gospel!

How does Haldane view Christ in his work as our propitiation? 'By a propitiation is meant that which appeaseth the wrath of God for sins and obtains His favour.'[2] In this way, he says, 'God was pacified towards believers in Jesus Christ, and made favourable to them, the demands of His law and justice being satisfied, and every obstruction to the exercise of His mercy towards them removed.'[3] On the nature of the believer's sanctification Haldane is equally clear: 'The sanctification of believers rests on the same foundation, and springs from the same source, as their justification, namely, their union with Jesus Christ … the one cannot exist without the other.'[4] So much for the objection that justification by faith alone breeds Antinomianism!

[1] Haldane, *Exposition of the Epistle to the Romans*, pp. 48-9.
[2] *Ibid.*, p. 150.
[3] *Ibid.*, p. 150.
[4] *Ibid.*, pp. 243-4.

It is worth noting that Haldane takes the view that Paul in Romans 7:14-25 refers to himself in a regenerate, not in a pre-regenerate, state. Hence, he argues, when Paul refers to himself with the words 'I am carnal' (Rom. 7:14), Paul must not be understood to be speaking of an unregenerate state: 'It does not imply that he was not regenerated, but shows what he was even in his renewed state ... Every Christian in this sense is carnal; in himself he is corrupt.'[1]

One text which has often been misunderstood is Romans 8:29: 'For whom he [God] did foreknow he also did predestinate ...' The danger is to suppose that God 'foreknows' in the sense of knowing in advance. The Arminian error is to imagine that God predestinates those whom he foresees are going to choose Christ. Haldane makes it clear that foreknowledge in this text refers to love on God's part: 'Those whom God foreknew—those whom He before loved, chose, acknowledged as His own—He predestinates ...' The Christian owes his salvation, not to his own free will, but to God's electing love. Here is a doctrine which humbles us all as believers and which ought to make us fall on our faces before Almighty God for his sovereign, undeserved love and kindness to his own dear people.

I would like to mention one final strand of teaching which Haldane gives us in this fine commentary. It is his interpretation of Romans 11 and the future of the Jewish people. We sometimes refer to this as the 'Puritan hope'. The view held by Haldane concerning the Jewish nation is one which has deeply influenced the present writer. He understands that the apostle, in chapter 11 of Romans, teaches us to expect that God will some day bring the Jewish nation to see that Christ is their true Messiah. Not all orthodox commentators have understood Romans 11 in this way. But surely this is the only adequate way to understand Paul's teaching at this point. Haldane interprets Romans 11:11 this way: 'His [God's] design in their stumbling was not that they should fall for ever, but rather that through their fall salvation should come to the Gentiles, and that, through this, the nation of Israel might ultimately receive the Messiah.'[2] Haldane clearly looked for the restoration of Israel some day in the future. He believed that one day God will graft the Jewish people as a body back

[1] *Ibid.*, p. 292.
[2] *Ibid.*, p. 532.

into his church. The Jews have been largely in a state of opposition to the Christian gospel since the beginning of New Testament times. But this will not continue forever. God will one day graft the Jews as a people back into his church and they will be richly blessed and will also be a rich blessing to the entire world. Haldane puts it like this: 'If the casting away of the Jews was such a blessing to the world, their recall will be a blessing unspeakably greater.'[1]

I must confess that this teaching deeply influences my own prayers. I have for years felt a deep love for the Jewish people and I have made it my frequent prayer that God will hasten their 'ingrafting', to use the Apostle Paul's word in Romans 11:23.

It is a pleasure to commend Haldane's *Exposition of the Epistle to the Romans* to readers young and old. This is a commentary in the English language which loves God's truth and most helpfully opens out this encyclopaedic Epistle of Paul.

Would that God would raise up a fresh generation of Bible-loving and theologically profound preachers who will open up God's word to our unbelieving age as Haldane did to his!

[1] *Ibid.*, p. 534.

12

Historical Theology
William Cunningham

Keith Underhill

MY AIM in drawing attention to this book is to get people to read it! It has a very prosaic and unpretentious title,[1] and when you find that it consists of two large volumes, totalling around 1,250 pages, you may not find it to be a very inviting prospect. But this book is so relevant to our day. Let me explain why.

Historical Theology was first published in 1862. It was reprinted by Banner of Truth in 1960 as a volume in what was originally called the Students' Reformed Theological Library. The reprint is prefaced by a valuable biographical introduction by Iain H. Murray.

William Cunningham was a gifted Christian. J. J. Bonar spoke of him as 'a great man who lived a great life',[2] and that is saying something when we consider that the mid-nineteenth century was an era when there were many bright stars in the galaxy of the Scottish church. Iain Murray, with the hindsight of a century, went so far as to say that Cunningham was 'one of the strongest and noblest sons of Scotland and one of the most illustrious divines that has ever lived since the days of the Apostle Paul'![3] His exceptional abilities were evident early in his student days. 'Nothing could exhaust his enormous appetite for study and he was never satisfied with a

[1] *Historical Theology: A Review of the Principal Doctrinal Discussions in the Christian Church since the Apostolic Age.*

[2] William Cunningham, *Sermons* (1872), Preface.

[3] William Cunningham, *Historical Theology*, vol. 1 (London: Banner of Truth, 1960), p. xx.

superficial view of any subject.'[1] In debate and controversy his speech was 'fraught with varied information, closely argumentative in its style, sharp in repartee, terrible in invective, merciless in its exposure of fallacies, and yet translucently clear in expression, without any flowers of rhetoric'.[2] He was able 'to seize leading principles and to state the essential points of difference between opposing systems of thought'.[3] It is such characteristics that make Cunningham's *Historical Theology* so valuable to the reader today.

In 1847 Cunningham became the Principal of the newly formed Free Church College in Edinburgh. Murray claims that the college rose to be the finest theological school in Europe, and that this was due in no small measure to the leadership of William Cunningham.

Cunningham was also a great preacher. Bonar considered that, except for the sermons of Jonathan Edwards, there were no sermons more eminently fitted to strike, wound, and then heal the heart.[4] His preaching surpassed his great reputation for argumentative skill, boundless reading, and intellectual prowess. And it had the same characteristics as his theological lectures: unadorned, to the point, rigorous, and direct.

Cunningham occupied the chair of church history at the Free Church College and had very particular views about how the subject was to be taught. The historian of the church, he believed, must contribute to the *theological* education of the student and therefore must not merely narrate the external events of church history. Not content simply to ask what was believed at different times in the church's history, Cunningham was above all concerned with the most practical and ultimate question in which the theologian is interested, namely, 'What is true?' 'The benefit to be derived from this method depends on compression and compendious handling; everything falls away excepting this question ... What was truly in debate? What was the real argument in the case? ... And what was it all worth when summed and sifted?' His biographers Rainy and Mackenzie in their day claimed they knew of no comparable work to Cunningham's

[1] *Ibid.*, p. viii.

[2] R. Rainy and J. Mackenzie, *Life of William Cunningham* (London: T. Nelson and Sons, 1871), p. 40.

[3] *Historical Theology*, vol. I, p. xxi.

[4] *Ibid.*, p. xxx.

Historical Theology.[1] One hundred years later Iain Murray reckoned that still nothing even approximating Cunningham's work in value had been written.[2]

As Cunningham surveys the history of doctrine he fully deals with the three main systems of error: Romanism, Socinianism, and Arminianism. In various forms they remain powerful alternatives to a truly biblical faith in the present day. Certainly Cunningham's *Historical Theology* has by no means lost its relevance for us today. If we believe, as Cunningham did, that the great doctrines of the faith were held and confessed by God's people in ages past, then Cunningham's work will greatly help us to understand the central issues involved in their maintenance and defence so that we in turn can stand firm for the truth in our generation. When it comes to theological study we do not need to 'reinvent the wheel': new teachings are often only the old heresies in new dress.

I bought *Historical Theology* in 1971 when I started seminary. But it was not until 1978 that I began to study the two volumes seriously and systematically when setting out on my life's work as a church planter in Kenya. At the beginning of my ministry I set apart an hour after lunch for theological study each day. For church history I chose Cunningham's *Historical Theology* and soon found that it complemented my love for systematic theology. Cunningham gave me an appreciation for his kind of church history which I soon discovered was much more than a mere knowledge of facts, dates, and biographies, edifying as these may be. In the context of what I was seeking to do in Kenya, the planting of a biblical, *i.e.*, a reformed church, church history as Cunningham taught it reminded me of the vital and foundational importance of purity of doctrine.

Early in my ministry in Nairobi I began the work of training pastors and I introduced them to the writings of William Cunningham. While there will be some difficulties to overcome by anyone attempting to study a nineteenth-century textbook (and that is especially true for those whose first language is not English), the rewards are well worth the effort. Convinced of the benefit to be gained by a close study of Cunningham's great work, I set approximately four hundred pages

[1] *Life of William Cunningham*, p. 229.
[2] *Historical Theology*, vol. i, p. xxii.

of his *Historical Theology* as required reading in both the systematic theology and church history units of our theological training course. Recently I was delighted to read the following testimonial about the value of studying Cunningham, written by one of my students:

> I particularly love that common thread holding Cunningham's *Historical Theology* together: God has always had a church on earth, a remnant. She has been threatened with extinction, buffeted by oppression and cruelty, yet true to her Master's words the gates of hell have not prevailed against her. Her footprints have indelibly remained upon the sands of time.

As an introduction to Cunningham's work I would encourage a new reader to dip into Cunningham's treatment of (1) the Trinity and (2) the will.

Cunningham on the Trinity

Cunningham deals very helpfully with what is a most complex subject and he does so in just forty pages.[1]

The doctrine of the Trinity was a battleground in the first centuries of the church's history and it is a doctrine that continues to be attacked in many quarters today. Cunningham clearly summarizes the long-drawn-out discussions that took place concerning this doctrine in the early church and shows how the truth of the doctrine of the Trinity was firmly established. He then presents the doctrine in two parts, showing firstly in what sense the three persons of the Trinity are equal, and secondly in what sense they are to be distinguished from each other. Cunningham excels in his ability of presenting the basic issues involved in this controversy, and in so doing allows us to see the truth in all its clarity. It was this ability that made his public disputation so powerful, and his writings so valuable.

Cunningham on the bondage of the will

A second section a new reader might explore is the helpful treatment of the bondage of the fallen human will and in particular Cunningham's answers to the objections raised concerning the total inability of sinful man to do anything spiritually good.[2] As is characteristic of

[1] *Historical Theology*, vol. 1, pp. 267-306.
[2] *Ibid.* pp. 588-613.

Cunningham (we must remember that he is writing *historical* and not *systematic* theology) he takes us back to basics and does not get lost in detail. He first notes that the basic objection comes not from any specific statement of Scripture to the effect that fallen man does possess such ability. Rather the objection is an inference drawn from what men often consider to be a general principle of Scripture, 'Responsibility implies ability.' This principle has two parts:

(1) God could not have addressed such commands to men unless they were able to obey them.[1]

(2) An ability to obey is necessary in order for there to be true responsibility.[2]

Before giving his response, Cunningham shows that there is conclusive evidence from Scripture for the fact of the bondage of the will. The objectors only bring forward 'general reasonings', so the key to the argument is: 'Is there anything in the general reasonings of the objectors above stated, that is so clearly and certainly *both* true and relevant, as to warrant us, on that ground alone,—*for there is no other*,—summarily to reject this evidence, or to resolve at all hazards to explain it away?'[3] Cunningham's insistence on what the central arguments are make his *Historical Theology* a work of great value. He puts aside much that is secondary to get to the heart of the matter.

In relation to the first part of the objection Cunningham takes objectors to task for asserting that God could not have any good reasons for commanding men if they were unable to obey. This is tantamount to claiming to judge all the reasons why God should do something. For example, man as created was obligated and able to obey the moral law, but his fall does not invalidate his obligation. Rather God continues to press the demands of his law on his creatures in order to convict them of their fallenness. As regards the commands to repent and believe for salvation, a knowledge of inability is designed to make sinners seek the grace of God, and is the instrumentality through which God imparts his strength.

Cunningham regards the second part of the objection as the real difficulty. It is one thing to state that God does command men

[1] *Ibid.*, p. 589.
[2] *Ibid.*, p. 590.
[3] *Ibid.*, p. 590.

to do what they are not able to do. But how can God hold men *responsible* for what they are not able to do? Moral responsibility is a given because it is scriptural. Yet inability is likewise plainly and explicitly taught in the Bible. Cunningham proceeds to evaluate the common explanation which distinguishes between natural and moral inability, and finds it doubtful.[1] He then puts forward the doctrine of the imputation of Adam's first sin to all his progeny as a more satisfactory explanation. Man 'is answerable for that inability itself, having, as legally responsible for Adam's sin, inherited the inability, as part of the forfeiture penally due to the first transgression'.[2]

This example of the way Cunningham deals with objections to an established doctrine, by showing where the real problems lie, is the unparalleled strength of Cunningham's *Historical Theology*. He sweeps aside 'straw men', exposes fallacies, and deals with the real issues.

Value of Cunningham for today

I cannot commend too highly a serious study of Cunningham's *Historical Theology*. It was written by a man who was renowned in his day as a skilled theologian, debater, and preacher. By careful argumentation he *persuades* the reader of the truth. He does not deal with irrelevant theological matters, but with the great issues, the foundational doctrines of the faith upon which our eternal welfare depends, and which have been hammered out in the course of history on the anvil of controversy.

[1] *Ibid.*, pp. 602-5.
[2] *Ibid.*, pp. 610.

13

The Great Christian Doctrine of Original Sin Defended

Jonathan Edwards

———————————

R. C. Sproul

IN 2002, a survey by the Barna Group polled Americans' understanding of religious issues.[1] The survey revealed a startling lack
of knowledge about the teaching of the Bible, as more than half
of those surveyed agreed with the following unbiblical statements:
praying to deceased saints can have a positive effect in a person's life
(51%); Satan does not exist, but is merely a symbol of evil (59%); and
anyone who is good enough or who does enough good can earn a
place in heaven (50%).

Earning overwhelming assent from those polled was this statement:
'When people are born they are neither good nor evil—they make a
choice between the two as they mature.' Seventy-four per cent said
they agreed.

Clearly, the myth that we have within us the power to be good is
alive and well. Thanks to the influence of secular humanism, which
teaches that people are basically good, generations of people are
growing up believing that sin is not deadly, that it is not inherent to
our nature, that it is just a little defect or flaw on the surface.

At one time I held similar beliefs, as I followed a Semi-Pelagian

---

[1] 'Americans Draw Theological Beliefs from Diverse Points of View', The Barna
Group, published October 8, 2002, accessed June 11, 2014, http://www.barna.org/
barna-update/article/5-barna-update/82-americans-draw-theological-beliefs-from-
diverse-points-of-view.

view of conversion. I rejected what Augustine called 'total moral inability', that my soul and my will were in bondage and dead to the things of God. Instead, I believed that although I needed the help of the Spirit to come to Christ, ultimately, I had an island of righteousness in me, and a little bit of power left to assent to and agree with the influence of the Spirit or to reject it. The final choice in the matter of salvation was mine.

Jonathan Edwards changed all that. I studied his classic work *The Freedom of the Will* in depth and found his arguments, especially on Romans 9, compelling and irrefutable. I fought him tooth and nail, but in the end, I was convinced that I had been teaching and believing what I wanted the Bible to say rather than what it actually said. To this day, I owe Edwards a huge debt of gratitude.

Edwards' most famous works are *Freedom of the Will* (1754), *Religious Affections* (1746), and his sermon *Sinners in the Hands of an Angry God* (1741). But I believe the church would be greatly served by paying more attention to one of his lesser-known works.[1]

In *The Great Christian Doctrine of Original Sin Defended* (1758), Edwards was not replying to any specific author, but he was moved to write what he called a 'general defence' of this important doctrine. He says of it in his preface: 'I look on the doctrine as of *great importance*; which every body will doubtless own it is, if it be *true*. For, if the case be such indeed, that all mankind are by *nature* in a state of *total ruin*, both with respect to the *moral evil* of which they are the subjects, and the *afflictive evil* to which they are exposed, the one as the consequence and punishment of the other; then, doubtless, the great *salvation* by CHRIST stands in direct relation to this *ruin*, as the remedy to the disease; and the whole *gospel*, or doctrine of salvation, must *suppose* it; and all real belief, or true notion of that gospel, must be built upon it.'[2]

Much of the controversy over human free will is waged in the context of speculative debate over the relationship of man's freedom

---

[1] Portions of this chapter are excerpted from R. C. Sproul, *Willing to Believe: The Controversy over Free Will* (Grand Rapids, MI: Baker, 1997), pp. 147-53. Used by permission.

[2] Jonathan Edwards, *The Great Christian Doctrine of Original Sin Defended: Evidences of Its Truth Produced, and Arguments to the Contrary Answered*, in *The Works of Jonathan Edwards, A.M.*, 10th ed., 2 vols. (1865; Edinburgh: Banner of Truth Trust, 1979), vol. 1, p. 145. The author's preface is dated 1757.

to God's knowledge, or to election and reprobation. For Edwards, the central issue of free will is rooted in the ancient controversy (as between Pelagius and Augustine) over the relationship of free will to man's fallen nature and ultimately to his redemption through the gospel. In a word, Edwards focuses on the broader issue of the necessity and sufficiency of grace. This same motive drove Martin Luther in his debate with Erasmus: the concern to see *sola fide* solidly rooted in *sola gratia*, to affirm that our fallenness is so severe that God and God alone could give us faith to trust in Christ. For Edwards, the greatness of the gospel is visible only when viewed against the backdrop of the greatness of the ruin into which the fall has plunged us. The greatness of the disease requires the greatness of the remedy.

Evidence for original sin

One interesting facet of Edwards' defence of the classical view of the fall and original sin is his attempt to show that, even if the Bible were silent on the matter, this doctrine would still be evident to natural reason. Since the phenomena of human history demonstrate that sin is a universal reality, we should seek an explanation for this reality. In simple terms the question is, Why do all people sin?

Even the most sanguine critics of human nature, those who insist that man is basically good, repeat the persistent axiomatic aphorism 'Nobody's perfect.' Why is no one perfect? If man is good at the core of his heart and evil is peripheral, tangential, or accidental, why does not the core of goodness in us win out over the evil that is not inherent in us? Even in the society in which we find ourselves today, in which moral absolutes are widely denied, people still readily admit that no one is perfect.

Consider this from a different angle: if humans are born with no default inclination to sin, one would think that at least fifty per cent of people in this world would end up sinless. But we all know that this is clearly not the case. There is clearly something morally deficient in every human being. The light of nature itself gives a hearty 'Amen' to what the Bible teaches so clearly.

People claim a commitment to moral relativism, but when someone steals from us, we cry foul. Suddenly the credo that 'everyone has the right to do his own thing' is challenged when the other person's 'thing' conflicts with my 'thing'. Edwards saw in the universal *reality* of sin manifold evidence for a universal *tendency* toward sin. Edwards states:

> If any should say, Though it be evident that there is a tendency in the state of things to this general event—that all mankind should fail of perfect obedience, and should sin, and incur a demerit of eternal ruin; and also that this tendency does not lie in any distinguishing circumstances of any particular people, person, or age—yet it may not lie in *man's nature*, but in the general constitution and frame of *this world*. Though the nature of man may be good, without any evil propensity inherent in it; yet the nature and universal state of this world may be full of so many and strong temptations, and of such powerful influence on such a creature as man, dwelling in so infirm a body, etc. that the result of the whole may be a strong and infallible tendency *in such a state of things*, to the sin and eternal ruin of every one of mankind.
>
> To this I would reply, that such an evasion will not at all avail to the purpose of those whom I oppose in this controversy. It alters not the case as to this question, Whether man, in his present state, is depraved and ruined by propensities to sin. If any creature be of such a nature that it proves evil in its proper place, or in the situation which God has assigned it in the universe, it is of an evil nature. That part of the system is not good, which is not good in its place in the system; and those inherent qualities of that part of the system, which are not good, but corrupt, in that place, are justly looked upon as evil inherent qualities. That propensity is truly esteemed to belong to the *nature* of any being, or to be inherent in it, that is the necessary consequence of its nature, considered together with its proper situation in the universal system of existence, whether that propensity be good or bad.[1]

Edwards then draws an analogy from nature to illustrate his point:

> It is the *nature* of a stone to be heavy; but yet, if it were placed, as it might be, at a distance from this world, it would have no such quality. But being a stone, is of such a nature, that it will have this quality or tendency, in its proper place, in this world, where God has made it, it is properly looked upon as a propensity belonging to its nature.

[1] *Ibid.*, p. 151, col. a.

... So, if mankind are of such a nature, that they have an universal effectual tendency to sin and ruin in this world, where God has made and placed them, this is to be looked upon as a pernicious tendency belonging to their nature.[1]

Edwards concludes that within the nature of man there is a propensity toward sin. This inclination is part of the inherent or constituent nature of man. It is natural to fallen mankind. When Scripture speaks of 'natural man', it refers to man as he is since the fall, not as he was created originally. The fall was a real fall and not a maintenance of the status quo of creation.

Concerning the *preponderance* of evil deeds over good ones, Edwards says, 'Let never so many thousands or millions of acts of honesty, good nature, etc. be supposed; yet, by the supposition, there is an unfailing propensity to such moral evil, as in its dreadful consequences infinitely outweighs all effects or consequences of any supposed good.'[2]

Edwards goes on to point out the degree of wickedness and heinousness that is involved in merely one sin against God. Such an act would be so wicked, because it is committed against such a holy being, that it would outweigh the sum of any amount of contrasting virtue. 'He that in any respect or degree is a transgressor of God's law', Edwards says, 'is a wicked man, yea, wholly wicked in the eye of the law; all his goodness being esteemed nothing, having no account made of it, when taken together with his wickedness.'[3]

At this point, Edwards echoes the sentiment of James, saying that to sin against one point of the law is to sin against the whole law[4] and, of course, the Lawgiver himself. Likewise, Edwards says works of obedience, strictly speaking, cannot outweigh disobedience. When we are obedient, we are merely doing what God requires us to do. Here we can be nothing more than unprofitable servants.

Edwards sees evidence for man's depraved nature in the propensity of humans to sin immediately, as soon as they are morally capable of committing actual sin. He sees further evidence in the fact that man

[1] *Ibid.*
[2] *Ibid.*, p. 152, col. a.
[3] *Ibid.*, p. 152, col. b.
[4] James 2:10-11.

sins continually and progressively, and that the tendency remains even in the most sanctified of men. Edwards also finds significant what he calls the 'extreme degree of folly and stupidity in matters of religion'.[1]

In a cursory look at human history, Edwards provides a catalogue of woes and calamities that have been perpetrated by and on the human race. Even the most jaded observer of history must admit that things are not right with the world. Then Edwards turns to the universality of death as proof for the universality of sin. In the biblical view, death came into the world through and because of sin. It represents the divine judgment on human wickedness, a judgment visited even on babies who die in infancy. 'Death is spoken of in Scripture as the *chief* of calamities', Edwards notes, 'the most extreme and terrible of all natural evils in this world.'[2]

The Bible and original sin

Edwards then turns his attention to the scriptural warrant for the doctrine of original sin. He pays particular attention to Paul's teaching in Ephesians 2.

> Another passage of the apostle, to the like purpose with that which we have been considering in the 5th [chapter] of Romans, is that in Ephesians 2:3— 'And were by nature children of wrath, even as others.' This remains a plain testimony to the doctrine of original sin, as held by those who used to be called orthodox Christians, after all the pains and art used to torture and pervert it. This doctrine is here not only plainly and fully taught, but abundantly so, if we take the words with the context; where Christians are once and again represented as being, in their first state, *dead in sin*, and as *quickened* and *raised up* from such a state of death, in a most marvelous display of free *rich grace and love*, and *exceeding greatness of God's power, etc.*[3]

With respect to the uniform teaching of Scripture, Edwards concludes:

[1] *Great Christian Doctrine of Original Sin Defended*, *Works*, vol. 1, p. 156, col. b.
[2] *Ibid.*, p. 173, col. a.
[3] *Ibid.*, p. 197, col. b.

As this place in general is very full and plain, so the doctrine of the corruption of nature, as derived from Adam, and also the imputation of his first sin, are both clearly taught in it. The *imputation of Adam's* one transgression, is indeed most directly and frequently asserted. We are here assured, that 'by one man's sin, death passed on all.' ... And it is repeated, over and over, that 'all are condemned', 'many are dead', 'many made sinners', etc. 'by one man's offence', 'by the disobedience of one', and 'by one offence'.[1]

Finally, Edwards argues for original sin from the biblical teaching regarding the application of redemption:

It is almost needless to observe, how evidently this is spoken of as *necessary* to salvation, and as the change in which are attained the habits of true virtue and holiness, and the character of a true saint; as has been observed of *regeneration, conversion, etc.* and how apparent it is, that the change is the *same.* ... So that all these phrases imply, having a *new heart*, and being *renewed in the spirit*, according to their plain signification.[2]

This, then, is the sum of Edwards' teaching on original sin: because we are fallen and in bondage to sin, we must be converted by the work of the Holy Spirit. The Spirit's work is the antidote to our corrupt condition, and it alone can bring us out of that condition.

For this reason, Edwards stressed the need to place confidence in the power of the word rather than in technique, methodology, or eloquence. While forceful delivery or emotional manipulation may elicit a response, too often there is the danger of false professions of faith. Edwards warned against thinking you have saving faith when you have not truly been converted, for it is through the word that the Spirit ordinarily brings about conversion.

This is crucial to remember in our day, when false professions are common, even in the church. The call for us is to be as faithful and accurate as possible in proclaiming the word, because through it the Spirit transfers people out of their fallen, dead condition and brings them into new life.

[1] *Ibid.*, vol. 1, p. 210, col. b.
[2] *Ibid.*, vol. 1, p. 214, col. a.

14

Evangelical Eloquence

Robert L. Dabney

Hywel Jones

WHEN R. L. Dabney's book was first reprinted in 1979 it bore the original title—*Lectures on Sacred Rhetoric.* Twenty years later this was altered to something more contemporary in an attempt to commend it to any who might have found the classical term 'rhetoric' unfamiliar or unacceptable. *Evangelical Eloquence* was chosen for this purpose because it was Dabney's own.[1] Now, almost two decades later, the term has reappeared in political and journalistic comment with the expression 'That's just rhetoric.'

Unlike the rhetoric of the first and the twenty-first centuries 'Sacred Rhetoric' neither embellishes nor exaggerates. Instead it allows the biblical text to regulate the form and the content of the sermon. 'It will communicate a peculiar earnestness, tenderness and authority. Its influence will extend to the structure, the style, the utterance and the gesture, making all more serious, more paternal, more elevated than they are in him who pleads the affairs of earth.'[2] In his own work on Homiletics, John A. Broadus described Dabney's book as 'a valuable and suggestive treatise on the theory of preaching, [containing] many judicious observations and sound principles'.[3]

---

[1] *Evangelical Eloquence* (Edinburgh: Banner of Truth Trust, 1999), p. 31, fn.

[2] *Ibid.*, p. 48.

[3] John A. Broadus, *On the Preparation and Delivery of Sermons.* Ed. E. C. Dargan. (Birmingham, Al: Solid Ground Christian Books, 2005), p. 548.

Dabney outlines his thesis as follows:

If this work has any peculiarities to which value may be attached, they are these: that the necessity of eminent Christian character is urged throughout as the foundation of the sacred orator's power, and that a theory of preaching is asserted, with all the force which I could command, that honours God's inspired word and limits the preacher most strictly to its exclusive use as the sword of the Spirit. If my readers rise from the perusal with these two convictions enhanced in their souls—that it is grace which makes the preacher, and that nothing is preaching which is not expository of the Scriptures—my work is not in vain.[1]

It is generally admitted that preaching had poor ratings in the nineteenth century. By preachers' giving an ear to the academy's refusal to recognize the text of Scripture as God's written word, his living and life-giving voice ceased to be heard in the church—and nowhere was this more evident than in college sermon classes where the hermeneutical confusion of the lecture room echoed loudly in the homiletical cacophony of the chapel.

The orthodox doctrine of Scripture has now been largely recovered and with it a hermeneutical approach that respects the canonical text. But the discipline of homiletics needs to be given a higher priority in both the evangelical and reformed world. The notion that preaching was something that could not be 'taught' but had to be 'caught' is still common among evangelicals and the reverse is common among the reformed. Among 'evangelicals' preaching often sat loose to the data of the biblical text and context and consequently a sermon could lack a firm biblical foundation. Among the 'reformed' a sermon was often more like an exegetical and doctrinal paper than a message from the Lord to his people. The former could do with becoming more didactic, especially as there is a growing aversion to theological training; the latter, more prophetic—and on both sides, more congregationally related. Dabney's book was an absolute Godsend to this writer because he had the privilege and responsibility of helping men on both sides of the Atlantic improve their preaching.

[1] *Evangelical Eloquence*, p. 7.

Robert Lewis Dabney was born in 1820 in the state of Virginia. Almost all of his nearly four score years were spent there and he loved the 'Old South' deeply. He farmed its soil and quarried its stone; he taught its children, managed an estate, preached to its soldiers and prepared its pastors. He was a close associate of 'Stonewall' Jackson and a respected leader in the Southern Presbyterian Church. He advocated moderation in the disputes between North and South before enlisting in the Civil War. Whether he ever completely recovered from the defeat of the Confederacy is doubtful. He composed many articles on the social and ecclesiastical questions of his day[1] and wrote a *Defence of Virginia* and *The Life and Campaigns of Stonewall Jackson*. Although he died in Texas he was buried in Farmville, Virginia, in full Confederate uniform. His guiding text, 'Prove all things; hold fast to what is good', was engraved on his tombstone.

His college studies at Hampden-Sidney were twice interrupted because the family plantation needed supervision following his father's early death. He graduated Master of Arts in 1842 and two years later began theological studies at Union Theological Seminary which he completed without interruption. In 1846 he was licensed to preach by West Hanover Presbytery, ministering first in his home church and then at Tinkling Spring from July 1847 to August 1853. He reconstructed the building and saw the work greatly revived. Broadus heard him preach there on John 4:35[2] and recorded that it was 'one of the most powerful sermons with which he was acquainted'.[3]

In 1853 Dabney was invited to lecture in church history and government at Union. Six years later he was moved to the chair of systematic theology—a discipline in which A. A. Hodge regarded him as being without equal.[4] Building on the other theological disciplines he lectured on *pulpit rhetoric* for almost twenty years.

[1] Several of the latter are found in, *Discussions: Evangelical and Theological*, 3 vols. (London: Banner of Truth Trust, 1967) and T. C. Johnson, *The Life and Letters of R. L. Dabney* (Edinburgh: Banner of Truth Trust, 1977).

[2] See 'The World White to Harvest: Reap, Or It Perishes', in R. L. Dabney, *Discussions*, vol. 1, pp. 575-95.

[3] Quoted in Sean Michael Lucas, *Robert Lewis Dabney: A Southern Presbyterian Life* (Philipsburg, NJ: P&R Publishing, 2005), p. 61.

[4] See his *Lectures on Systematic Theology* (Edinburgh: Banner of Truth Trust, 1985).

Rhetoric was a staple of education in the Graeco-Roman era and notable thinkers such as Aristotle, Cicero and Quintilian wrote on the subject. Dabney was well aware of this and quotes from them, sometimes supplying translations. He also refers to the writings of J. W. Alexander[1] and W. G. T. Shedd[2] but did not think that a book which was suitable for his class-work existed. He therefore resolved 'to attempt the construction of such a course as would be an adequate guide to an evangelical Protestant preacher'.[3] At the request of many he eventually put his lectures into written form but they still retain an oral character and contain striking expressions and graphic illustrations.

There are twenty-four lectures in this book which address fourteen subjects. Most of them relate to the preacher and to his sermons. The first two lay the foundation for all that follow. In the first the idea that Paul was outlawing all rhetoric in 1 Corinthians is disposed of by means of the records of Paul's own preaching which was 'honest, simple, modest and (self) disinterested' in contrast to the 'tricks of logic and diction' of the Greek sophists and also by differentiating between 'art' and 'artifice'. For Dabney there was 'a true art of preaching which [was] not only lawful and honest, but sacredly obligatory'.[4] A survey of the history of preaching follows with a list of some factors which contributed to its decline.

In the second he identifies the minister's mission as that of 'preach[ing] the gospel for the salvation of souls'.[5] Such preaching should connect 'all the powers of the speaker's soul' with those of 'the hearer' via 'a particular species of eloquence'. It is 'the emission of the soul's energy through speech'.[6] It necessitates 'sincere, eminent piety' on the part of the speaker[7] and special attention is given to this matter in a subsequent lecture. Dabney depicts this earnestness in a memorable illustration:

[1] J. W. Alexander, *Thoughts on Preaching* (Edinburgh: Banner of Truth Trust, 1975).

[2] W. G. T. Shedd, *Homiletics and Pastoral Theology* (New York: Scribner, Armstrong & Co. 1867).

[3] *Evangelical Eloquence*, p. 6.

[4] *Ibid.*, p. 16.

[5] *Ibid.*, p. 41.

[6] *Ibid.*, p. 32.

[7] *Ibid.*, p. 40.

The preacher's task may be correctly explained as that of (instrumentally) forming the image of Christ upon the souls of men. The plastic substance is the human heart. The die which is provided for the workman is the revealed word; and the impression to be formed is the divine image of knowledge and true holiness. God, who made the soul, and therefore knows it, made the die. He obviously knew best how to shape it, in order to produce the imprint he desired. Now the workman's business is not to criticise, recarve, or erase anything in the die which was committed to him; but simply to press it down faithfully upon the substance to be impressed, observing the conditions of the work assigned him in his instructions. In this view, how plain is it, that preaching should be simply representative of Bible truths and in Bible proportions! The preacher's business is to take what is given him in the Scriptures, as it is given to him, and to endeavour to imprint it on the souls of men. All else is God's work.[1]

The next twelve lectures deal with 'the structure, the style, the utterance and the gesture' of such sermons. They concentrate on the *Distribution of Subjects* (the arrangement of material); *the Text*; the *Cardinal Requisites of the Sermon*, namely textual fidelity, unity, instructiveness, evangelical tone or unction (not the same as animation but 'gravity and warmth united'), *Movement, Point* and *Order*. Over the years what Dabney says about *Movement, Point and Order* has proved to be particularly useful to students. Adhering to a single theme and unfolding it he constructs an address that combines lucid purpose with memorable effect. Another of Dabney's analogies reinforces this. He writes:

The pointed or incisive discourse may be likened as to its framework to the ancient war-ship [galley]. Its weapon of offence was its beak [prow]. Let us suppose that the architect had left the ponderous mass of pointed metal which formed this beak lying in some accidental position amidst the timbers of the ship, and all those timbers a disorderly heap of rubbish merely thrown together and set adrift upon the sea as a raft. The impact of this shapeless pile instead of piercing the opposing trireme, would only have dissolved itself into fragments; and the intended prow would probably have sunk out of sight without even coming into the feeblest contact with the enemy's

[1] *Ibid.*, p. 37.

hull. The architect, therefore, commits no such folly. He places the beak at the forefront of his structure. He causes the chief beams of its framework to converge to its base, and frames them into it. He adjusts the ribs and braces to support these in turn, so that there is not one piece of timber in the whole ship which does not lend its strength, either directly or remotely, to sustain the prow immovably in its place. And now, when the triple banks of rowers raise their chant and strain at their oars all in concert, they launch the pointed beak into the adversary's side with the *momentum* of the whole ship's weight.[1]

Nine lectures follow which deal with more formal matters, namely the component parts of a sermon and how they should be arranged namely *Constituent Members of the Sermon* and the *Sources, Rules and Division of Argument* (supporting evidence). Dabney does not insist that these should all be followed rigorously but only that to some degree they should be present in the preacher's mind in the details of his preparation. In a lengthy footnote[2] he treats Romans 3:20 by way of an example of what such preparation should involve. Reformed preachers who want to include good works along with faith as instruments of justification and evangelicals who try to preach *sola fide* without making use of the law of God should read those pages.

There are two lectures on the most important subject of *Persuasion* which is not something to be added to exposition but wedded to it. The whole sermon should be persuasive in character. This cannot be done without emotion being kindled, both in the speaker and in the hearer. Dabney is well aware that 'an appeal to feeling' is often made at the expense of truth and he regards that as reprehensible and dangerous. But some emotions are part of human nature as divinely created. They are 'moral' and 'spiritual' and so are consonant with the truth and inseparable from a proper reception of it. They are all present in fallen man and when roused by the truth they echo the verdict of the conscience in its favour so that the whole man responds to God. Persuasion is 'spiritual logic' and 'of this art … he is the greatest master who seems to have none'.

Two lectures each on *Style* and on *Action*, one on *Modes of Preparation* and one on *Public Prayer* bring the work to a conclusion.

---

[1] *Ibid.*, pp. 126-7.
[2] *Ibid.*, pp. 226-9.

Style is 'grammatical purity (correctness), perspicuity, energy and especially seriousness'. *Action* includes 'utterance' (variation of pitch and volume) and 'gesture' that is appropriate but unselfconscious. *Preparation* is done by one of three ways, namely 'writing, writing and memorising and extemporising'. In Dabney's view reading a manuscript 'can never, with any justice, be termed preaching'. Extemporising is endorsed with the cautionary note that more premeditation should be done because less will encourage diffuseness and confusion in the actual delivery of the message. 'Writing and memorising' is what Dabney favours. This he explains as producing a manuscript of two-thirds of the sermon and familiarising oneself with the 'geography of the manuscript' thus leaving room for 'a commerce of eye and countenance between the speaker and his hearers, by which they mutually stimulate each other. The mind thus roused, having the advantage of its previous premeditation and thorough knowledge of the subject, grasps it with more vigour than it had ever done in solitude. Indeed all the powers of the soul are now exalted … the emotions of the hour dictate an action natural, flexible and animated.'[1]

The final lecture is given to *Public Prayer* because 'the principles which regulate pulpit eloquence apply also to [its] devotional parts'.[2] The whole of worship is to express 'the transcendent weight of eternal things' and to resist 'the tendencies of man towards the sensuous and forgetfulness of the spiritual life'.[3] The lecture contains a section of the neglected *Directory of Public Worship of the Westminster Divines* and also acknowledges the work of Samuel Miller, Archibald Alexander's colleague at Princeton.[4]

Dabney's great concern was that sermons should accord not only with the content of the biblical text but also with its literary features so that the preached material might resound with God's voice. He believed that there was a kind of human speech which suited God's word. It was structured but also spirited; clear but never cold; strong and yet sweet; humbling yet exalting. In his view 'the state of the pulpit

[1] *Ibid.*, p. 334.
[2] *Ibid.*, p. 345.
[3] *Ibid.*, p. 42.
[4] Samuel Miller, *Thoughts on Public Prayer* (Philadelphia: Presbyterian Board of Publications, 1849).

may always be taken as an index of that of the Church. Whenever the pulpit is evangelical, the piety of the people is in some degree healthy; a perversion of the pulpit is surely followed by spiritual apostasy in the Church.'[1]

[1] *Evangelical Eloquence*, p. 27.

15

Tracts and Letters

John Calvin

Ian Hamilton

I N EARLY 1969 a friend gave me a copy of Robert Haldane's *Exposition of the Epistle to the Romans*. I was a young Christian and had just started university in Glasgow. A little later, I came across John Murray's *Redemption Accomplished and Applied*, and so began a lifelong love affair with such books.[1] Murray's book especially was a turning point in my young Christian life. I hadn't realised how deep and broad and glorious the gospel is!

As I approached my final year at university I had to choose a dissertation topic. Although my degree was in economic history I was resolved, if possible, to write on 'John Calvin and the Struggle for the Reformed Faith in Geneva'. My professor was kindly indulgent and because he knew my heart was set upon studying theology agreed to my somewhat surprising dissertation title. A year or so earlier I had read a brief biography of Calvin, *The Man God Mastered*, by Jean Cadier. I was intrigued and then somewhat overwhelmed as I read of Calvin's courage and faith as he sought to serve the gospel of God's grace in the most turbulent of times. Since then I have owed more to Calvin, under God, than to any other writer in shaping and filling my understanding of the Christian life and, more importantly, in shaping and filling my understanding of who God is.

Calvin was a remarkable Christian man. He was a theologian without compare ('The Theologian' according to Philip Melanchthon). He was a wonderful biblical commentator. He wrote great theological

[1] See above, pp. 79ff., and below, p. 201ff., for more about these two titles.

treatises. But Calvin was first and foremost, certainly in his own eyes, a pastor. It is in his *Tracts and Letters*[1] that, perhaps most memorably, we see the heart of Calvin the pastor, and it was a large and capacious heart.

Over the past thirty-four years I have aspired to be a faithful pastor in Christ's church, serving two congregations, Loudoun Church of Scotland and Cambridge Presbyterian Church. During those years Calvin has been a model I have sought to emulate (along with two or three living models!). It is my hope that the following excerpts will highlight the faithfulness, courage, generosity and catholicity of this man that God mastered, Christian qualities that the Banner of Truth Trust has sought to promote through its books.

The Christian pastor as a servant

When Calvin was effectively dismissed from Geneva in 1538, he left without any sense of rancour or bitterness. Something of his humble spirit is seen in the letter he wrote shortly after he had been exiled: 'Here, therefore, with the most fervent salutation written by my own hand, do I supplicate the Lord Jesus, that he may protect you in his holy fortress of defence; that he may heap on you his gifts more and more; that he may restore your Church to due order, and specially, that he may fill you with his own spirit of gentleness, so that in the true conjunction of soul we may every one bestow ourselves in the promoting of his kingdom. Your most devoted, servant J. C.'[2] Would that every faithful minister dismissed from his congregation could exhibit the same spirit!

It was this same humble, servant spirit which brought Calvin back to Geneva in 1541. In the previous year, when Calvin's friends urged him to return to Geneva he gave them an 'over my dead body' response. In May of 1540, he wrote to Pierre Viret, 'I read that passage in your letter, certainly not without a smile, where you shew so much concern about my health, and recommend Geneva on that ground. Why could you not have said at the cross? For it would have been far preferable to perish once for all than to be tormented again in that place of torture. Therefore, my dear Viret, if you wish well to me,

---

[1] John Calvin, *Tracts and Letters,* 7 vols. (Edinburgh: Banner of Truth Trust, 2009).
[2] *Ibid.,* vol. 4, p. 149.

make no mention of such a proposal.'[1] The following year, however, he returned; why? He wrote to William Farel in August 1541, 'As to my intended course of proceeding, this is my present feeling: had I the choice at my own disposal, nothing would be less agreeable to me than to follow your advice. But when I remember that I am not my own, I offer up my heart, presented as a sacrifice to the Lord ... Therefore I submit my will and my affections, subdued and held-fast, to the obedience of God; and whenever I am at a loss for counsel of my own, I submit myself to those by whom I hope that the Lord himself will speak to me.'[2] Here we encounter the 'real' Calvin. He was not his own; he had been bought with a price. Calvin's personal emblem was a picture of a flaming heart held up in a hand with the inscription: '*Cor meum tibi offero, Domine, prompte et sincere*'—'My heart I offer to you, O Lord, promptly and sincerely.' This is a heart gripped by the gospel of God's grace in Christ (Rom. 12:1-2).

The Christian pastor as a defender of the faith

In his letter to Emperor Charles V, prefacing his treatise *The Necessity of Reforming the Church* (1543), Calvin sought to explain why he and others, following Luther, were pursuing the work of Reformation: 'If it be inquired, then, by what things chiefly the Christian religion has a standing amongst us, and maintains its truth, it will be found that the following two not only occupy the principal place, but comprehend under them all the other parts, and consequently the whole substance of Christianity, viz., a knowledge, first of the mode in which God is duly worshipped; and, secondly, of the source from which salvation is to be obtained.'[3] Calvin's concern for right doctrine was principally animated by his concern that God should be worshipped according to his revelation in Holy Scripture and not according to the traditions and ingenuities of men. The 'regulative principle' was born not out of a desire to be prescriptive, but out of a desire to worship God the way he commands us to worship him.

Calvin was also deeply concerned to recover the sovereignty of God and his grace in salvation. He was appalled by the semi-Pelagianism

[1] *Ibid.*, vol. 4, p. 187.
[2] *Ibid.*, vol. 4, pp. 280-1.
[3] *Ibid.*, vol. 1, p. 126.

of Rome's teaching on salvation. This is perhaps nowhere more passionately expressed by Calvin (while still in exile from Geneva!) than in his 1539 *Reply to Sadoleto*: 'You, in the first place, touch upon justification by faith, the first and keenest subject of controversy between us. Is this a knotty and useless question? Wherever the knowledge of it is taken away, the glory of Christ is extinguished, religion abolished, the Church destroyed, and the hope of salvation utterly overthrown.'[1] No pastor more faithfully laboured to defend the sovereignty of God's grace—not only for the sake of God's glory but also for the good and security of his flock. As we will see, Calvin was an instinctive ecumenist, but he was first and foremost a man committed to guarding the gospel (1 Tim. 6:20). This concern brought the Banner of Truth Trust into existence in the late 1950s and continues to shape the choice of books to be published.

The Christian pastor's preaching focus

Calvin the pastor never wearied of telling his congregation to get out of themselves and into Christ. In the *Institutes* he wrote, 'We have taught that the sinner does not dwell upon his own compunction or tears, but fixes both eyes upon the Lord's mercy alone.'[2] Calvin was always pleading with his people to look away to Christ. In October 1555, he wrote to five prisoners at Chambéry, who were waiting to be executed for their evangelical faith: 'If you feel in yourselves too much infirmity, have recourse to him who has every virtue in his hand.'[3] In an earlier letter to them on September 5, 1555, Calvin wrote, 'the main point is to collect all your thoughts in order to repose in his paternal goodness'.[4] Calvin was unwearying in seeking always to point his readers and hearers to Christ. Is this not the burden of pastoral ministry, to point God's people in all of their weaknesses and extremities away from themselves to our Lord Jesus Christ?

It was this gospel note that struck me so forcibly when I first read *Redemption Accomplished and Applied*. I cannot thank the Banner of Truth Trust enough for publishing this remarkable book (and I do

[1] *Ibid.*, vol. 1, p. 41.
[2] *Ibid.*, vol. 4, p. 3.
[3] *Ibid.*, vol. 6, p. 233.
[4] *Ibid.*, vol. 6, pp. 221-2. The five wrote to Calvin, 'Sir, and most honoured father, we have received your letters of the 5th September, which have greatly consoled us.'

mean 'remarkable'). Living, experiential Calvinism is anchored in the Saviour who is *extra nos—outside of ourselves*.

The Christian pastor's catholic spirit

Calvin's pastoral heart is seen in his instinctive ecumenism. This commitment to godly ecumenism is witnessed in his justly famous letter to Archbishop Thomas Cranmer: 'This other thing also is to be ranked among the chief evils of our time, viz., that the churches are so divided, that human fellowship is scarcely now in any repute among us, far less that Christian intercourse which all make a profession of, but few sincerely practise ... Thus it is that the members of the Church being severed, the body lies bleeding. So much does this concern me, that, could I be of any service, I would not grudge to cross even ten seas, if need were, on account of it.'[1] Calvin concludes his letter, 'Adieu, very distinguished Archbishop, deserving of my hearty reverence. May the Lord continue to guide you by his Spirit, and to bless your holy labours.'

Calvin also pursued peace and unity among the Protestant churches by his pastorally wise advice to churches pursuing scriptural purity in worship. In his letter to the English at Frankfurt in January 1555, Calvin urged them to recognise the perilous times they were living in and to lay aside 'contentions about forms of prayer and ceremonies'. Calvin was not saying that these matters are of no importance. He was, however, reminding the English exiles not to behave 'as if you were at ease and in a season of tranquillity, and thus throwing an obstacle in the way of your coalescing in one body of worshippers'; and, he adds, 'this is really too unreasonable'.[2]

Calvin is clearly sympathetic to the concern of the exiles. He speaks of the ceremonies they are being required to submit to as 'silly things'; however, 'silly things that might be tolerated'. He tells the exiles that regarding matters such as 'external rites', he himself is 'indulgent and pliable'; though at the same time he is quick to add, 'I do not deem it expedient always to comply with the foolish captiousness of those who will not give up a single point of their usual routine.' The exiles, and all believers, should be aiming 'at something purer' (that is, a

---

[1] *Ibid.*, vol. 5, pp. 347-8.
[2] *Ibid.*, vol. 6, pp. 117-8.

church shaped by the teaching of Holy Scripture alone). But this, Calvin is quick to acknowledge, will take time and 'faults' will not 'be corrected on the first day'.

The same patience is seen in his letter to Edward Seymour, Duke of Somerset (Lord Protector of England from 1547–49). Calvin expressed his concern that the Reformation in England was proceeding all too slowly, but continued, 'I willingly acknowledge that we must observe moderation, and that overdoing is neither discreet nor useful; indeed, that forms of worship need to be accommodated to the condition and tastes of the people. But the corruptions of Satan and of Antichrist must not be admitted under that pretext.'[1]

This letter is a timely reminder to Reformed Christians today to resist the temptation to make every hill of difficulty a hill to die on. The public unity of Christ's church should occupy a greater place in our hearts and minds than it presently appears to do. Reading the *Tracts and Letters* could be a word in season, challenging us to be proportionate in our espousal of the distinctives of the Reformed faith.

Calvin's letters constantly reflect his godly generosity of spirit and his readiness to stand alongside fellow Christians, even those like Cranmer who were not pursuing reformation in the church with the zeal that he would have liked. This generosity did not hinder him, however, from confronting even close friends with strong words of admonition. In a letter to his close friend Philip Melanchthon, Calvin wrote, 'Though you shrink from noisy contests, yet you know what Paul prescribes by his example to all the servants of Christ. Certainly you cannot desire praise for greater moderation than that which was evidenced in him. When he then, who was endowed with so much forbearance, passed intrepidly through seditions, we cannot give way where the circumstances in our times are by no means so painful. But, in one word, you should maturely consider whether your too obstinate a silence may not leave a stain on your reputation in the yes of posterity. ... If a means of pacification is sought for, our only hope lies in a conference; which I doubt not but you desire, but which I could wish that you called for more courageously.'[2] Sadly the

---

[1] *Ibid.*, vol. 5, p. 193.
[2] *Ibid.*, vol. 6, p. 337.

conference that Calvin hoped for never materialised. Melanchthon kept silent.

The *Tracts and Letters* give us an immediate access into Calvin's heart and mind. Far from being an aloof, unyielding, censorious Christian, Calvin exhibited a tenderness and generosity of spirit, along with a godly passion for truth that endeared him to friends of the gospel and anathematised him to enemies of the gospel.

One feature that surfaces again and again in Calvin's letters is his deep sense of his own weakness and need of God's help. He wrote in his *Short Treatise on the Lord's Supper*, 'If we consider our life to be placed in Christ, we must acknowledge that we are dead in ourselves; if we seek our strength in him, we must understand that in ourselves we are weak ...' Here, perhaps, is the key to Calvin's usefulness. He was no spiritual superman; he was a weak man who understood that all his strength lay in God. As Paul reminded the church in Corinth, it is when we are weak that we are strong.

So, read Calvin's *Tracts and Letters* and find yourself confronted with a godliness of spirit that will by turns shame you, humble you, challenge you, and inspire you to live more to the praise and glory of our great God and Saviour Jesus Christ.

16

The Work of the Holy Spirit

Octavius Winslow

Iain D. Campbell

B Y A HAPPY providence, my desire to write on Octavius Winslow's *The Work of the Holy Spirit* for this collection of essays
coincided with the publication of a new biography and study
of Winslow in the United States of America.[1] The author, Tanner G.
Turley, summarises Winslow's career in a sentence that justifies any
study of him anywhere: 'The profound goal of Winslow's ministry
was to proclaim Christ in all of His glory and see His people love
him supremely.'[2]

Winslow knew that without the Holy Spirit, such a goal is
impossible to attain. In the preface to his book on this subject,
Winslow writes: 'All that we spiritually know of ourselves, all that we
know of God and of Jesus, and His Word, we owe to the teaching
of the Holy Spirit; and all the real light, sanctification, strength and
comfort we are to possess on our way to glory, we must ascribe to
him.'[3]

Originally published in 1840 under the title *The Inquirer Directed
to an Experimental and Practical View of the Holy Spirit*, the first
Banner of Truth edition of Winslow's work was published in 1961,
and has been reprinted several times.

---

[1] Tanner G. Turley, *Heart to Heart: Octavius Winslow's Experimental Preaching*
(Grand Rapids, MI: Reformation Heritage Books, 2014).

[2] *Ibid.*, p. 41.

[3] Octavius Winslow, *The Work of the Holy Spirit* (Edinburgh: Banner of Truth
Trust, 1991), p. 1.

Who was Octavius Winslow?

Turley summarises Winslow's career in the following paragraph:

> Winslow served the church for nearly forty-five years as a pastor, preacher, and prolific author. He shepherded two congregations in New York City for the first five years of his ministry and spent the next forty in the English towns of Leamington Spa, Brighton and Bath. Though he served Baptist churches most of his life, he finished his ministerial career in the Church of England. He exercised a prolific ministry, publishing more than forty books, with most being printed multiple times.[1]

Winslow was born in London to Thomas and Mary Winslow in 1808. His mother, whose memoir he would write, had been converted just before he was born. Winslow had every reason to be thankful to God for her, and for the Christian influences she brought to bear on an otherwise ungodly home. 'If there was one feature in the religious life of Mrs Winslow', he writes, 'more distinct and palpable than any other, and which, as her Christianity ripened, became a yet more strongly developed, firmly rooted, and all-controlling principle of her life, it was the profound homage with which her soul bowed to the supreme authority of God's revealed word.'[2] That same submission to God's word is everywhere evident in Octavius Winslow's writings.

As was common in domestic life in that period, Thomas and Mary Winslow experienced illness, financial privation and death in their family circle. Their circumstances led them to the United States in 1815, shortly after which the father and an infant child died. Changes in circumstances led to a return to England, then back to New York where, during a revival in 1824, Octavius was converted to Christ.

During the years 1827 to 1833, as his biographer puts it, 'Winslow confessed his faith in Christ, experienced the call to the ministry, pursued theological education, and was ordained.'[3] Like his mother, Winslow had become a Baptist, and his first pastorates were in New York, in Central Baptist Church from 1833 to 1835, and in Second Baptist Church from 1836 to 1838. He married Hannah Ann Ring in

---

[1] *Heart to Heart*, p. 1.
[2] *Life in Jesus: A Memoir of Mrs Mary Winslow* (London, 1866), p. 88.
[3] *Heart to Heart*, p. 20.

1834, and returned to England five years later. They had a large family of five sons and six daughters, two of the daughters dying in infancy.

Winslow was pastor of Warwick Street Chapel in Leamington Spa from 1839 to 1857, and in many ways this was his most effective and productive period of ministry. There followed a pastorate in Kensington Chapel in Bath, from 1857 to 1867, followed by a strange turn of ecclesiastical direction when he became minister of a Nonconformist (and non-Baptist) church in Brighton. Two years later, in 1870, he was ordained a deacon in the Church of England, and served as an Anglican minister until his death in 1878.

The change in denominational and ecclesiastical affiliation has proved enigmatic; his biographer simply says that 'Winslow's transition to the Church of England has been clouded in mystery',[1] and makes a good effort at analysis. One factor may have been that, although Winslow preached at the opening of the Metropolitan Tabernacle on 4 April 1861, he distanced himself from some of Spurgeon's more caustic criticisms of Anglican clergymen, and retained a high regard for evangelical clergy within the Church of England. The distancing was highlighted by Spurgeon's criticisms of Winslow's work on Psalm 130.[2]

Notwithstanding these differences, Winslow's writings breathe a warm, irenic, gospel spirit; this, together with a high view of Scripture and a deep reverence for the Puritan approach to theology and piety, means that, as a writer, Winslow's material has sat well with the ethos of the Banner of Truth Trust. Five of his titles are still available from the Trust: *Personal Declension and Revival of Religion in the Soul*, *No Condemnation in Christ* (on Romans 8), *Help Heavenward*, *Soul-Depths and Soul-Heights* (on Psalm 130), and *The Work of the Holy Spirit*.

The Holy Spirit: an experimental and practical view

I am not sure when I first came across Winslow's work on the Holy Spirit, but two things struck me when I first read it: the biblical nature of its contents, and the simplicity of its style.

---

[1] *Ibid.*, p. 50.
[2] See T. Nettles, *Living by Revealed Truth* (Fearn, Ross-shire: Christian Focus, 2012), p. 446.

The first is indispensable, of course, to any treatment of the Holy Spirit and his work. The Spirit who gave the word in the first instance is revealed in it; we could have no knowledge of the person and work of the Spirit apart from the self-disclosure of God in the Bible. So as Winslow deals with various aspects of the doctrine of the Holy Spirit, he ransacks the text of both the Old and New Testaments. There is biblical quotation on virtually every page. That reason alone is sufficient to commend Winslow's work.

But what ought not to be forgotten is that in the mid-nineteenth century, this was not the popular topic it has become today. In the preface to his work on the same subject, Sinclair Ferguson alludes to the fact that trends in the charismatic and Pentecostal movements are such that the topic of the Holy Spirit is dealt with in a vast number of publications; he suggests that the pendulum has swung too far in the direction of 'an obsession with the powers of the Spirit', and that this, the most glorious theme in the world, is 'now well-worn'.[1]

It was not, however, in danger of being 'well-worn' when Winslow produced his book, which makes his treatment all the more worthy of our attention. For, no matter how many movements of religious experience change our perception of theological issues, we must always return to the foundation of the Bible. In that Winslow is both a sure guide and a good example.

But no less important is the simplicity of his style. He is by no means simplistic; his treatment is no shallow, surface view of the topic of the Spirit's person and work. But it is a straightforward, clearly mapped-out, easy-to-follow treatment, in which the precision of Winslow's thought is expressed in an engaging and arresting style.

That is an indication to us that he writes as a preacher, engaging his hearers with a view to their instruction, conversion and growth in personal holiness. His aim, as the original title suggests, was to be 'practical' and 'experimental', not to turn the doctrine of the Holy Spirit into a dry and arid locus of theology, but to make it applicable to the daily walk, conversations and battles of ordinary Christians. In other words, 'he made the relevance of every doctrine clear so his hearers might be sanctified'.[2]

---

[1] Sinclair B. Ferguson, *The Holy Spirit* (Leicester: IVP, 1996), p. 11.
[2] *Heart to Heart*, p. 141.

The argument of *The Work of the Holy Spirit* is clear and straightforward. Winslow begins by affirming both that the Holy Spirit is a distinct person, and that he is God. The first of these is necessary to guard against the view that the Spirit is a mere religious influence. If it is possible to blaspheme the Spirit (*Matt.* 12:31-2); if the Spirit is a servant (*John* 15:26-7); if the powers of speaking, revealing and witnessing are attributable to him; if he can be vexed, grieved and resisted, then he is a person.

Further, if the Spirit can be given the names of God, as well as the attributes which belong to God alone, such as eternity, omniscience, and so on, then we can only conclude that he is God. This, for Winslow, is the bedrock of our experience of salvation:

> so long as this doctrine is brought home with convincing power to the soul that the Holy Spirit is a distinct person from, yet co-essential, co-equal and co-eternal with the Father and the Son, then we have the comforting assurance that the experience of truth in the heart, of which He is the Author and we the subjects, is a supernatural work—the work of God the Holy Ghost.[1]

Winslow then moves on to argue that it is the work of the Holy Spirit to bring new life into the soul of man. He must impart life (as a 'Quickener', from the older translation of *John* 6:63) before he can improve life as a Sanctifier and Comforter. Winslow denies the validity of the position of baptismal regeneration; no church ordinance is the source of spiritual life. Nor is a mere change of habit in the individual, or even a profession of faith.

Nor, he argues in one of the most searching passages in the book, do gifts equal graces: 'great gifts', Winslow warns, 'may exist in union with great impiety'.[2] If the Bible's testimony to man's fallen condition means anything, it means that we have no power either to convert ourselves or to co-operate with the Spirit in our conversion. We need the sudden, sovereign, gracious and effectual work of the Holy Spirit in our hearts. By it, we are able to respond to the call of the gospel, and as a result of it, we are new creatures in Christ Jesus, known by the fruits of holiness, repentance over sin and victory over the world.

---

[1] Winslow, *The Work of the Holy Spirit*, p. 27.
[2] *Ibid.*, p. 40.

Winslow's discussion of the conflict with sin in the regenerate man is superb, as is his comfort to those who are burdened by the sin they discover in their own souls:

> The Lord has wisely, we must acknowledge, so ordained it that sin should yet remain in his people to the very last step of their journey. And for this he has graciously provided His word as a storehouse of promises, consolations, cautions, rebukes, admonitions, all referring to the indwelling sin of a believer. The covenant of grace—all its sanctifying, strengthening, invigorating and animating provision— all was designed for this very state. The gift of Jesus—all his fulness of grace, wisdom, strength and sympathy, his death, resurrection, ascension and advocacy, all this was given with a special view to the pardon and subjection of sin in a child of God.[1]

The pastoral and practical application of doctrine continues in Winslow's discussion of the Spirit indwelling a believer. The old temple stood as witness to the presence of God with his people; to make that presence permanent required the incarnation, the tabernacling, of the Son of God in our nature. 'On the dignity of [Christ's] person, finished righteousness, perfect atonement, all-sufficient grace and inviolable faithfulness, believers "as lively stones, are built up a spiritual house", for the everlasting indwelling of God the Holy Ghost.'[2]

The Spirit thus enters into our hearts at regeneration, and manifests God's glory within our souls, dwelling in us as the Spirit of grace and comfort and holiness, permanently indwelling the believer. 'There may be periods', says Winslow, 'when you are not sensible of the indwelling of the Spirit … do not forget that even then, dejected saint of God, when all is dark within and all is desolate without, then the Holy Spirit, the Sanctifier, and the Comforter and the Glorifier of Jesus, dwells in you, and shall be with you forever.'[3]

Winslow's chapter on sanctification is a consistently grace-focused and Christ-centred discussion on how we are to grow to be like God himself. In it, he is continuously urging us to keep our attention on the work of Christ, but never allowing us to slip into self-reliance or

[1] *Ibid.*, p. 76.
[2] *Ibid.*, p. 96.
[3] *Ibid.*, p. 101.

complacency. The balance of biblical truth is maintained; sanctifying us is the work of the Holy Spirit in its entirety, but we are reminded that we must feed on the word of God, and battle against sin daily.

On the sealing of the Spirit, Winslow argues that as a seal authenticates a letter, so the Christian is sealed by God. His definition of the sealing is that 'it is that act of the Holy Spirit by which the work of grace is deepened in the heart of the believer, so that he has an increasing and abiding conviction of his acceptance in Jesus and his adoption into the family of God'.[1] He equates it with the 'full assurance and understanding of faith',[2] and argues that it progresses in stages, as, beginning at regeneration, the Spirit then gives more of himself to the believer, and that it is the duty of the believer to seek it: we must not rest, says Winslow, 'until our rest is found in a clear, unclouded, immovable and holy assurance of our being in Christ; and this is only experienced in the sealing of the Spirit'.[3]

There is, however, a difficulty over this. The tense of the Greek participle translated 'sealed' in Ephesians 1:13 suggests a once-for-all action, not a work proceeding in degrees. There is considerable Puritan pedigree for Winslow's position, and it has been popularised in recent times by Dr D. Martyn Lloyd-Jones.[4] While not denying the truth of the material on assurance in Winslow's discussion, it does seem preferable to argue that the seal is the very definition of what a Christian is, rather than a subsequent assurance of sonship which varies in degrees.

On the Spirit as a Witness, as the Author of Prayer and as a Comforter, Winslow is at his best, marrying the rich doctrine of the New Testament to the daily experience of the child of God. 'More valuable and precious', he writes, 'is one grain of the truth of God experienced in the heart than the whole system occupying a place only in the judgement' (pp. 156-7). As a tender and sympathetic Comforter, the Spirit ministers to God's people in their sins and sorrows, reminding them of the Father's love and of the Son's loving care.

[1] *Ibid.*, pp. 138-9.
[2] *Ibid.*, pp. 139-40.
[3] *Ibid.*, p. 150.
[4] See D. W. H. Thomas, 'Spirit-baptism and the Clash of the Celts' in *The People's Theologian* (Fearn, Ross-shire: Christian Focus, 2011), pp. 153-71, and the discussion in Ferguson, *The Holy Spirit*, pp. 180-2.

Why we need Winslow today

If Sinclair Ferguson is correct that the pendulum has swung to the extreme of us being in danger of having too much written and published on the subject of the Holy Spirit, then we—we all, but particularly we preachers—need to return to the clear biblical parameters of our doctrine and discussion. In this, Winslow is a sure guide, for at least three reasons.

First, he insists that there is no doctrine of Scripture which is not essentially trinitarian. Time and again Winslow reminds us that the doctrine of the Holy Spirit belongs to the mystery of the being of God who is tri-personal. That forms the backdrop and foundation to every element of revealed truth. Creation, providence, atonement and salvation—these are all doctrines which emerge from the will and the work of the triune God. Any emphasis on the Holy Spirit which fails to do justice to the character of God is necessarily weakened; as a teacher of the Bible, Winslow's strength is that he brings us back to our trinitarian foundations.

Second, he underscores that there is no proper understanding of the gospel that is not essentially covenantal. Whether we express the gospel in explicitly covenantal terms or not, the good news of salvation is not just that Jesus has done something that saves; it is that through him the covenant of grace binds us to God and God to us. That note runs through Winslow's work. It is the reason we can entertain assurance. It is the place where our souls find refuge: 'we cannot imagine an exigency, a trial, a difficulty or a conflict which is not amply provided for in the covenant of grace.'[1]

Third, he emphasises that there is no experience of grace that is not entirely Christ-centred and focused. In Winslow's thought, doctrine and experience dovetail. Neither is at the expense of the other. Objectivity and subjectivity coalesce, and the depth of God's self-revelation calls to the depth of our experience, as deep calls to deep. Such a presentation of truth will deliver us from the shallow faith of much that passes for evangelicalism, and will warn us against a barren intellectualism. I cannot imagine a more pressing concern for the Reformed faith at the present time.

[1] Winslow, *The Work of the Holy Spirit,* p. 205.

17

The Apostles' Doctrine of the Atonement

George Smeaton

Jerry Bridges

I T IS ironic and somewhat amusing to me that I should be
invited to write a chapter on my favourite Banner of Truth book.
I grew up in what I describe as a semi-Arminian Baptist church.
It wasn't that I was taught that particular doctrine of salvation. I simply absorbed it. I had never even heard of Calvinism or Reformed
theology.

When I was thirty years old and in Christian ministry, a friend
asked me to read a small booklet entitled *The Doctrine of Election*. I
was shocked and deeply offended by its teaching. My reaction was
that my friend had gotten into heresy. I put the book aside without
even considering its message. The next day in an unusual way, the
Holy Spirit opened my understanding to see that the doctrine of
election is indeed true, and that I was a believer because God chose
me in Christ before the foundation of the world (Eph. 1:4).

Shortly after that I left for Europe on a transatlantic passenger
ship. During the five days' voyage I read through the New Testament
and saw the doctrine of election taught repeatedly throughout its
pages.

I don't remember how I learned of Banner of Truth books. Probably
it was through my friend back in the United States. But I discovered
a Christian bookshop near where I was living, and they carried all the
Banner's books in print at that time. My first purchase was Robert
Haldane's *Exposition of the Epistle to the Romans* in October 1961.
Other Banner commentaries soon filled my small bookshelf, and

by the time I returned to the States in 1963, I was committed to Reformed theology.

In 1991, the Banner of Truth published George Smeaton's book, *The Apostles' Doctrine of the Atonement*, the subject of this chapter. George Smeaton (1814–89) was a Scottish theologian and minister of the Church of Scotland. He was among the numerous ministers who left the Church of Scotland in 1843 to form the Free Church of Scotland. He was a student of the great Thomas Chalmers and was a classmate to such well-known men as Robert Murray M'Cheyne and the Bonar brothers, Andrew and Horatius. In 1857, he was appointed Professor of Exegetical Theology at New College, Edinburgh.

The Apostles' Doctrine of the Atonement is actually the second of a two-volume set on the atonement. The first, *Christ's Doctrine of the Atonement*, covers all that Christ taught about his atonement as recorded in the four Gospels. The second volume covers all that the apostles taught on the same subject in the remainder of the New Testament. Together these two volumes cover all that the New Testament teaches about Christ's atonement.

Without meaning to diminish in any way the importance of Christ's teaching, I would say the second volume covering the apostles' teaching is the more valuable for a thoroughly biblical understanding of the atonement. This is because the apostles wrote after Christ's accomplishment of the atonement, and were further enlightened by the Holy Spirit's infallible teaching.

To me Smeaton's book has two strengths. The first and most obvious is its thoroughness. He exegetes every passage from Acts to Revelation that teaches on the atonement. The second strength is his continued emphasis on the federal headship of Christ and his office as our representative before God in both his sinless life and his sin-bearing death. There are other excellent books that teach on our union with Christ, but Smeaton's book, by its very nature, is gloriously repetitive.

If an author on any other subject were so repetitive, we would soon put the book aside with the thought that he had said all he is going to say in the first chapter, and in subsequent chapters is just repeating himself. This is not the case with Smeaton's work. Rather by following Paul and other writers as they address different churches and different situations, he gets to the same truth from many different routes. He is like a wedding photographer who will take two dozen pictures of the bride in different poses and from different angles, and all of them are good. So Smeaton's continual emphasis on the representative nature of Christ's life and death from different perspectives gradually builds into a theological crescendo that gets the reader excited about the gospel.

This representative nature of Christ's life and death is taught most clearly in Romans 5:12-19, where Paul draws the contrast between Adam as the federal head of the entire human race and Christ as the federal head of his people, of all who trust in him. Smeaton, along with other earlier writers, makes the point that in all of human history, God has dealt judicially with only two men, Adam and Christ. All the rest of us are represented before God by one or the other.

This representative position of both Adam and Christ is utterly unique. It cannot be illustrated by analogy, for example, to legislators in a representative form of government. It is an absolute representation. What Adam did, all who are in Adam did. What Christ did, in both his sinless life and sin-bearing death, all who are in Christ did.

Smeaton's treatment of the righteousness of God (Rom. 1:17 and 3:21-22) is quite helpful in these days when the advocates of the 'New Perspective on Paul' insist that the righteousness of God is his own inherent righteousness, and not that accomplished by Christ and imputed to those who trust in him. Smeaton writes that it means 'the righteousness of which God is the author'. And again, 'this righteousness is the finished work of Christ, considered from the viewpoint of the divine approval'. It is a real righteousness lived out in a real world over thirty-three years. It is just as much a reality as sin.

Smeaton writes, 'The Son of God made flesh, and obedient in life and death, is our righteousness before God. Scripture knows of only ONE righteousness uniting God and men and the world has never seen another.' And again, '[This righteousness] is made ours not less truly than if we ourselves had rendered it, in consequence of the legal oneness formed between us and him.'

We are said to be made the righteousness of God in him. This is remarkable: we are made all that Christ was; he is the Lord our righteousness (Jer. 23:6), and we are made the righteousness of God in him (2 Cor. 5:21).

In another place, he says, 'The immediate effect of receiving the righteousness of God is the sentence of absolution, called the justification of our persons. ... This sentence is complete at once, and capable of no addition; and it has a twofold side,—the absolving of the man from any charge of guilt, and the pronouncing of him absolutely righteous, because in the possession of this righteousness of God.'

Most contemporary presentations of the gospel stress the fact that Christ died for us. This is true, but it fails to convey the truth that we are so united to Christ that we may say, Christ died for us; or we died in him. We may say he was crucified for us, or we were co-crucified with him. But to say we were co-crucified with him does not indicate a separate parallel act on our part. Rather as Smeaton so strongly emphasizes, 'We have but one public representative, corporate act performed by the Son of God, in which we share as truly as if we had accomplished that atonement ourselves.'

It is such statements that get me so excited. In effect Smeaton is saying, 'When Christ lived a perfect life, we lived a perfect life. When Christ died on the cross we died on the cross.' All that Christ did in his sinless life and sin-bearing death he did as our representative before God, so that God counts his righteousness as our righteousness and his death as our death.

My favourite verse in all the Bible is 2 Corinthians 5:21. So I was eager to see what Smeaton would say about it. Here are brief excerpts from the book on this great text:

The source of the whole atonement is traced to God, who is said to make him [sin]. The contrast is '[he] knew no sin.' That is Jesus was judged by God as completely faultless, and as never having had one feeling at variance with the divine will and law.

This sinless one, judged by God as one who knew no sin, is described as having been made sin. By God's appointment he was made sin, not in mere semblance, but in reality, not before men, but before God, on the great foundation of a federal unity between him and his people. He was, as it were, the embodiment of sin or incorporated guilt; and we may well affirm that never was so much sin accumulated upon a single head. He was not made sin in a vague, indefinite abstract way; but the very sins of which we are painfully conscious in the moment of conviction—that is, our own sins of nature and life—were laid on him, or transferred from our head to his. He bore their burden; and this rendered it possible to visit him with the recompense due to sin, and with its necessary punishment, which would otherwise have been impossible.

The end for which Christ was made sin was, THAT WE MIGHT BE MADE THE RIGHTEOUSNESS OF GOD IN HIM. The apostle again uses the abstract term, as in the previous clause. We need not dwell on the phrase 'the righteousness of God', which we already expounded at large. Let it suffice to say that here the one clause of this verse explains the other. We are made the righteousness of God in the same way in which Christ was made sin. The antithesis of the two clauses is in the highest degree important. They are both objective; they are both by imputation, not by infusion. We are, through Christ's vicarious obedience, made the righteousness of God. And this is found only in him objectively, and as we are united to him by a living faith.

Galatians 2:20 is another of my favourite verses of Scripture. In the context of verses 15-21, Paul is writing about our justification; not our sanctification. And in that context he says, 'And the life I now live in the flesh I live by faith in the Son of God who loved me and gave himself for me.' Smeaton's remarks are valuable at this point:

> Obviously, that is not the language of faith for attaining justification, but the language of a man already justified, and glorying in a sense of acceptance and the experience of grace. The spiritual life of a Christian finds its activity on the same object to which the anxious inquirer first came for pardon, with this difference, that it is now accepted in its special destination: 'who loved ME, and gave himself for ME'.

This leads to a subject very seldom taught but one which every believer needs to learn: that is, to live in the present reality of one's justification. My observation is that most Christians view belief in the gospel as a one-time event by which we are saved. After that our day-to-day relationship with God is based on our own obedience rather than the perfect obedience of Christ.

The truth is, however, that we need to live by the gospel every day. In a sense the gospel is like the manna for the Israelites in the wilderness. They could not store it up. It had to be gathered daily.

To use another metaphor, living daily by the gospel is like rowing a boat upstream against the current. The moment we take our oars out of the water we begin to drift back toward a works-righteousness relationship with God.

And so a final word for ministers. Smeaton's book is intimidating to the average believer with its five hundred pages of dense nineteenth-century prose. But it is a *valuable* book. In fact, it is not an overstatement to say it is a *necessary* book since it sets before us so clearly and emphatically that our righteousness is to be found only in Christ, not in ourselves.

My observation is that most sermons are preached and most Christian books are written to teach us how to live out the Christian life in our everyday world. But as is often observed, the *imperative* (how we ought to live) should always follow the *indicative* of what Christ has done for us in his sinless life and sin-bearing death. Unfortunately we so often neglect the indicative.

By contrast Smeaton gives us a heavy dose of the indicative. So those of us who are ministers or teachers of God's word need to absorb the message of Smeaton's book and restate it to our audiences of today in language that they can understand and incorporate into their Christian lives.

18

A Body of Divinity

Thomas Watson

Walter J. Chantry

THOMAS WATSON'S *A Body of Divinity* (along with his *The Ten Commandments* and his *The Lord's Prayer*) consists of sermons on the Westminster Shorter Catechism.

From the earliest days of Christendom churches have used creeds or catechisms as forms of words expressing articles of belief considered necessary for the wellbeing of the Christian church and for the understanding of its members. They represented foundational knowledge to be expressed before baptism or before confirmation of membership in churches. Those who were in the process of learning these creeds were called 'catechumens'.

Although many outstanding saints who loved the Scriptures laid a foundation for the great Protestant Reformation, we think of that historical season as occurring in the sixteenth and seventeenth centuries. The Reformers, from Martin Luther through to the members of the Westminster Assembly, devoted a great amount of time to composing confessions of faith and catechisms.

The Westminster Confession and Catechisms were published with an epistle entitled, 'To the Christian Reader, Especially Heads of Families'. It was signed by numerous clergymen who participated in the Westminster Assembly, including Thomas Watson. How these Reformers intended their catechisms to be used becomes clear from their epistle.

First, they viewed their catechisms' doctrines as '... the first principles of the oracles of God' (Heb. 5:12) which teachers of others must know. They urged fathers to master these truths that they might be equipped to teach their children. The lament of the Lord that 'My people are destroyed for lack of knowledge' (Hos. 4:6) is mentioned to impress on parents that catechizing their children is essential to the future godliness of their churches and to the future good character of their nations' citizens. Of course all of that is in addition to their children's eternal blessing in Christ. The catechism was to be a tool to 'Train up a child in the way he should go: so that when he is old, he will not depart from it' (Prov. 22:6), a biblical command with promise every parent should cherish.

When this expectation of parental diligence in teaching the catechism at home is enhanced by the frequent use of the catechism in church meetings by clergy and other teachers, we realize how much emphasis the Reformers and Puritans attached to doctrinal training in homes and churches. There is no more useful guide or commentary on the Shorter Catechism to assist any teacher or preacher of this recommended course of study at home, in the pulpit, or in classes and discussions within the church.

Thomas Watson's *A Body of Divinity* is a series of sermons which he presented to his London congregation on Sunday afternoons. These sermons were no 'bare-bones' rehearsal of questions and answers. Rather the sermon material is filled with Bible passages which support the catechism's answers. The preaching was also attended with a multitude of illustrations and applications of the truth being taught. Watson even put into his hearers' minds questions which they might ask in light of the biblical teaching, and he answered those questions.

From Watson's *A Body of Divinity* we catch the warm and earnest spirit of this delegate to the Westminster Assembly. Thus we also have an example of the manner in which the catechism should be taught.

However, the great importance of this book is that it enables us to understand the end to which the Westminster Divines were driving. These men of God were convinced of the saying of our Lord Jesus Christ: 'If ye continue in my word, then are ye my disciples indeed; and ye shall know the *truth* and the *truth* shall make you free' (John 8:31-32, emphasis mine). Ministers and parents must heed the exhortation of Paul to Timothy (1 Tim. 4:13), 'Till I come, give attention to reading, to exhortation, *to doctrine*' (emphasis mine). 'Hold fast the form of sound words, which thou hast heard of me' (2 Tim. 1:13).

Within their churches and their members' homes the men of the Assembly wanted to form a culture of repeated teaching of sound biblical doctrine. Their reasoning was that children would hear these things from parents, and they would hear the same teaching from pastors and teachers; thus the truths taught would be reinforced. Being 'Reformed' is more than having some sense that God is sovereign. Being 'Reformed' also involves the ordering of homes, churches and schools so as to stamp upon the minds and hearts of believers and their children the doctrines of Holy Scripture. It is an atmosphere of piety which ever echoes the summary of our mutually held faith.

When *A Body of Divinity* was republished in 1958 it had the effect of sending some of us scurrying to find and to dust off old copies of confessions and catechisms once used by various Protestant denominations. This new-found interest spurred conversation in the church about these various summaries of Bible truth. Some members of our households began teaching the catechism to small children. Now, after our children have taught their children, we delight in hearing even our great-grandchildren recite answers to the first questions of *The Children's Catechism*, just as they are learning to speak!

But alas, this had not been the culture or form of piety in which we had been raised. Now a very different culture began to emerge in both homes and churches, as the works of our fathers in the faith were rediscovered.

What had happened during the years between the sixteenth and seventeenth centuries and the times of our lives in the twentieth century to make catechisms and catechetical teaching fall out of favour with the church in the United States? In our colonial and early American years many immigrants from Reformation-era denominations settled on our continent. For example, English and Scottish Presbyterians, French Huguenot, and Dutch Reformed families were among those who arrived during that time. Additionally many early Baptists taught the Westminster standards in all but a few points.

Meanwhile churches in Europe did not remain static. The Netherlands had the Arminian controversy with which to contend. The French endured the Amyraldian conflict. None of these theological disruptions was entirely kept from American shores. Doctrinal positions suffered assaults from competing positions. Later, German so-called 'higher criticism' of Scripture would have its impact on 'the New World'. Yet America had its own theological upheavals.

To be sure, many Presbyterian churches in the colonies and during the early days of our national history continued to uphold the doctrine and practice of the catechetical piety of the Westminster tradition. Throughout the years of our Civil War until the time of the First World War many Presbyterians held fast to the Westminster Confession and Catechisms and the practice of upholding homes and churches undergirded by Reformation teaching. Because of this, Princeton Seminary stood by its doctrinal standards for some time after other schools and denominations had turned aside to other systems of doctrine (largely to theological liberalism). For example, it was because of their parental and church reformational piety in teaching and practice that both Charles and A. A. Hodge held on to their historic doctrine, thus keeping Princeton anchored in its historic doctrine for a longer period of time than men and institutions in other denominations.

But even Princeton and the large Presbyterian denomination were swamped by 'Modernism' in the early twentieth century. However, under the leadership of J. Gresham Machen, who was also raised in the piety *and* theology that Westminster had instilled, a number of Presbyterian churches did hold firmly to the Westminster standards. At this day a denomination of churches has grown to sizeable numbers which remains faithful to the teaching of the Hodges and Machen and their Westminster forefathers.

New England, of course, had Puritan and Reformed ancestors. But New England became the leading proponent of 'Revivalism' in America. As this tradition developed in the years after Jonathan Edwards the schools and leaders who promoted large evangelistic crusades began to tamper with the theology once held by New Englanders. Much of the doctrinal adjustments surrounded the view of man's will and its susceptibility to certain persuasions in evangelistic crusades.

In addition, from New England came the raising of many social issues; these began to be heard from pulpits as well as evangelistic preaching. The following are a few matters that arose, though there were others:

- The call to free all slaves some years prior to the Civil War;

- A movement for women's suffrage with regard to political voting;

- From New England was also launched a temperance movement (forbidding the use of all alcohol);

- An anti-Masonic cause.

Later, 'Fundamentalists' would include in their evangelistic efforts the teaching of dispensationalism and an attack on Darwinian evolution. Such intrusions of academic and social issues certainly caused attention to be diverted from foundational evangelistic doctrines. This was occurring at the very time that the gospel was being reduced to a few items of truth combined with methods of persuasion in order to win numerous converts.

Some 'evangelists' would say that they had no time for doctrinal discussion. They were too busy winning as many souls as possible. How revealing this is of a failure to understand that salvation comes to those who know the truth!

Still other 'evangelists' did not want any controversy which might trouble the rising waters of their gathering crowds. Many doctrinal matters must be avoided, they thought, for the sake of peace, so that all 'Christians' would participate in the evangelistic crusade.

Were the Westminster divines correct that the atmosphere of home and church are most conducive to a movement of God in their communities? And were they correct to believe that instilling doctrine from cradle to grave is what people need?

In the Revivalist movement it was not said, but the impression was given, that it was not a catechism of truth which was needed by sinners. Instead one large, exciting gathering with famous speakers using an 'invitation system' was the way to go. An emotional experience could do without extensive biblical doctrine.

As these large crowds assembled with an expectation of emotional engagement, a spirit of ecumenism also grew. Even Charismatic and Roman Catholic clergy were involved in the 'crusades'. Professing 'converts' were sent to churches where biblical truth was not upheld.

Although their statistics and appearances do not rival those of the remaining mega-gatherings which imitate the older revivalism, today there are growing numbers of churches and homes within the U.S.A. that are employing the catechisms of the Reformation era.

One of my favourite sections of Watson's teaching in *A Body of Divinity* is his treatment of questions 36-38 of the Shorter Catechism. The questions are:

Q. 36: What are the benefits which in this life do accompany or flow from justification, adoption, and sanctification?

Q. 37: What benefits do believers receive from Christ at death?

Q. 38: What benefits do believers receive from Christ at the resurrection?

Unless there is repeated teaching on these parts of the catechism in your church, there is likely to be a neglect of these emphases of the word of God. Many Christians and ministers give much more attention to their lives in this world than they give to their expected experiences in the much longer-lasting world to come, which they *will* experience.

These meditations underscore Jesus' instruction to 'Seek *first* [emphasis mine] the kingdom of God and his righteousness' (Matt. 6:33), and to 'lay up for yourselves treasures in heaven' (Matt. 6:20).

19

Diary of Kenneth A. MacRae

Iain H. Murray (Ed.)

John J. Murray

I CAME to know the Rev. Kenneth MacRae towards the end of his life and ministry. My acquaintance with him came through my father who was an elder in the Dornoch, Sutherland, congregation of the Free Church of Scotland. Mr MacRae, who was then minister of the Free Church of Scotland congregation in Stornoway, Isle of Lewis, became one of the best-known preachers in the Highlands in the 1940s and 1950s. He frequently preached at Communion seasons throughout the area. Through these visits my father came to know him and was greatly attracted to his preaching.

After I moved to Edinburgh in 1954 I became aware of the beginnings of a recovery of the doctrines of grace through Reformed books, first from the U.S.A. and then from the reprints of the Banner of Truth Trust. I was so captivated by the enterprise and surprised at the lack of appreciation for such books among my peers that I began, in April 1959, to publish a magazine called *Eternal Truth* (price 6p). I sent a copy of the first issue to Mr MacRae. He wrote back on 21 April 1959:

> I am delighted to receive a copy of *Eternal Truth* which you so kindly sent me … No doubt you are aware of a similar production, *The Banner of Truth*, brought out by a namesake of your own, Mr Iain Murray. If you could send me 60 copies each quarter I could get them sold at 6 ½ p each (to cover postage).

A letter of 5 May followed:

In one day—today—the sixty copies which you sent me were swept off my hands and not a few would-be buyers were left disappointed. I think you'd better send me another forty copies … will you please send on one hundred copies of each issue as long as I am here.

Ten days later there was a request for another forty!

After moving to London in 1960 to join Iain Murray in the work of the Banner of Truth Trust, I became an elder in the Free Church of Scotland congregation there. As the pastorate was vacant, ministers from Scotland would supply the pulpit for a month at a time. When I discovered that Mr MacRae had been invited to speak at the first Banner of Truth Ministers' Conference at Leicester in July 1962, I wrote to ask him if he would preach in the London congregation on the Sundays before and after the conference. He readily agreed and later, when giving details of his travel, he wrote: 'I hope I shall not disappoint you in London. My hands are so full with local concerns that I cannot find time for preparation for my English engagements.' In the end Mr MacRae preached at four services in English, and two short services in Gaelic, at the London Free Church in connection with the Communion season. On the Sunday after the Leicester Conference he also preached for Iain Murray at Grove Chapel, Camberwell.

Mr MacRae at the first Leicester Conference

It could be said that the first Banner Ministers' Conference in July 1962 brought together three stalwarts of the Reformed faith: Professor John Murray, Rev. W. J. Grier, and Mr MacRae. The preacher from Stornoway was in his element at the conference and gave two lectures on subjects near to his heart: 'Teaching Essential to Evangelical Preaching', and 'The Danger of Compromise in Preaching'. Among the forty men who attended, twelve were from Scotland. Back in Stornoway after the conference, Mr MacRae, addressing his people on 'The Present Prospects of the Reformed Faith', reported that he had seen in England 'a little cloud like a man's hand' (1 Kings 18:44). Reflecting on the conference he wrote to a friend:

The earnestness and spiritual unity of those young fellows who gathered at Leicester was for me a real tonic and encouraged me greatly. So far, the movement towards the Reformed Faith may be weak and largely unorganised, but that there is such a movement cannot be questioned, and in it, by God's grace, there are tremendous possibilities. Worm Jacob may yet thresh the mountains. May the Lord grant it so!

When Mr MacRae died in Stornoway on 5 May 1964 the crowd wishing to attend his funeral was so large that two separate services had to be held simultaneously, one in the main Free Church building and the other in the Seminary in Francis Street, and both were packed to capacity. The press reported that at least a thousand men took part in the procession to the graveyard. 'Hundreds of women lined the streets, many of them weeping.'

Background to the book

It was when Iain Murray was on a subsequent visit to Stornoway that he was shown the large boxes of personal manuscripts and notebooks left by Mr MacRae. In an appendix to the published *Diary* forty-one diaries and journals are listed! The preparation of the material for publication was a monumental task which took eleven years to complete. The skilful way in which Iain Murray selected and wove together a series of diaries, fragmented in some cases and rather uneven in their entries, with the use of historical background, additional biographical material and explanatory notes resulted in a volume of exceptional quality.

Value for Christians

1. *The* Diary of Kenneth A. MacRae *is a fascinating read for anyone interested in the course of Scottish history and culture of the early to mid-twentieth century.* Mr MacRae was a great lover and keen observer of nature. He was an enthusiast for walking and mountaineering. He loved the hills and glens of his native Ross-shire. He regularly comments on the scenery around him on his frequent travels. He had a fascination too for vehicles and the *Diary* records some hilarious adventures he had with his motorcycles and cars. His observations on World War I, during his early ministry in Lochgilphead, and World War II, while resident in Stornoway, make fascinating reading. Although what is contained in the published *Diary* does not make

many references to family life in the MacRae household, we are given a brief glimpse of his effort at relaxation with his daughter.[1]

2. *The volume is also a commentary on the state of Christianity in Scotland, and particularly its decline over a fifty-year period.* Mr MacRae had an uncommon ability to assess the number of people present at a service or meeting and these figures are studiously recorded in the *Diary*. One can readily gauge the decline in church attendance. However, there is much to encourage the reader in the accounts of the revivals he experienced, first in the Isle of Arran (1916), then in Kilmaluag, Isle of Skye (1923–24), and latterly in different districts in the Isle of Lewis. Mr MacRae was a shrewd observer of revivals and especially of the phenomena that accompanied them at times. The *Diary* captures the spiritual tone and prevailing culture of the Highlands and of the Hebrides in better days.

3. *In the publication of a* Diary *we are not surprised to discover much of the opening of the heart of the individual concerned.* Mr MacRae recounts his conversion experience: 'I hereby set on record that since the Lord in his sovereign mercy entered my heart on the lonely summit of Bell's Hill in the Pentlands on that memorable afternoon—9 August 1909—I have ever sought to serve him as my only Lord.' The spiritual pilgrimage of Mr MacRae embodies what were the main characteristics of Highland religion in its best days—conviction of sin, the fear of God, searching for evidences of grace in the life, attendance on the preached word, and spiritual conversation and fellowship with fellow believers. There was a distrust of all religion in which the Spirit of God was not evidently present. Such expressions as 'Degree work seems to destroy all spirituality' (p. 39) and 'The worldliness, the materialism of Argyllshire is strangling me' (p. 146) reveal the heart of the man.

4. *The* Diary *is a testimony from first to last about the influence of good books on the development of the Christian life.* It was the reading of the *Diary of Andrew Bonar* that convinced Mr MacRae of the usefulness of keeping a diary. On Monday 23 January 1922 he wrote:

> The perusal of the *Diary of Dr Andrew Bonar* has made me aware of how much spiritual benefit may be derived from the keeping of a

[1] Iain H Murray, ed., *Diary of Kenneth A. MacRae* (Edinburgh: Banner of Truth, 1980), p. 221.

diary. Daily the soul thus is brought to a personal and present scrutiny of its own state and condition. Such an exercise, especially in the case of one such as I am, prone to be entirely engrossed with duties and pressing interests, is bound to be beneficial.

Other entries include: 'Brainerd's *Diary* I find most helpful';[1] 'Reading *Life of Whitefield* tonight. Would that I had his consecration, his faith, his humility, his selflessness and his power!'[2] One of the most constant exhortations of MacRae to his people was that they be diligent in the circulation of Christian literature, both books and booklets. In this respect as in others he led by example. He encouraged every effort to spread the doctrines of grace. In the second year of his long pastorate in Stornoway he records: 'At the close [of a lecture] opened my congregational library and gave out about 70 volumes. The people seemed quite interested and eager.'[3]

Value for ministers

1. *The ministry of Mr MacRae, spread as it was over half a century, gives much insight into the trials, challenges, and consolations of a faithful pastor.* Many an entry in this *Diary* will find an echo in every minister's soul. There are reflections on the more sombre aspects of pastoral experience: 'I wish I were a better man and a more spiritual minister. I am a secret grief to myself';[4] 'A minister spiritually dead is the most pitiful creature on God's earth';[5] 'I had liberty but it was that awful mechanical icy liberty which distresses me more than the stammering lips. Again they listened very well but who can expect any blessing to attend a heart hard as rock and cold as death';[6] 'I have been ill, very ill, with influenza, and am only now beginning to recover. I needed this illness; it has shown me myself and the hollowness of my ministry— what pride, self-complacency! What self-seeking! How little of the Spirit of Christ, of faithfulness, of true humility!'[7]

[1] *Ibid.*, p. 193.
[2] *Ibid.*, p. 264.
[3] *Ibid.*, p. 266.
[4] *Ibid.*, p. 225.
[5] *Ibid.*, p. 37.
[6] *Ibid.*, p. 82.
[7] *Ibid.*, p. 188.

Then there are the consolations: 'Oh what a glorious night I have had! What joy, what delight, what glimpses of the beauty of my Redeemer! I got very great liberty in the prayer, and then how the dry sermon was transformed for me';[1] 'I cannot help observing of late what I have often observed before—that my freedom in public does not depend on my thoroughness in preparation but upon the spirituality of my mind.'[2]

2. *There are valuable observations that should guide young ministers in particular:* 'A further lesson I have derived from that *Diary* [of Andrew Bonar], and also from M'Cheyne's *Memoirs,* is that one's own soul must receive the *first* interest, and then the congregation. Here I have been altogether wrong from the outset of my ministry. I have worn myself out labouring for my people, preaching, visiting, writing, without end, and I have starved my soul by my neglect to such an extent that I almost forgot I had one. And the result of all this feverish output of energy has been meagre in the extreme. My method has been all wrong and must be changed. More prayer, more personal soul exercise, more retirement, must be my method henceforth, and then haply I may look for fruit in my public ministrations';[3] 'I must not lose sight of the preacher's golden rule "Never preach a sermon which has not sufficient in it—used of the Spirit—to lead a soul to Christ."'[4]

3. *Mr MacRae is a model of the diligent pastor.* He keeps a record of services, the number in attendance, the pastoral visits conducted and so on. The statistics given on page 205 of the *Diary* would put many of us who have been in the ministry to shame. He reached out to the non-churchgoers in the community: 'Spent a most enjoyable day in Totscore. Gave a brief exhortation in every house upon a text which I judged to be suitable to the state of each family, and thus was able to bring the truth to twenty-three individuals capable of comprehending it, nine of whom either cannot or will not go out (to the church) to hear it';[5] 'Had a big day today, visiting in Laxdale.

[1] *Ibid.,* p. 81.
[2] *Ibid.,* p. 186.
[3] *Ibid.,* p. 165.
[4] *Ibid.,* p. 38.
[5] *Ibid.,* p. 163.

Had worship in 30 houses.'[1] It was faithfulness in his message and his evangelistic effort that made him look for fruit from his labours, and at an early stage in his Lewis pastorate he reckoned that around one hundred people had made profession of faith under his ministry.[2]

4. *In the eyes of some Mr MacRae was a controversial figure,* exposing the failings of the government to uphold the law of God and pointing out some of the trends that were taking place in the national Church of Scotland and even within his own denomination of the Free Church. His views on a wide variety of issues are described in the *Diary*. But he was no lover of controversy for its own sake. The love which he had for the good of souls and his zeal for the glory of God led him to engage in aggressive evangelism as much as in timely warnings about the errors and declension that endangered spiritual life. There are many today who regard the stand he took at different times as both timely and wise. But even in dark days his own convictions about a sovereign God made him hold on in the belief that 'the tide will turn'.

This is a volume that can be read through or dipped into. Even those unacquainted with Scottish church history and the distinctives of Highland Christianity will find the book profitable because of the editor's explanatory notes and background information. Many contemporary illustrations greatly enhance the book. I have heard many ministers speak of the benefit it has been to them. They found it a balm to the soul. Among the books which Dr Lloyd-Jones read in the last year of his life was the *Diary of Kenneth A. MacRae*. Though suffering from much physical weakness, he was able nevertheless to say, 'I am enjoying it tremendously.'

[1] *Ibid.,* p. 251.
[2] *Ibid.,* p. 298.

20

Christian Leaders of the Eighteenth Century

J. C. Ryle

————

Peter Barnes

I STUDIED history at the University of Sydney in the 1970s where, so far as I could discern, the history faculty seemed to be divided, for the most part, between devotees of some brand or another of Marxism and those who viewed history as having no real meaning, as events that just happened, one thing after another. Elsewhere, one occasionally came across Christian attempts at understanding history, but they were invariably premillennial dispensational efforts at explaining the Cold War—and not altogether convincing.

Reading Augustine's magisterial *City of God* was enough to convince me that a biblical and Christian view of history was possible, and Ryle's treatment of the leaders of the eighteenth-century evangelical revival showed how this could be done in a specific context. Furthermore, it showed how it could be done in a way that was faithful and clear, and yet not simplistic nor inaccurate. In the one work, Ryle manages to be true both to history and to Christian spirituality. The result is edification based on a clear presentation of truth.

J. C. Ryle

The long life of John Charles Ryle (1816–1900) covered most of the nineteenth century. It was a time when, for all its apparent strength, the evangelical faith was losing its grip on English society. Ryle himself commented in 1890 that 'Never, perhaps, since the days of Celsus, Porphyry, and Julian, was the truth of revealed religion so openly and unblushingly assailed, and never was the assault so speciously and plausibly conducted.'[1]

In fact, the trends of the times were becoming obvious thirty years earlier with the publication of *Essays and Reviews* in 1860. Six of the seven essayists were clergymen of the Church of England. The two areas of the faith that were especially called into question were the authority of the Old Testament and the doctrine of hell. The church as a whole hesitated to respond in a decisive way, although Ryle himself denounced these biblical critics as 'spiritual robbers' who take away the bread of life and do not even leave a stone.[2]

Ryle was born into a household that could be best described as respectable rather than evangelical. He was educated for almost seven years at Eton, where he captained the cricket team. He went on to study at Oxford, where G. H. Liddell taught him Greek, and where he took ten wickets in a match against Cambridge in 1836. However, he was converted in 1837 when he went to a parish church, the name of which he could not remember later, and heard a public reading of Ephesians 2:8—not a sermon or a tract, just the reading. He went on to draw much help from William Wilberforce's *A Practical View* (1797), and gave up dancing and billiards which he loved. His family barely tolerated his change of heart, but their reaction only confirmed Ryle in his convictions.

By the end of 1841, Ryle was made a deacon and was placed in charge of the Chapel of Ease in Exbury where he visited house to house, and gave out tracts, as well as beef tea to those with scarlet fever, and port wine to those with typhus. In 1843 he moved to St Thomas', Winchester, and five months later left for Helmingham, Suffolk. For spiritual help, he turned increasingly to the Puritans, especially Richard Baxter, and wished that more had, like William Gurnall, remained inside the national church after the Great Ejection of 1662. His views remained evangelical and episcopal: 'There is no warrant for staying away from assemblies and councils merely because

---

[1] J. C. Ryle, *Charges and Addresses* (1903; Edinburgh: Banner of Truth Trust, 1978), p. 205.

[2] Eric Russell, *That Man of Granite with the Heart of a Child: Biography of J. C. Ryle* (Fearn: Christian Focus, 2001), p. 86.

we happen to be a minority'[1]—a view which his friend Charles Spurgeon did not hold, particularly as the Down-Grade Controversy unfolded after 1887.

All through his Christian life, Ryle maintained the practice of rising early to study the Bible, and to underline words of special significance to him. As a preacher, his height gave him an imposing presence, and he had a strong voice and a clear delivery. His writing style was simple and epigrammatic, and especially suited to the writing of tracts. In fact, one woman expressed her disappointment at his preaching because she understood it![2]

By 1870 he was rural dean of Hoxne, with oversight of twenty-five parishes, then he was moved on to become dean of Salisbury in 1879. However, he was almost immediately made the bishop of Liverpool, and remained in that office until his death at the turn of the century, having surprised himself, and others, by living so long.[3] He adopted as his motto the text of John 17:17, 'Thy word is truth.'[4] On his grave were marked two texts: 2 Timothy 4:7 and Ephesians 2:8. Bishop Chavasse was to characterise him most wonderfully as 'that man of granite with the heart of a child'.[5]

Throughout his ministry Ryle stated that his aim was to be 'as broad as the Bible, neither less nor more'.[6] In 1884 he saw three dark clouds facing the Established Church of England: those who wanted to Romanize the Church of England; those who wanted to liberalise their understanding of 'the grand old doctrines' of Christianity; and those who wished to disestablish and disendow the state church.[7] The first two groups were dubbed the 'Rits' and the 'Rats' by Benjamin Disraeli, meaning the Ritualists and the Rationalists.

Ryle's preaching and writing were similar in style: warmth and simplicity combined in a way not always found in preachers who

[1] *Ibid.*, p. 127.

[2] *Ibid.*, p. 201.

[3] E.g. Ryle, *Charges and Addresses*, p. 235, where he says in 1890 that this 'may possibly be the last Charge I may ever be allowed to deliver'; also p. 286 for 1893.

[4] Ryle, *Charges and Addresses*, p. xi (where it is mistakenly given as John 17:7).

[5] Marcus L. Loane, *John Charles Ryle 1816-1900* (London: Hodder and Stoughton, 1983), p. 113.

[6] Russell, *Man of Granite*, p. 109.

[7] Ryle, *Charges and Addresses*, pp. 82-85.

write or writers who preach. In writing his work on the eighteenth-century Christian leaders, he introduced the book by adopting an understated laconic stance: 'If anyone can name better men, he knows more than I do' (p. iv). Overall, his prose was vigorous and punchy, and J. I. Packer was to refer to the 'rib-jabbing drumbeat of Ryle's style'.[8]

Contents of the book

In *Christian Leaders of the Eighteenth Century*, Ryle gives valuable biographies of eleven evangelical leaders whom God used during the revival. These men were George Whitefield, John Wesley, William Grimshaw, William Romaine, Daniel Rowland, John Berridge, Henry Venn, Samuel Walker, James Hervey, Augustus Toplady, and John Fletcher. At the beginning of the eighteenth century England was in a sorry condition. The Christian faith was ridiculed in many places, while the 'spirit of slumber was over the land' (p. 19). The great jurist, Sir William Blackstone (1723–80), commented after hearing the preachers of London, that no more Christianity was preached than could be found in the writings of Cicero (p. 15).

Such a situation was transformed, and England was spared the ravages of what took place in the French Revolution. Yet this transformation did not come about by Acts of Parliament, the passing of laws, media outrage, or the laments of church leaders. Rather, God raised up evangelists who preached a common message: the sufficiency and supremacy of Scripture; the total corruption of human nature; Christ's death as the only satisfaction for sinners; justification by faith in Christ alone; regeneration by the Holy Spirit; the need for personal holiness; and the reality of heaven and hell. This message was proclaimed everywhere, simply, fervently, and directly, by men who were convinced of its truth. It is a wondrous story, worthy of our deep attention.

Ryle pays tribute where it is due to George Whitefield as the first in order of merit (p. 31). More than any other human agency, Whitefield was behind the rise of Evangelicalism and the demise of infidelity (p. 47). Ryle may be less than helpful in claiming that Whitefield

[8] Cited in Vaughan Roberts, 'J. C. Ryle: "Evangelical Churchman"' in *Churchman*, Spring 2014, p. 26, n. 5.

never used the indefinite expression 'we' in his preaching (p. 52)—for Calvin most certainly made use of it—but the point remains that people need to be convicted of sin. No one preached the gospel more vividly than Whitefield, personifying the Arabian proverb that 'He is the best orator who can turn men's ears into eyes' (p. 52). Ryle himself had an ear for a memorable turn of phrase. When a woman declared her admiration for a minister with more talents than grace, William Grimshaw reproved her: 'I am glad you never saw the devil' (p. 146).

Ryle was quite willing to give his opinion on various aspects of the lives of the evangelists. Hence he describes the Orphan House of Bethesda somewhat unfairly as 'a design of very questionable wisdom' (p. 36). Also, Whitefield's marriage 'does not seem to have contributed much to his happiness' (p. 41). It is not obvious that it contributed much to his wife's happiness either! He married a woman whom he barely knew, and who was ten years his senior. She was a widow named Elizabeth James, and she had been romantically connected to Howell Harris. Indeed, it was Harris who arranged a meeting between Whitefield and Elizabeth. On their week-long honeymoon Whitefield preached twice a day. Later, when their only child who survived childbirth—a four-month-old son—died, Whitefield preached three times before the funeral.

As a loyal Anglican, Ryle is critical of Whitefield's saying that 'Archbishop Tillotson knew no more of the gospel than Mahomet' (p. 60)—a statement that was perhaps inaccurate without being wildly so. At other times Ryle was not afraid to be incisive. Noting the ejection of Daniel Rowland from the curacy of Llangeitho in 1763, Ryle exclaimed: 'A more unhappy, ill-timed, blundering exercise of episcopal power than this, it is literally impossible to conceive!' (p. 192).

A shrewd observer of the human condition, Ryle observed with regard to Fletcher's being laid aide with consumption (tuberculosis) from 1776–81: 'His one employment was that most wearing and depressing one, the search for health' (p. 413). He was acutely aware, no doubt from experience, that ministerial jealousy is one of the clergy's besetting sins: 'Nowhere, perhaps, will you find men so slow to recognize the gifts of others, and so quick to detect their faults, as in the ranks of preachers of religion' (p. 303).

How the book informs, balances, corrects, and strengthens its readers

Ryle sought to combine spiritual truth with a spirit of charity. He criticised the eighteenth-century Anglican hymn-writer and fierce controversialist Augustus Toplady: 'he is frequently more systematic and narrow than the Bible' (p. 379). Ryle explained: 'Arminianism seems to have precisely the same effect on him that a scarlet cloak has on a bull' (p. 380). To Toplady, an Arminian was akin to a Roman Catholic and a heretic, but in 1898 Ryle entertained the President of the Methodist Conference at the palace in Liverpool, and told him: 'If we cannot remove the hedges that separate us, let us keep them as low as we can and shake hands over them.'[1] Ryle makes the practical suggestion and laments that Toplady engaged in too many controversies when he could have written more hymns (p. 383). Elsewhere in the book, Ryle—who was a 'four-point Calvinist' rather than a 'five pointer'—pays due respect to two Arminians: John Wesley and John Fletcher. He regards them as true men of grace who aimed, in Wesley's words, 'to reform the nation, particularly the Church, and to spread Scriptural holiness over the land'.[2]

The sturdy bishop had enough historical sense to suspect that some of the wilder stories about William Grimshaw were probably apocryphal (p. 140 n.) and enough pastoral sense to warn that unless a man is 'a Grimshaw', he ought not to imitate him (pp. 143-4).

Regarding John Berridge at Cambridge where he drank in Socinianism, Ryle lamented: 'How hardly shall resident Fellows of colleges enter the kingdom of God!' (p. 221). Such a criticism was an indication of Ryle's willingness not to be shackled by Victorian notions of what constituted being a respectable gentleman. He also defended itinerant ministries even when they were opposed by the bishops, and supported Berridge's doing so even when his bishop demanded that he desist. In Berridge's view, and in Ryle's, the Great Commission of Matthew 28:19-20 was a higher charge (p. 232). Yet Ryle does not lose his perspective or discernment, and notes that Berridge's collection of hymns, entitled *Zion's Songs*, constitutes 'very poor' poetry which is at times 'painfully ludicrous' (p. 239).

[1] Loane, *Ryle*, p. 106.
[2] Cited in A. Skevington Wood, *The Burning Heart* (Exeter: Paternoster, 1976), p. 74.

The book is full of wise spiritual lessons given by means of historical illustrations. Ryle did not try to explain more than he could, and contented himself with saying that 'there is some hidden secret about pulpit power which baffles all attempts at definition' (p. 196). So, for example, sermons which are excellent to listen to may not read well—notably those of Henry Venn (pp. 205-6, 287). Not everything is recorded by historians for posterity, for 'Spiritual work done in rural parishes is, perhaps, less "seen of men" than any work within the province of the Christian ministry' (p. 228).

Value of the book

Ryle makes much of the fact that the eleven evangelical preachers were all ministers of the Church of England. Eight of them were university men—from Oxford (Wesley, Whitefield, Romaine, Hervey, and Walker) or Cambridge (Grimshaw, Berridge, Venn). Rowland and Fletcher never went to university while Toplady went to Trinity College, Dublin. Four of them never married: Berridge, Hervey, Toplady, and Walker. A number of them were converted after their ordination, with Berridge even formerly being a prayerless denier of Christ's deity.

Most of all, Ryle urges that the Church of England return to the same evangelical doctrines and life that God so blessed and used in the eighteenth century. Ryle's work is a strong reminder to us that God is true, his word is true, his gospel is forever, and no matter how bleak our present conditions in both church and society, God is able to glorify his name and add greatly to the number who are being saved. He is the God who gives life to sinners dead in trespasses and sins, acquits them, and transforms them into the image of his beloved Son.

21

The Works of Richard Sibbes

Mark Dever

A CHOICE service has been done for the church of Jesus Christ by the reprinting of the collected works of Richard Sibbes (1577–1635). During the decade 1973–83 the seven-volume set of Alexander Grosart's nineteenth-century compilation was reprinted and made available to now a fourth century of readers.[1] Richard Sibbes preached these sermons (as almost all of his printed works began) in Cambridge and London during the reigns of King James I and King Charles I. Those published in his lifetime make up volume 1 of this collection, while the other six volumes are collections of his sermons printed after his death. Sibbes had left many of his sermon notes corrected and prepared to two sets of friends—one set in Cambridge for those preached there, and one set in London for those preached there. It was then left up to these literary executors, and others, which of his sermons would be published.

Everything we have today is from those works first published in the seventeenth century. Of Sibbes' unpublished material nothing can be said. The only records of his sermons are of those that have been printed. Starting with *The Bruised Reed* in 1630, Sibbes' sermons were frequently published and republished throughout the remainder of the century. In his own remaining years, *The Bruised Reed* went through five editions. Soon after his death, especially 1637–39, Sibbes' other sermons flooded the presses. For the next twenty years or so, almost annually some new work of Sibbes would find its way into print, or some earlier printing would be re-edited. Many of these same volumes were translated into Dutch and published in the

[1] Vol. 1, 1973; vol. 5, 1977; vol. 3, 1981; vol. 7, 1982; vols. 2, 4, 6, 1983.

Netherlands during these years. In the following century, German translations of a few works were also published.

Shortly after the restoration of the monarchy in England, the demand for Sibbes' works in English seemed to fall off. After a few new editions in 1662 and 1664, nothing more of Sibbes appeared in English for a century. Often godly literature finds an initial audience and usefulness—often among those who personally knew the author, or knew those who did. But later, the works seem to fall away and out of sight, until a new wave of interest picks up the old works and gives them renewed life. Is it any surprise that the evangelical awakening in the middle of the eighteenth century would revive interest in such literature?

And so it was that after a century of no new editions or printings of Sibbes' works, in 1768, *The Soules Conflict with Itself* and *The Bruised Reed* came out again in Glasgow, published together in a single volume. In the remainder of the eighteenth century, volumes of Sibbes' sermons were also published in England, and, for the first time, in the United States (in Newport, Philadelphia, and Wilmington).

Every decade of the nineteenth century saw some work or other of Sibbes being printed, usually multiple works. It wasn't just *The Bruised Reed*, but it was also *Divine Meditations*, *A Fountain Opened*, and, of course, *The Soul's Conflict*. In 1809 W. Baynes published the first attempt to collect Sibbes' works together in a multi-volume set. In those three volumes, all of Sibbes' major works could be found. From Berwick and Aberdeen to Philadelphia, presses poured forth copies of Sibbes to edify the eager reader. This all culminated in Alexander Grosart's collection in seven volumes called *The Complete Works of Richard Sibbes*, published from 1862 to 1864. With that edition, the appetite for Sibbes' works again seemed to be sated for a century.

This is where the Banner of Truth Trust's edition comes in. For over fifteen years, starting in the late 1950s, the new publishing house had been reprinting works from the seventeenth, eighteenth, and nineteenth centuries that had formerly shown great power to build up the church, but which had become neglected and even unknown. The decision was made to add the works of Sibbes to those works already reprinted. So in 1973, a reprint of volume 1 of the seven-volume Grosart edition came from the presses, with a commendation on the front fly-leaf by J. I. Packer, and a four-page 'Publisher's Preface' dated January 15, 1973 (presumably written by Iain H. Murray). In it, the renewed demand for Puritan works was noted, and the argument made that some of the leading works of Sibbes should now be printed (*e.g. The Bruised Reed* and *The Soul's Conflict*), along with those of John Owen and John Flavel. At the time, the publisher wrote that 'the re-issue of the remaining six volumes of Nichol's edition of Sibbes is not ... currently contemplated'.[1] On June 16, 1976, in a 'Publisher's Preface' to a now-reprinted volume 5, the following explanation was given: 'the steady demand for Volume 1 has encouraged us to proceed'. Still the publisher said that there was no current plan for the re-issue of all seven volumes. Then in 1981 came forth a re-issued volume 3, mentioning that volumes 1 and 5 had been 'highly appreciated'. That volume must have found similar appreciation, because in quick succession, the rest of Sibbes' *Complete Works* came out: volume 7 in 1982, and in 1983 all the remaining volumes.

It was while this reprinting was going on that the publisher's hopes—and Grosart's before, and the various original editors', and initially Sibbes' own hopes—were fulfilled in the life of this present writer. William Nigel Kerr, professor of church history at Gordon-Conwell Theological Seminary, approached me in September of 1982. We were in the seminary library, and a lecture had just been given by a noted author of the day. He asked me what I thought. Being only twenty-two years and a few days old, I was reluctant to share my evaluation with a godly man of his wisdom and scholarship and age (he was then nearing seventy). After he lovingly coaxed out of me my concerns, he smiled approvingly and, through a short conversation, asked about the subject of my research project in his seminar. I suggested that, of the four possible subjects, I should probably do Bunyan because he was a Baptist. Owen would be desired by all, and I had misgivings about Baxter. The only other alternative was a Puritan I'd not heard of, 'Richard Sibbes'. At this Kerr's eyes lit up,

---

[1] *The Works of Richard Sibbes* (Edinburgh: Banner of Truth Trust, 1973), vol. 1, p. xiii.

and he guided me—did he physically pull me?—over to the section of the library where the nineteenth-century Grosart edition of Sibbes' works was. He pulled out the first volume, opened it to *The Bruised Reed* and asked me to sit down and start reading it. I did. And I was so taken by it that I purchased one of the new Banner of Truth reprints of it, took it home, and started reading it to my wife. She loved it! And we were both edified by these sermons all over again, 350 years after they were first preached in London in 1630. Such is the miracle of book publishing!

Since then, the Banner of Truth has brought out a number of Sibbes' works in the Puritan paperback series. Here in our church's internship programme, each man who goes through the programme is required to read *The Bruised Reed* and to write a reflection paper on it. *The Bruised Reed* is not the only thing Sibbes wrote, of course, but its themes and qualities well reflect the best of Sibbes' works that we have left to us. In them, Christ is central, his glory is great, his wrath is terrible, and his mercy is overwhelming. 'There is more mercy in Christ than sin in us.'[1] 'Let us not be cruel to ourselves when Christ is thus gracious.'[2] In Sibbes' preaching, mercy is plentiful and sweet, but never cheap and assumed. Every time fresh heights of God's grace are scaled, fresh aspects of God's love are relished. In these volumes, systematics are preached and theology edifies. The reader can be instructed in every topic from angels (an extensive section in vol. 5, pp. 496-504) to God's use of human means. 'Divers ways how God delivers from the lion's mouth ... By stirring up one lion against another; as the Persians against the Babylonians, Grecians against Persians, Romans against the Grecians, and the other barbarous nations, as the Goths and Vandals, against them; so whilst lions spit their fury one upon another, the sheep are quiet. Thus the Turks and other enemies have kept popish princes from raging and tyrannising over the church to the height of their malice.'[3]

The first-time reader of Sibbes could benefit from following the order of the Banner's reprinting. Start with Sibbes' best-known works in volume 1. They have been celebrated and cherished for a reason!

---

[1] *The Bruised Reed, Works*, vol. 1, p. 47.
[2] *Ibid.*, p. 66.
[3] *The Saint's Safety in Evil Times: Manifested by St Paul, Works*, vol. 1, pp. 317-8.

Then go on to volume 5 where shorter sermons on Paul's letters are easily read in brief sittings. By this point, the reader will have become sufficiently acquainted with Sibbes himself to know what he's looking for when he picks up a volume. All seven volumes have their glories. The Memoir in volume 1 should not be overlooked. Nor should the 'Description of Christ', the sermons Sibbes was preaching right before he preached the sermons that made up *The Bruised Reed*. Volume 2 well captures how Sibbes' own heart was ravished with the love of Christ from texts in the Song of Solomon and Hosea. Volume 3 is over five hundred pages of close and careful commentary on 2 Corinthians chapter 1. This volume alone should correct any impression that the Puritans as a class were *eisegetes* rather than *exegetes*. Sibbes was a careful, even meticulous student of God's word.

Volume 4 contains some deep work of theology by Sibbes. In 'The Excellency of the Gospel above the Law', he deals carefully with election and effectual calling, as well as many other issues. The sealing of the Spirit is carefully considered in 'A Fountain Sealed' (vol. 5). Is there a better example of Sibbes' typically Puritan patient mediation than his concentration on John 17:26 in his sermon 'The Matchless Love and Inbeing', reprinted in volume 6? And in volume 7, we find among many others, Sibbes' final two sermons, in the last of which he preached—one week before he died—'It is the growing Christian that is the assured Christian.'[1]

If one theme can be said to predominate throughout the works of Sibbes, it is most certainly the comfort there is to be found in the grace of God in Christ. This comfort is not a mere sentimental empathy (though empathy itself is strong), but it is that which puts courage and strength in us for the conflict.

When comfort is wanting, Sibbes said, 'We must judge ourselves … by faith, and not by feeling; looking to the promises and word of God, and not to our present sense and apprehension.'[2] Like John Calvin, Sibbes, too, had taught that even the best actions of the believer 'need Christ to perfume them'.[3] Relying too much on works is always a danger in the human heart. One 'cause of disquiet is, that

---

[1] Second Sermon, *Works*, vol. 7, p. 353.
[2] *Bowels Opened*, *Works*, vol. 2, p. 103.
[3] *Bruised Reed*, *Works*, vol. 1, p. 50.

men by a natural kind of popery seek for their comfort too much sanctification, neglecting justification, relying too much upon their own performances'.[1] When corruption is so strong that one can see nothing of sanctification, the believer should remember that one's salvation did not come from assurance, and that

> God can see somewhat of his own Spirit in that confusion, but the spirit [of the believer] itself cannot. Then go to the blood of Christ! There is always comfort. ... Go ... to the blood of Christ, that is, if we find sin upon our consciences, if we find not peace in our consciences, nor sanctification in our hearts, go to the blood of Christ, which is shed for all those that confess their sins, and rely on him for pardon, though we find no grace; ... before we go to Christ it is sufficient that we see nothing in ourselves, no qualification; for the graces of the Spirit they are not the condition of coming to Christ, but the promise of those that receive Christ after. Therefore go to Christ when thou feelest neither joy of the Spirit, nor sanctification of the Spirit; go to the blood of Christ, and that will purge thee, and wash thee from all thy sins.[2]

Though 'The evidence indeed to prove our faith to be a true faith, is from works, ... the title we have is only by Christ, only by grace.'[3] This was to be the ultimate basis of assurance for the Christian, because 'We are more safe in his comprehending of us, than in our clasping and holding of him. As we say of the mother and the child, both hold, but the safety of the child is that the mother holds him.'[4]

The present author can add his own testimony to that of Dr Martyn Lloyd-Jones that sometimes 'what you need is some gentle tender treatment for your soul'. Sibbes' books, Lloyd-Jones testified, 'quietened, soothed, comforted, encouraged and healed me'.[5] Too

[1] *The Soul's Conflict with Itself, Works*, vol. 1, p. 138.

[2] *A Learned Commentary or Exposition upon the First Chapter of the Second Epistle of St Paul to the Corinthians, Works*, vol. 3, p. 464; cf. pp. 476-7; *Bowels Opened, Works*, vol. 2, p. 157; *Divine Meditations and Holy Contemplations, Works*, vol. 7, p. 211; *Soul's Conflict, Works*, vol. 1, pp. 124, 212-3; *Witness of Salvation, Works*, vol. 7, p. 378.

[3] *The Faithful Covenanter, Works*, vol. 6, p. 5.

[4] *Bowels Opened, Works*, vol. 2, p. 184.

[5] D. M. Lloyd-Jones, *Preaching and Preachers, 40th Anniversary Edition* (Grand Rapids, MI: Zondervan, 2011), pp. 186-7.

often Reformed theology is presented as cold and harsh, but in the preaching of Sibbes' staccato phrases and pithy summations, the warmth and love of God's grace to us in Christ breaks upon the reader's heart and soul afresh.

Richard Sibbes never married. He spent his life living communally in Cambridge (as a fellow of St John's College, then as Master of St Catharine's) and in London (as Preacher of Gray's Inn), teaching and preaching. There was no national church he had reformed like Luther or Cranmer or Knox. He had no son like Thomas Goodwin had, to carefully prepare his biography and arrange his many papers. His memory would live only in those who heard him preach, or those, who through later publishers, have 'heard' him on the page. As Sibbes preached, 'There is a power in hearing the word to transform us into the obedience of it.'[1] That transformation is what happened initially by God's Spirit in the seventeenth century, and, thankfully, is happening still in the twenty-first century.

---

[1] Sibbes, *Demand of a Good Conscience, Works*, vol. 7, p. 481.

22

The Diary and Life of Andrew Bonar

Marjory Bonar (Ed)

———————————

Andrew Swanson

O F HOW many books can it be said that they can be read with great profit by a young man just setting out on his ministry, read twenty years later with further profit, then yet again with the greatest blessing of all, by the same man when he is a seventy-year-old retiree? This has been my experience as I recently re-read Andrew Bonar's *Diary and Life*, which was first published by the Banner of Truth Trust in 1960.[1] What is it about this book that makes me wish to recommend it?

It is a modern phenomenon to have a mentor to whom we are accountable, someone we respect and trust enough to be able to share our lives with transparency. The corresponding phenomenon in the nineteenth century was the use of a diary in which one reflected on one's life with equal honesty. The advantage of the latter is that future generations can also benefit from the struggles and insights of a godly man. Whilst a good spiritual mentor can be a great blessing, sad to say not every believer enjoys such a privilege. However, for a very modest outlay any literate believer can gain immense spiritual benefit from the purchase and prayerful reading of this classic, and make it a lifelong companion that can be re-read every ten years or so.

———————————

[1] A new re-typeset edition of this work was published by the Trust in 2013. It will also be available through the Trust's website as an ebook.

General content and layout

Originally, this diary was contained in two small volumes written in Byrom's shorthand, with continuous entries for sixty-four years from 1828–92, until just a few weeks before the diarist's death. The diary as we now have it was first published at the earnest request of many of Andrew Bonar's congregation and personal friends, under the excellent editorial supervision of his daughter, Marjory Bonar.

The Banner of Truth edition divides into two distinct parts: 'Diary' (about 380 pages) and 'Reminiscences of His Life' (another 134 pages). The Diary is divided into seven chapters giving us the spiritual landmarks of Bonar's life.

1. Conversion and College Life, 1828-1834

2. Work in Jedburgh and Edinburgh, 1835-1838

3. Collace, 1838-1856

4. Early Years in Finnieston, 1857-1864

5. Ministry in Glasgow, 1864-1875

6. Labours More Abundant, 1876-1888

7. Closing Years, 1889-1892

Bonar's spiritual preparation and ministry as outlined in these chapter headings took place during sixty years of one of the most interesting and fruitful periods of Scottish church history. This is one reason why the book can be so highly recommended. It means that by reading Bonar's *Diary*, not only do we learn a lot about his own spiritual pilgrimage but also we are introduced to some of the mighty acts of God that took place during these years. Likewise, we are introduced to some of the spiritual giants raised up by God in those days with whom Bonar enjoyed intimate friendship and fellowship.

In particular, the names of William Chalmers Burns, Thomas Chalmers, Alexander Duff, John Milne, and Robert Murray M'Cheyne represent the outstanding galaxy of spiritually gifted men raised up by God to bring blessing not only to Scotland but also to other parts of the world, such as China and India. Incidentally, on a similar time scale, God had raised up in England men of the spiritual calibre of J. C. Ryle (1816–1900), C. H. Spurgeon (1834–92) and Hudson Taylor (1832–1905) whose lives overlapped Bonar's ministry in Scotland. Indeed, Bonar notes in his *Diary* the death of Spurgeon on February 6th 1892, while he himself passed on to glory a day before that same year ended.

Although part two of the book, his daughter's 'Reminiscences of His Life', is only about a third as long as the 'Diary', it is covered in nine chapters. She sums up the aim of her reminiscences as follows:

> The succeeding chapters of this book have been written to bring out in detail some parts of our father's life and character, to show, not a perfect man, but one who more than most around him bore on his forehead the impress of holiness.[1]

The resulting portrait presents a winsome, godly, Christ-exalting life and ministry more than worthy of emulation.

An appreciation of Bonar's Diary and Life

My initial reason for reading this book was a follow-up to Bonar's superb *Life of Robert Murray M'Cheyne*. It was such a blessing I felt that anyone who could produce such a valuable book was someone I needed to know better. One paragraph of John J. Murray's introduction hooked me:

> The main lesson we learn from the life of Andrew Bonar, as indeed from all the great saints of God, is that what is real in the life of man has more affinity with the solitude of the closet than with the stir of outward things. If reality in religion is to be reached again by the present generation of Christians, then the outward must occupy less of our time and the inward more. There must be more privacy than Christians seem now to think needful; there must be more waiting upon God in the secret place; there must be more unbroken fellowship with the Father and the Son.[2]

That sums up perfectly what to expect if you read this book. What is revealed in these pages is well summarised by Marjory Bonar:

> the revelation of the life of one who prayed always, who prayed everywhere, who the nearer he came to the other world, was every

---

[1] Majory Bonar, ed., *The Diary and Life of Andrew A. Bonar* (Edinburgh: Banner of Truth Trust, 2013), p. 294.

[2] *Ibid.*, p. xi.

day more constantly enjoying closer intercourse with it. He led his congregation in prayer at a Sabbath-day service, or, an evening prayer meeting, often it seemed as if he had forgotten the presence of any other, and were speaking with his unseen God and Saviour 'face to face, as a man speaketh unto his friend'. His diary does not reveal much of the bright, joyous, happy spirit which was so characteristic of him but his letters are pervaded by it, as was his whole life and conversation. We think of him now as having entered into the joy of the Lord, in whom on earth he rejoiced 'with joy unspeakable and full of glory.'[1]

The first chapter is almost exclusively concerned with a clear testimony of his spiritual pilgrimage from darkness to light. It begins with the following entry: 'I felt myself unsaved, and felt a secret expectation that in the course of my studies in divinity I might be brought to the truth.'[2] Almost two years later another entry tells us: 'I am still without Christ and without hope.'[3]

Shortly after this he began to read with great profit William Guthrie's *The Christian's Great Interest*. On Sunday 17th October 1830 he wrote in the margin of his diary 'Assurance begun' alongside the following entry: 'This is the first beam of joy ... yet it is scarcely more than a hope.' It was nearly another year before he could write with greater confidence: 'Happier far this year than last, because now I know that Christ loves me.'[4] Doubtless, that long, deep conversion experience was foundational to all that follows.

From the remainder of the *Diary* I noted the following fifteen major topics Bonar touches on:

1. His prayer life

2. His friends

3. Deaths of relatives, friends and brothers in ministry

4. The second coming of Jesus Christ

5. Books that he read and found helpful

---

[1] *Ibid.*, p. xv.
[2] *Ibid.*, p. 1 (Aug. 21, 1828).
[3] *Ibid.*, p. 6 (Sun. Aug. 8, 1830).
[4] *Ibid.*, p. 11 (Mon. Aug. 1, 1831).

6. Remarks on preaching and pastoral care

7. Lessons he learned through the work of the ministry

8. His concern for conversions

9. His concern for and experience of revival

10. His involvement in mission to the Jews

11. Self-examination

12. His correspondence

13. Personal references and his family life

14. Some notable events in Free Church of Scotland history

15. His ministry of writing

These topics are not listed in order of importance but, if they were listed in order of how frequently he touched on them, the following topics would head the list:

1. *His prayer life.* In spite of frequent resolves to improve this, an ever-deepening awareness of its privilege and vital importance, many remarkable answers and occasions when he was deeply conscious of the felt presence of the Lord, he always felt he still had so much more to learn in the school of prayer.

2. *The second coming of Christ.* This was not simply a truth he enjoyed proclaiming, it was a reality he trusted in and longed for. While some are unable to share his premillennial view of this event all believers would be more spiritually minded if they shared his hope in and longing for the Lord's return.

3. *Self-examination.* Throughout the *Diary* there is frequent reference to searching self-examination with a corresponding humiliation and penitence over his sins and shortcomings.

These certainly are the topics I have been most challenged and blessed by. Since they are foundational to all who desire true godliness, this book deserves a wider readership than gospel ministers. If nothing else this book provides an accurate portrait of the kind of minister for which the church ought to be pleading with God to give. Indeed, although this book was initially published for the benefit of Andrew Bonar's congregation and personal friends, much of it must have an especial appeal for men who are either aspiring to, or actually involved in, Christian ministry.

Young ministers will gain great help from the amazing variety of lessons Bonar himself learned in his own ministry. All his remarks on preaching and pastoral care warrant careful consideration. His love for his flock and his concern for the unconverted are deeply moving as well as very challenging. Unfortunately, some of the books he read and found helpful are no longer in print today, but most can be obtained in one way or another, and may be read with appreciation and profit. Between the first and second part of the Banner of Truth edition of his *Diary and Life* there is a list of his own writings of which at least six are published by the Banner of Truth Trust and still in print—they are very worthwhile reading.

It hardly needs saying that all the other topics mentioned above will have a particular appeal to the varied interests of individual readers. I found his concern for conversions, desire for and experience of revival, along with involvement in mission to the Jews, both very interesting as well as humbling and painfully searching—how little I really know of these things! On the other hand, some of his thoughts on revival are a source of huge encouragement and hope. Others will rejoice, as I do, in the beauty of his godliness, as illustrated by the friends he loved, his correspondence, and especially his family life. No appreciation of Bonar's life would be complete without mentioning two more topics that further illustrate why I commend this book so highly.

1. His ministry of writing

Few ministers have the gift and ability to write such a classic as Bonar's *Life of M'Cheyne*—it is hard to believe that such a beneficial biography could have been written by a busy pastor in almost exactly twelve weeks. He also wrote other biographies, and edited two editions of Samuel Rutherford's *Letters* and at least ten other books, not to mention a huge correspondence. In the midst of a very demanding pastorate one wonders where he found the time to accomplish so much. His daughter Marjory asks the same question: 'How he found time for all he read and wrote, and studied, it is difficult to say'; but she then adds this insightful comment, 'But the hours of prayer, which nothing was allowed to hinder, made the other duties as they came, easy and light.'

Another question we might ask is why so many people were blessed by his written ministry. After reading Bonar's *Diary* there is only one satisfactory answer: this ministry was bathed in prayer. Time and again entries in his *Diary* mention prayer in this connection. He prayed for help to write, then sought God's blessing upon his readers.

2. His great bereavement

All through his ministry we find moving references to the loss of loved ones. In the early days his great loss was that of his good friend Robert Murray M'Cheyne. On the day his dear friend died Bonar wrote in his *Diary*:

> Never, never yet in all my life have I felt anything like this ... It is a blow to myself ... My heart is sore ... Life has lost half its joys, were it not the hope of saving souls. There was no friend whom I loved like him.[1]

Forty-one years later, on the anniversary of M'Cheyne's death, he wrote: 'This is a day of many memories. Friends in glory; and some of us spared wonderfully ...'[2]

On April 1, 1860 Bonar experienced the grief of losing his son Andrew at the tender age of two. However, four years later on October 15, 1864, the great bereavement of his life came with the sudden death of his wife after only twelve years of marriage.

> O what a wound! Last night most suddenly, after three hours' sinking, my dear, dear Isabella was taken from me. Lord, pour in comfort, for I cannot. It needs the Holy Ghost to work at such a time. Lord, what innumerable kindnesses Thou gavest me through her: a true wife, a true mother, a true mistress, a true friend. She passed away so gently that, till I held her and touched her cheek, I could scarcely believe it was death. I have needed this affliction. It brings to my remembrance sins of many, many kinds: neglected prayer, neglected thanksgiving, self-indulgence, my life too much a life for myself and family. Lord, let me not love Thee less, but more, because of this stroke, and from this day may I work more for the ingathering of souls.[3]

[1] *Ibid.*, p. 69 (Sat. Mar. 25, 1843).
[2] *Ibid.*, p. 254 (Tue. Mar. 25, 1884).
[3] *Ibid.*, p. 168 (Sat. Oct. 15, 1864).

Undoubtedly this was a major landmark in his spiritual life and, in the years of grief that followed, his walk with God was closer than ever. The whole of chapter 5, which details how the Lord upheld Bonar at this time, will repay close attention. I know of at least one brother in the ministry who found tremendous comfort from this portion of Bonar's *Diary* as he grieved over the loss of his wife.

As I bring this appreciation to a conclusion it is hard to find words that adequately express the blessing this book has been to me during the last few weeks. Maybe the best I can offer is to say that as I have viewed this portrait of Bonar I have seen a man who grew in the grace and knowledge of God all his days. Like Enoch, he walked with God till he was not, for God took him. My hope is that many will read—maybe some re-read—this book and reach the same conclusion as I: is there any reason why you and I cannot follow Bonar's example and do the same?

23

Revival Year Sermons (1859)

C. H. Spurgeon

Stuart Olyott

I T WAS the early summer of 1960 and I was seventeen. Having been converted a little over two years earlier, I was now the member of a small independent Baptist church without a pastor where I was learning to love the Lord, to love his word, to love his day, to love his people, and to love working for him as a Sunday School teacher and, more recently, as an occasional preacher. Doctrinally, however, I was all at sea. Then into my hands came a small book of ninety-six pages which set my compass and decided the course of my whole adult life. It was *Revival Year Sermons* by C. H. Spurgeon, which, in commemoration of the 1859 Revival, had been published by the Banner of Truth Trust the previous year.

Charles Haddon Spurgeon (1834–92) became a pastor at seventeen and was the most influential gospel preacher of the nineteenth century, exercising the greater part of his ministry in the Metropolitan Tabernacle, London. Millions of people the world over still read his sermons today, as well as his lectures, commentaries, and devotional books. When he lay dying in the south of France, 'half Europe' waited anxiously for news of him. But I knew nothing of this; nor did I know anything of the multitudes converted under his ministry, of the Pastors' College which he founded, or of the countless charitable causes for which he was responsible.

But I had heard his name. When I asked a Christian friend why he was called Haddon, he simply replied that his parents had named him 'after Spurgeon'. Not only so, but the Lord had saved me through the sermon of an unnamed preacher in a chapel in Colchester, Essex, which I was attending as a visitor. Sometimes when I spoke about this, people would say 'how like Spurgeon!' And now I was the member of a church in Chester where a small bust of 'C. H. Spurgeon' was on prominent display every Sunday, even though no one ever told me who the bearded gentleman was!

At this point I was told by the Chester Auxiliary of the National Sunday School Union that I had won a prize in the annual Scripture exam and that I could choose any books I wanted up to a total value of 12s 6d (62½p). Curiosity about 'Spurgeon' moved me to use six shillings (30p) of this princely sum in requesting *Revival Year Sermons* which I had recently seen advertised. And so the invisible hand of Providence gave to me a book which would change me for ever.

Revival Year Sermons consists of a ten-page introduction written by 'The Publishers', followed by five representative sermons of C. H. Spurgeon preached at the Surrey Gardens Music Hall during 1859. This was the third successive year that his congregation, having outgrown its chapel, had met there on Sunday mornings. On successive Sundays throughout this period this great building was filled with between 5,000 and 9,000 people. Even in Spurgeon's remarkable ministry, 1859 was an exceptional year, during which he preached with unusual power and witnessed an extraordinary number of conversions.

The introduction

The introduction to the book filled me with awe and moved me to prayer as it outlined the spiritual awakening of 1859 and placed the sermons in their historical context. For the first time, I learned that there is such a thing as revival. No one had ever told me that there are times when the Spirit of God is poured out in unusual measure, when Christ's church is wonderfully refreshed by his presence, filled with prayer and new zeal, and moved to take bold initiatives in spreading the gospel. Nor did I know that there is such a thing as anointed preaching which fills congregations with expectancy, leaves them breathless, and results in large numbers of conversions. Oh, how I longed to hear such preaching! It was the obvious need of the hour. And how I yearned that perhaps one day I might preach like that myself!

I also learned from the introduction that 'the strength of Spurgeon's ministry lay in his theology'. The gospel he preached was not the one that was being proclaimed in any of the circles with which I was acquainted. I read that he believed in 'the five great points commonly known as Calvinistic' and found out what they were. It excited me to discover that these truths were the spring from which flowed all his evangelistic preaching and appeals. Not only so, but there was a connection between the proclamation of these truths and the outbreak of revivals, and this was proved by an appeal to church history. What counts at all times is not the man, nor the methods, but the purity of the message. The sermon that honours God, God will honour.

If preachers are powerless, it is because they do not know what the gospel is. They are either ignorant of real gospel Calvinism, or are afraid of it. They are not committed to the truth which God has revealed and therefore he does not own them. 'In proportion as a ministry is truthful, God can bless it.' We cannot invite the Holy Spirit to set his seal to a lie. It is ridiculous to think that we can have God with us, while we wander from the truth. Spurgeon's opinion was that 'there is no such thing as preaching Christ and him crucified, unless we preach what nowadays is called Calvinism. It is a nickname to call it Calvinism; Calvinism is the gospel, and nothing else.'

I determined there and then that I would give more than ordinary attention to the five sermons that I was about to read. And if their Calvinism did indeed prove to be true to the word of God, then I would be unashamed to preach those truths myself, and to do so evangelistically, whatever others might say about it. This was an important point to me, for had not the previous leader of our youth group been removed from his position 'because he was teaching Calvinism'?

The sermons

When I began to read the sermons I was thrilled. The first one, on Psalm 44:1 and entitled 'The Story of God's Mighty Acts', enthralled me and gave me an appetite for church history that has never left me.

After rehearsing God's mighty acts in the Old and New Testaments, Spurgeon surveys times of spiritual awakening through the centuries, as well as making references to what was currently happening in Ulster (the northernmost province of Ireland). Such times of special blessing come suddenly, and the Lord usually brings them about by insignificant instruments who are strong in faith and prayer. The sermon proceeds to answer common objections to the idea of revival, stirs us to praise for the past and prayer for the future, shows us why the means of grace are often without effect, warns us against self-dependence, and closes with an urgent evangelistic plea.

'The Blood of the Everlasting Covenant' (Heb. 13:20) is the title of the second sermon. This taught me that God will not deal with us except through a covenant, and gave me a theological foundation where previously I had had none. The sermon is about the covenant of grace and speaks of its covenanting parties, its stipulations, those who benefit from it, and what motives lie behind it. The covenant is everlasting, 'the oldest of all things', and is sure, immutable, and will never run out. The blood of the Saviour is the fulfilment of the covenant, the bond of the Father, an evidence to us, and the glory of each person of the Trinity. As someone who had only ever heard Arminian preaching, I remember being struck by the sentence, 'And why should election frighten thee? If thou hast chosen Christ, depend upon it he has chosen thee.'

The text for the third sermon is Ezekiel 36:27, which is called 'The Necessity of the Spirit's Work'. No one can be saved unless the Holy Spirit works in them. By nature man is spiritually dead and hostile to all that is good and right, so the Holy Spirit must change his will and the bias of his heart. In and of themselves, the preaching of the word of God, and baptism and the Lord's supper, can do no good to anyone without the Spirit of God. The covenant of grace is ineffectual until the Spirit applies it. And who but the Spirit can create repentance and faith, humiliation of heart, submission to the Lord in loss and tragedy, and indifference to earthly joys? This sermon produced in me the conviction that there was no place for anything slick or clever in our presentations of the gospel. It does not matter if we come across as weak or foolish, as long as our plain preaching of the word is accompanied by the Holy Spirit.

'Predestination and Calling' (Rom. 8:30) follows as the fourth sermon. This introduced me to the whole subject of assurance. Those who have been called can know for certain that they have been predestined. The general call is sincerely addressed to all, but man is so opposed to God that no one responds to it unless the Holy Spirit makes this call effectual. Spurgeon illustrates the effectual call by vividly narrating the experiences of five biblical characters. By appealing to a selection of biblical texts he then shows how the effectual call causes sinners to walk the way of holiness, heavenly-mindedness, communion with Christ, and spiritual liberty. If you have been called, you can comfort yourself in the knowledge that you must have been elected. The Lord will never rescind this call, so, whatever you may feel about yourself, you are safe and will soon be in heaven. Examine yourself, therefore, to see whether you have been called.

The final sermon is 'The Minister's Farewell'. This was Spurgeon's last sermon at the Surrey Gardens Music Hall and he knew that it was likely that he would never see many of his hearers again. He looks at the Apostle Paul's parting words in Acts 20:26-27 before addressing the people before him in a strikingly tender and urgent manner. The apostle was pure from the blood of all men because he had not shunned to declare to them all the counsel of God. In the same way, we must preach in its due proportion every truth that the Scriptures contain. We must do this in simple language, not failing to address the particular sins of our time and of our hearers. If we do this, we will be criticized on all sides. It does not matter. Only the whole counsel of God will meet people's true needs. Those who harp on about one doctrine, thus losing the biblical balance, produce nothing but evil and spiritual ruin. If we would know the Lord's blessing, we must preach the gospel as a whole.

Spurgeon then tells the congregation that he is aware of his personal failings, and yet he has not failed to declare to them all the counsel of God. Nor has he failed to exhort, entreat and invite sinners to come to Christ. If any hearer is finally lost, it will not be the preacher's fault. He then proceeds to the most extended plea to the unconverted that I have ever read or heard, asks his hearers to pray for him, and returns to his evangelistic plea before closing.

Reflections through the years

I am very thankful to the Lord that I was introduced to the doctrines of grace through this wonderful book. As a result, these doctrines have always been to me living truths which exalt the God of Scripture, powerfully impact human lives, and stir up tender, urgent, moving appeals to men and women to close in on Jesus Christ. Yes, I have had to spend long hours studying the Bible and various theological works to improve and refine my understanding of these truths. But Spurgeon's preaching has spared me from any temptation to look on these doctrines in a dry, formal, and merely academic manner.

I have returned to *Revival Year Sermons* many times through the years, and always with considerable profit. Again and again this book has reminded me not to be squeamish about the truth. If we are the Lord's servants, we cannot spend our lives looking over our shoulders at others. He has not given us any commission to worry about what people may be saying about us. He has entrusted his gospel to us, and it is wonderful. It is not for us to add to it, to take away from it, or to qualify it in any way. We are to proclaim what he has revealed, and that is all.

But we are to be careful how we do it, and it is here that Spurgeon helps us again. As he speaks he is absorbed with his hearers and with their eternal welfare. He therefore speaks to them with obvious love, with astonishing bluntness and directness, and with pastoral sensitivity. He is aware of their questions, objections and preoccupations. He sympathizes with their burdens. He knows their joys, their fears and their temptations. He is no stranger to their daily lives. And so he speaks to them plainly, and constantly directs every one of them, converted and unconverted alike, to the Lord Jesus Christ, who is quite obviously the love of his life. As in all his works, it is Spurgeon that we read, but it is the Saviour that we see.

24

Human Nature in Its Fourfold State

Thomas Boston

Cor L. Onderdelinden

IN MY imagination, I picture myself in Simprin, a small village in the Scottish Borders. Everything around me exudes calm. In these peaceful, rural surroundings my thoughts hark back to times long ago. At a crossroads on the A6112, heading towards Swinton, I stand beside the ruins of a little church dating from the twelfth century: Simprin Old Parish Church.

It is a ruin now, with only one sandstone wall left standing on the remains of the old foundations. This is the place where, in 1699, Thomas Boston began his gospel ministry. It is a parish Boston neither desired nor chose. God saw to it that he accepted the call to Simprin. It was the Lord's leading that took him to this insignificant, minor parish. The manse was a tumbledown shack, the parish benefactor was penny-pinching, and the people were poor; accordingly, his income was low. It was here that God placed a man of great gifts and talents. For talented he certainly was, richly endowed with gifts of head and heart; knowledge and grace went hand in hand in his life.

John Macleod, in his *Scottish Theology*,[1] wrote of Thomas Boston: 'He is one of the brightest lights in the firmament of the Reformed Church in Scotland.' He also quotes Jonathan Edwards, who calls Boston 'a truly great divine'. Boston was a compassionate pastor and preacher who wrote a remarkable book that ranks among the

---

[1] John Macleod, *Scottish Theology* (Edinburgh: Banner of Truth Trust, 1974), p. 146.

spiritual masterpieces of his generation, comparable with Luther's *Commentary on Galatians*, John Bunyan's *Pilgrim's Progress*, and Joseph Alleine's *Alarm to the Unconverted*.

Boston was not destined to become a celebrated city minister, nor did he obtain a lectureship or professorship at a university. The Lord allotted Simprin to him. This is where he wrestled with God for the salvation of the souls entrusted to his care. Here, too, is where he prayed for the blessing of grace to rest upon his preaching, and for the genuine conversion of his hearers to the Lord Jesus Christ. The spiritual climate of Simprin was barren and moribund; there was great ignorance regarding spiritual life. Many parishioners were coarse and indifferent. Most were strangers to both the doctrine and the practice of piety. Boston was concerned above all else to win souls for Christ. As a minister of Christ he knew what his task was: 'Feed the flock of God which is among you, taking the oversight thereof' (1 Pet. 5:2).

It was here in isolated Simprin that the foundation was laid for Boston's *magnum opus*: *Human Nature in Its Fourfold State*.[1]

It was in that church, no larger than 60 by 15 feet, that he commenced preaching on who and what is man as he appears before a holy and righteous God. This was no cheap emotional storytelling ministry, but clear biblical preaching that announced the realities of sin and grace, law and gospel, death in Adam and life in Christ; and a preaching in which there was honesty with regard to man's eternal destiny—heaven or hell. This was a trumpet that gave no uncertain sound. This was serious work and so Boston engaged himself in prayer and study for many hours each day.

In order to structure the life of his congregation, he observed a strict pattern in his work. In the two years in which he toured parishes as a probationer while awaiting a call, he compiled his thoughts on gospel ministry in a book later published as *A Soliloquy on the Art of Man-fishing*[2]—his title chosen with reference to Matthew 4:19, 'Follow me, and I will make you fishers of men.' He called this book

---

[1] Thomas Boston, *Human Nature in Its Fourfold State* (London: Banner of Truth Trust, 1964).

[2] Thomas Boston, *The Art of Man-fishing* (Fearn, Ross-shire: Christian Focus, 1998).

his 'scribble', but it was much more than that. It was a model for his own ministry of the word.

The people were stirred by his simple, clear sermons. He was equally faithful in his pastoral visitations. Tradition has it that at the time of his arrival, the congregation numbered just eighty-eight. As time went by, however, this number increased so that the little church could barely contain Boston's many hearers. Communion services were particularly packed.

In the introduction to his *Memoirs*,[1] we read of his thorough organization of his parish. There was a forenoon and an afternoon sermon every Sabbath. There was a Sabbath evening meeting for the study of the Westminster Catechisms. Every Tuesday, there was a friendly gathering for praise and prayer at the manse, and every Thursday there was a midweek service. Rounds of instruction in the catechisms were held at stated intervals at locations throughout the parish. Every household was regularly visited. Friday and Saturday he spent in preparing his sermons. How many hours did Boston spend in private prayer and family worship? Often he wrote: 'I spent this day in fasting, prayer and meditation.' He could not, dared not, take any decisions without first seeking the Lord's approbation.

The Lord greatly blessed this faithful labourer among his 'handful', as he often refers to his flock. His sound and biblical preaching proved useful to the people. They had been ignorant, but at last they received with meekness the engrafted word. Repentance and faith was the fruit.

No drama, no orchestra, no entertainment was used, but plain preaching. His preaching was richly blessed by the Holy Spirit. The Apostle Paul wrote in Romans 10:17, 'So then, faith cometh by hearing, and hearing by the word of God.' This is a great lesson seen in the preaching of Thomas Boston: it is just this kind of preaching which we find in his sermons, and especially in his *Fourfold State*, that is the great need nowadays.

In 1707, Boston accepted a call to a larger congregation in the parish of Ettrick, but the circumstances there were not much better than those he had first encountered in Simprin. He laboured in

[1] *Memoirs of the Life, Time and Writings of Thomas Boston* (Edinburgh: Banner of Truth Trust, 1988).

Ettrick with the same application, earnestness, and burning zeal as he had in Simprin, and remained there until his death in 1732. His last sermon, preached as 'a dying man to dying men', was delivered from the manse window, his hearers standing outside.

His book

Only after a considerable number of problems in Boston's life had been overcome did the book *Human Nature in Its Fourfold State* appear in 1720, at the urging of a friend.[1] A second, comprehensively revised, edition was published in 1729. It was thereafter reprinted many times, including translations into Gaelic and Welsh.

This book is the gleanings of a thorough and industrious study. It is a simple, practical, and memorable summary of Christian doctrine. In it, Boston's vast knowledge of the reformers and Puritans is evident. As far back as Augustine, theologians had spoken of the *status quadruplex*[2] or 'four stages of man' division of spiritual states; reformation theologians who had followed suit included Zanchius, Turretin, and Ursinus.

N. Walker wrote: 'The book is a whole body of divinity. But what distinguishes it from such theological systems as are set forth by professors before their students is this, that, being addressed in the shape of sermons to country people, it is, in the first place, more popular in its form, and, in the second place, warmer and fresher in its spirit.'[3] Not surprisingly the book caught the attention of many who lived far beyond the borders of Boston's parish of Ettrick.

Boston describes in the work the four 'states' of humanity. These are:

- The State of Innocence, or Primitive Integrity;
- The State of Nature or Entire Deprivation;
- The State of Grace or Begun Recovery;[4]

[1] Andrew Thomson, *Thomas Boston, His Life and Times* (Fearn, Ross-shire: Christian Focus, 2004), pp. 93-94.

[2] Philip Graham Ryken, *Thomas Boston as Preacher of the Fourfold State* (Edinburgh: Rutherford House, 1999) pp. 67ff.

[3] Jean L. Watson, *The Pastor of Ettrick: Thomas Boston* (Edinburgh: James Gemmell, 1883), p. 84.

[4] William Addison wrote: 'Begun Recovery is a splendid alternative title!' *The Life and Writings of Thomas Boston of Ettrick* (Edinburgh: Oliver and Boyd, 1936), p. 168.

• The Eternal State or the State of Consummate Happiness or Misery.

What Boston is in fact doing in his treatment of these themes is setting out a 'touchstone of grace', conscious as he is of a great amount of chaff amongst the wheat, and well aware that not all who confess Christ with the mouth are true Christians. He clearly distinguishes between an historical faith and a true saving faith, and shows how the appearance of godliness is different from the substance of godliness.

The key issue in the book is the question of how the Lord transfers sinners from their wretched state of nature into the state of grace. 'I am now to show how the branches are cut off from the natural stock, the first Adam, and grafted into the true vine, the Lord Jesus Christ.' 'The cutting-off of the branch from the natural stock is performed by the pruning-knife of the Law, in the hand of the Spirit of God, Gal. 2:19: "I through the law am dead to the law."' This cutting-off typically occurs step by step. When a person becomes aware of being lost, he or she seeks to be righteous in God's sight by works of the law. This is an attempt to work out a righteousness for oneself through self-effort and duty. Fallen man reaches no further than the broken covenant of works; whatever he does, he is and remains in Adam and outside of Christ.

What is needed for this fallen sinner is a divine miracle: God himself must act. For this, God uses his holy law, which the Spirit of God impresses upon the soul of the sinner. Whether at once or by degrees, the converted sinner is by a process of continual discovery broken, cut off from his old existence, and brought to the feet of the Lord Jesus Christ. Boston compares this work of the law with twelve strokes of the axe or truncations. This is how the sinner is convicted of the inadequacy and shortcomings of all that springs from within. The old man of sin must be entirely cut off from Adam. As long as that old man remains bound to Adam, the sinner remains under the righteous wrath of God and the curse of the law. The troubled sinner discovers that the law is spiritual. All that is outside God's grace and mercy, and that is outside the blood and righteousness of Christ, is damnable in God's sight. For this reason, man must learn to smell the stench of death in all his own works and self-righteousness, in order that he may desire only that which comes from God by grace, namely forgiveness and reconciliation through the work of the Saviour, the Lamb of God that takes away the sin of the world. The sinner learns to despair of himself on the one hand and to look to God's grace on the other. The strokes of the axe are necessary to make room for Christ. After the twelfth stroke of the axe, the sinner is totally cut off and lies at the feet of the Lord Jesus. Christ then embraces the sinner and the sinner the Saviour. It is at this point that a poor sinner and a rich Christ come together. It is our being in Christ, or our not being in him, that determines our eternal destiny. He who is in Christ and believes in him and lives off his power will hear at the end of this brief life, 'Come, ye blessed of my Father.' Those who live and die outside of Christ will hear: 'Depart from me, ye workers of iniquity.'

Not many people believe in hell nowadays. Many no longer even agree that heaven exists. Shortly, when each person comes to die or if the Day of Judgment comes first, all will have to give an account to a holy and righteous God. Then where shall eternity be spent: in the state of consummate happiness or the state of consummate misery?

With his whole heart, Boston desired that his hearers and readers would be assured of the state of consummate happiness and that they would escape the consummate state of misery by way of genuine conversion. He knew that both of these states know no end!

Boston's inner life

We know that Boston struggled with many problems in his family. He himself was not of a strong physical constitution, his wife[1] suffered from depression, and of his ten children six died in infancy.

In his book *The Crook in the Lot*,[2] we see how Boston in all his afflictions exercised faith in God and trusted his providence, grace, and power. He humbled himself under the sovereign and omniscient will of God. He knew by experience that those who humbled themselves under God would be lifted up in due time. As the Lord promised his people: 'I will be with thee; I will not fail thee, nor forsake thee' (Josh. 1:5). God was his refuge and strength, a very present help in trouble (Psa. 46:1).

---

[1] Thomas Boston married Katharine Brown on July 17, 1700.

[2] Thomas Boston, *The Crook in the Lot, or the Sovereignty and Wisdom of God Displayed in the Afflictions of Men* (Morgan: Soli Deo Gloria Publications, 2001).

An example of one of his Personal Covenants[1] shows us his faith in the triune God.

I, Mr. Thomas Boston, preacher of the gospel of Christ, being by nature an apostate from God, an enemy to the great JEHOVAH and so an heir of hell and wrath, in myself utterly lost and undone, because of my original and actual sins, and misery thereby; and being, in some measure, made sensible of this my lost and undone state, and sensible of my need, my absolute need of a Saviour, without whom I must perish eternally; and believing that the Lord Jesus Christ, the eternal Son of the eternal God, is not only able to save me, by virtue of his death and sufferings, but willing also to have me (though most vile and ugly, and one who has given him many repulses), both from my sins, and from the load of wrath due to me for them, upon condition that I believe, come to him for salvation, and cordially receive him in all his offices; consenting to the terms of the covenant.

Therefore, as I have at several opportunities before given an express and solemn consent to the terms of the covenant, and have entered into a personal covenant with Christ; so now, being called to undertake the great and weighty work of the ministry of the gospel, for which I am altogether insufficient, I do by this declare, That I stand to and own all my former engagements, whether sacramental, or any other way whatsoever; and now again do renew my covenant with God; and hereby, at this present time, do solemnly covenant and engage to be the Lord's and make a solemn resignation and upgiving of myself, my soul, body, spiritual and temporal concerns, unto the Lord Jesus Christ, without any reservation whatsoever; and do hereby give my voluntary consent to the terms of the covenant laid down in the holy scriptures, the word of truth; and with my heart and soul I take and receive Christ in all his offices, as my PROPHET to teach me, resolving and engaging in his strength to follow, that is, to endeavour to follow his instructions.

I take him as my PRIEST, to be saved by his death and merits alone; and renouncing my own righteousness as filthy rags and menstruous cloths, I am content to be clothed with his righteousness alone; and live entirely upon free grace; likewise I take him for my ADVOCATE and INTERCESSOR with the Father: and finally, I take him as my

---

[1] *The Complete Works* (Stoke-on-Trent: Tentmaker Publications, 2002), vol. 2, p. 671 .

KING, to reign in me, and to rule over me, renouncing all other lords, whether sin or self, and in particular my predominant idol; and in the strength of the Lord, do resolve and hereby engage, to cleave to Christ as my Sovereign Lord and King, in death and in life, in prosperity and in adversity, even for ever, and to strive and wrestle in his strength against all known sin; protesting, that whatever sin may be lying hid in my heart out of my view, I disown it, and abhor it, and shall in the Lord's strength, endeavour the mortification of it, when the Lord shall be pleased to let me see it. And this solemn covenant I make as in the presence of the ever-living, heart-searching God, and subscribe it with my hand, in my chamber, at Dunse, about one o'clock in the afternoon, the fourteenth day of August, one thousand six hundred and ninety-nine years.

What we can learn from Boston's life and book

We, no less than Boston, must give good account of all that we undertake in the ministry. Well might we say with Spurgeon: 'Are we feeding the sheep or amusing the goats?' This is a question that calls for serious consideration. Let Boston's life and work spur us on to persevere in the ministry even in the most disheartening of situations. 'Preach the word; be instant in season, out of season; reprove, rebuke, exhort with all longsuffering and doctrine' (2 Tim. 4:2). Under all the difficult conditions Boston encountered, he continued to preach, visit, catechize, and diligently shepherd the flock of God. In all things he was a faithful minister of the gospel and a sincere servant of the Lord Jesus Christ. May we be found as faithful as he in the place where God has set us, and may we be used to the saving and blessing of lost sinners, as we too warmly invite and earnestly call them to Christ the Saviour just as Boston did.

It may be that a ministerial student or a recently ordained preacher, an inexperienced evangelist or newly sent missionary is reading these words. Are you, too, finding disappointment heaping up on disappointment? Are your hearers dismissive and not receptive to the gospel? Are you seeing little fruit in your work? Are you frequently encountering godlessness, carelessness, indifference, and immorality? Thomas Boston was familiar with all these discouragements (there is nothing new under the sun!). But don't give up! Pray and preach,

preach and pray. Be faithful to your calling and to the One who sent you. Endure hardship as a good soldier of Jesus Christ (2 Tim. 2:3).

If I think of the parishes of Simprin and Ettrick, what comes to mind is the illustration of the valley of dry bones in Ezekiel 37. Called to prophesy, Ezekiel had to pray for the Holy Spirit. God himself worked the miracle, using the prophet's ministry as the divinely appointed means. Ezekiel merely did as he had been commanded—and the Lord blessed it. Ezekiel's God lives still. Although Boston was not Ezekiel, he did as Ezekiel had done before him, and his work was not without blessing. And will this same Lord refuse to bless your work which is performed in prayerful dependence upon him?

Boston's domestic situation was an immense burden to him, but here too the Lord confirmed his promise: 'My grace is sufficient for thee: for my strength is made perfect in weakness' (2 Cor. 12:9).

I trust and pray that Boston's life and book will appeal to you sufficiently for you to take it up and read him. The scope of this chapter does not permit me to consider his life in the context of his times. One could certainly draw profitable lessons from the stand he made in the political and ecclesiastical controversies of his day, particularly in the Marrow Controversy that raged in the Scottish church.

On the other hand, Thomas Boston's *Memoirs* and his *Human Nature in Its Fourfold State* are excellent first choices for those looking to familiarize themselves with this great theologian and preacher. The latter in particular is a timeless classic and is just as applicable to the generations that will follow us as those that have gone before—useful for the renewal and revival of the church, to the glory of God and the salvation of sinners from perdition!

25

Letters of Samuel Rutherford

Andrew A. Bonar (Ed.)

Joel R. Beeke

ALTHOUGH he did not write letters for publication, Samuel Rutherford's *Letters* are his most popular work. They were originally collected and published by Robert MacWard, a former student, and later edited in the nineteenth century by Andrew A. Bonar.

Rutherford's *Letters*, including several abridgements, have been reprinted more than eighty times in English, fifteen times in Dutch, and several times in German, French, and Gaelic. Even Richard Baxter, one of Rutherford's most persistent critics, said that of 'such a book of letters the world never saw the like'. C. H. Spurgeon considered these letters closer to being inspired writings than anything else ever written. They are still treasured today for their beautiful presentation of both Reformed doctrine and the spiritual experience of the believer.

I have kept a copy of Rutherford's *Letters* on my nightstand for more than twenty years. I love to dip into these passionate letters before falling asleep. Countless times they have enabled me to end my day in our blessed Immanuel, whose portrait Rutherford paints with such clarity and colour as no other writer of which I am aware. When I am discouraged about my own lack of progress in sanctification or disheartened by circumstances in church or nation, I find that a letter of Rutherford's has an uncanny way of redirecting me to Christ the King enthroned upon his holy hill in Zion, as the Guarantor that we as believers will be 'more than conquerors through him that loved us' (Rom. 8:37). Many times these precious letters of Rutherford have lifted my soul out of the horrible pit and miry clay of spiritual despondency, and set my feet upon the Rock, Christ Jesus, and established my goings in him (Psa. 40:2).

Samuel Rutherford (1600–61) was born in Nisbet, Roxburghshire, and educated first at Jedburgh, then at the University of Edinburgh, where he excelled in Latin and Greek and graduated Master of Arts in 1621. He began his academic career at Edinburgh in 1623, and two years later he married Euphame Hamilton.

In 1627, Rutherford was appointed minister in the small rural parish of Anwoth by the Solway in Kirkcudbrightshire. His years there were fraught with affliction. The comfort his letters have brought to thousands was forged in the crucible of personal losses, particularly the loss of his wife, who died in 1630 after suffering intensely for thirteen months. Rutherford also experienced great personal trials. Due to political oppression he was banished to Aberdeen in 1636, having been deprived of his ministerial office and forbidden to preach anywhere in Scotland. The University of Aberdeen at that time was a bastion of Arminianism, committed to episcopacy, and strongly opposed to the Presbyterian faith which Rutherford held dear. Being separated from his congregation was a severe trial for Rutherford. Yet, in contemplating the bonds which he suffered as a prisoner of the Lord, Rutherford declared, 'I am his over-burdened debtor. I cry, "Down with me, down, down with all the excellency of the world; and up, up with Christ!"'[1]

Rutherford wholeheartedly embraced the covenanting cause in Scotland, signing the National Covenant in 1638. Soon the way opened for him to return to his post in Anwoth. The reforming Glasgow Assembly of 1638 appointed him professor of theology in St Mary's College, St Andrews. He accepted the position reluctantly and only on the condition that he be allowed to preach at least once every Lord's Day. In 1640, Rutherford remarried. His second wife was Jean M'Math, 'a woman of great worth and piety'. He had one daughter, Agnes, from his previous marriage, and six more children from the second, all of whom predeceased him. Two of the

---

[1] Samuel Rutherford, *Letters of Samuel Rutherford* (repr., Edinburgh: Banner of Truth, 1984), p. 419.

children died in infancy before Rutherford left Scotland to attend the Westminster Assembly of divines as one of the six influential Scottish commissioners or delegates. Two more children died while he and his wife were in London.

When the Assembly had concluded its work in 1647, Rutherford returned to St Andrews where he was appointed principal of St Mary's College and, in 1651, rector of the university. He spent the last fourteen years of his life teaching and preaching in St Andrews. Not long before his death Rutherford suffered renewed persecution at the hands of the restored Stuart monarchy. In 1661, a charge of high treason was brought against him and he was deprived of his ministry, his university chair, and his stipend. Summoned to answer the charges against him, the dying Rutherford told the officers of the crown, 'Tell them I have got a summons already before a superior Judge and judicatory, and I behove to answer my first summons, and ere your day come I will be where few kings and great folks come.'[1] He died peacefully on March 30, 1661, in St Andrews. Some of his last words were, 'I shall live and adore Christ; glory to my Redeemer forever. Glory, glory dwelleth in Emmanuel's land.' To his fellow ministers he said, 'Dear brethren, do all for Christ. Pray for Christ. Preach for Christ. Beware of men pleasing.'

An able scholar and disputant, Rutherford was preeminently a preacher and pastor. Not that he was a perfect man: on the one hand, he was godly and humble; on the other, he was a man of strong emotions who occasionally lost his temper and heaped abuse on his opponents. Rutherford once told his friend David Dickson, 'I am made of extremes.' Yet his life was marked by a profound diligence to honour his 'marriage vows' to Christ and, as a minister of the gospel, to espouse others to their one Husband (2 Cor. 11:2). This pastoral spirit shines throughout his letters, where we see Rutherford's heart displayed. He had a jealous love for his flock. He wrote to his congregation at Anwoth, 'My witness is above; your heaven would be two heavens to me, and your salvation two salvations.'[2] He provides a remarkable example of ministering to the saints—one which pastors would do well to emulate today.

[1] Cited in John Howie, *The Scots Worthies* (repr., Edinburgh: Banner of Truth, 1995), p. 236.
[2] Rutherford, *Letters*, p. 439.

Most (220 out of 365) of Rutherford's letters were written during his banishment in Aberdeen. While his freedom to preach was 'violently plucked ... away',[1] his pen was loosed. Indeed, Rutherford's letters are largely sermonic. He 'preferred the preaching of Christ ... to anything, next to Christ himself'.[2] The warmth and earnestness that he would have expended on his pulpit labours was encapsulated on the written page. These letters flow out of the sweet times of communion with Christ that Rutherford experienced in Aberdeen. 'I never knew by mine nine years of preaching, so much of Christ's love, as he has taught me in Aberdeen', he wrote. 'Sweet, sweet have his comforts been to my soul; my pen, tongue, and heart have no words to express the kindness, love, and mercy of my Well-beloved to me, in this house of my pilgrimage.'[3]

Generally, the fibre of Rutherford's letters is woven with two threads: the depths of the glory of God in Christ, and the blessedness of the Christian in Christ. Rutherford was captivated by the wonders of the exalted Christ for unworthy sinners:

> Set ten thousand thousand new-made worlds of angels and elect men, and double them in number, ten thousand, thousand, thousand times; let their heart and tongues be ten thousand thousand times more agile and large, than the heart and tongues of the seraphim that stand with six wings before him (Isa. 6:2), when they have said all for the glorifying and praising of the Lord Jesus, they have but spoken little or nothing.[4]

This doxological emphasis sets forth the true blessedness of the Christian, which Rutherford attempted to communicate to his recipients. 'I have', he writes, 'neither tongue nor pen to express to you the happiness of such life as in Christ.'[5] Though his path led him through hardship and trial, Rutherford's firm belief was that 'it is a king's life to follow the Lamb'.[6] The Christian today may greatly benefit from looking at life in the same way. In addition, the *Letters*

[1] *Ibid.*, p. 438.
[2] *Ibid.*, p. 182.
[3] *Ibid.*, pp. 227, 357.
[4] *Ibid.*, pp. 365-6.
[5] *Ibid.*, p. 47.
[6] *Ibid.*, p. 638.

display a number of other themes. There are at least four that are especially germane for the minister of the word to model in his own ministry.

Submission to God in all trials. Rutherford's counsel is profoundly sympathetic, addressing the young, the old, those who had lost children or spouses, and those who were going through 'divers temptations' (James 1:2). His pastoral sensitivity flowed out of his own experience. He knew what it was to be 'exercised with the wrestlings of God',[1] and was thus well equipped to speak to those who suffered in like manner. His letters frequently called believers to courage and to a faith which would 'teach you to kiss a striking Lord'.[2] Yet he was not ignorant of the struggles of faith. He prayed for himself, and also for others: 'I would I had a heart to acquiesce in his way, without further dispute.'[3]

The basis for striving after this submission was knowing God's sovereign and fatherly hand of providence. 'The wicked may hold the bitter cup to your head, but God mixeth it', Rutherford wrote.[4] In light of this, Rutherford's goal was to bring men to say, 'If God had done otherwise with me than he hath done, I had never come to the enjoying of this crown of glory.'[5] Suffering and difficult trials are often the Father's way of purging his precious children of their sins. 'My goldsmith Christ', he writes, 'was pleased to take off the scum, and burn it in the fire. And, blessed be my Refiner, he hath made the metal better.'[6] Such a submission is not mere philosophical resignation—it is joyous subjection! The Christian realizes that Christ's 'account-book is full of my debts of mercy, kindness, and free love towards me'.[7] Thus, he says, what cross is too heavy, or what trial too grievous?

Redeeming the time. Rutherford was keenly aware that though life at times seemed long and tedious, it is, as James says, 'only a vapour, that appeareth for a little time, and then vanisheth away'

[1] *Ibid.*, p. 49.
[2] *Ibid.*, p. 97.
[3] *Ibid.*, p. 510.
[4] *Ibid.*, p. 54.
[5] *Ibid.*, p. 52.
[6] *Ibid.*, p. 272.
[7] *Ibid.*, p. 296.

(James 4:14). Thus he charges his readers, 'Misspend not your short sand-glass, which runneth very fast; seek your Lord in time.'[1] The duty of the Christian is to exercise diligence in all things, and to seek the Lord while he may be found (Isa. 55:6). Rutherford's urgency is particularly evident in one letter, in which he admonishes a young person: 'Do nothing but that which ye may and would do if your eye-strings were breaking, and your breath growing cold.'[2]

With eternity knocking at the gate, Rutherford called on Christians to run the race set before them with much 'violent sweating and striving'.[3] Cater not to the natural desires of the flesh, which is a 'sluggard' and 'loveth not the labour of religion'.[4] Rather, he says, 'Haste, haste, for the tide will not bide.'[5]

Longing for heaven and being loosed from the world. The Christian is to live as a pilgrim on the earth who looks with fervent desire for his future glory in heaven. As Rutherford notes, 'If contentment were here, heaven were not heaven.'[6] Believers should expect to be restless in this life and dissatisfied with the world. The Lord all the while labours by his Spirit to loosen his children's grip on the earth. 'Build not your nest here', Rutherford exhorted, 'for God has sold the entire forest to death. … This world is a hard, ill-made bed; no rest is in it for your soul.'[7]

Instead, seek for the eternal rest above. 'Love heaven; let your heart be on it.'[8] Rutherford often expressed his deep longing to be in 'Immanuel's land' (cf. Isa. 8:8). So must the believer live his life, knowing 'that ye are as near heaven as ye are far from yourself, and far from the love of a bewitching and whorish world'.[9]

Being ravished with love for Christ. Above all, Rutherford's chief delight was to speak of the beauty and glory of Christ, and the greater part of his letters focus the minds of his readers on the sweetness of

[1] *Ibid.*, p. 277.
[2] *Ibid.*, p. 307.
[3] *Ibid.*, p. 541.
[4] *Ibid.*, p. 559.
[5] *Ibid.*, p. 346.
[6] *Ibid.*, p. 129.
[7] *Ibid.*, p. 514.
[8] *Ibid.*, p. 310.
[9] *Ibid.*, p. 527.

Christ. Throughout the letters there are frequent allusions to and quotations from the Song of Solomon. He was enraptured with the love of his Beloved. He says repeatedly that he was sick with the sweetness of Christ's love (cf. Song of Sol. 2:5 and 5:8).[1] His heart ached: 'I am so in love with his love, that if his love were not in heaven, I should be unwilling to go thither.'[2] If Rutherford longed for heaven, then, it was only because 'the Lamb is all the glory of Immanuel's land' (the refrain of Anne R. Cousin's famous poem mined from the riches of Rutherford's *Letters*).[3] Indeed, he exclaims, 'If comparison were made betwixt Christ and heaven, I would sell heaven with my blessing, and buy Christ.'[4] Thus, 'Sell all, and buy the Pearl.'[5] 'I think now five hundred heavy hearts for him too little.'[6] Such earnest declarations fill the pages of his letters. Truly, though, they spring from the ineffable happiness of one who got 'Christ for nothing'![7]

The reformed spirituality of Rutherford's *Letters* could be summed up in this citation: 'I am in as sweet communion with Christ as a poor sinner can be; and am only pained that *he* hath much beauty and fairness, and *I* little love; *he* great power and mercy, and *I* little faith; *he* much light, and *I* bleared eyes.'[8] The *Letters of Samuel Rutherford* set forth the King in his beauty, and lead the reader to lament with their author: 'Oh that I could win nigh him, to kiss his feet, to hear his voice, to feel the smell of his ointments! But oh, alas! I have little, little of him. Yet I long for more.'[9]

---

[1] See, for instance, *ibid.*, p. 352.

[2] *Ibid.*, p. 215.

[3] Anne R. Cousin, 'The Sands of Time Are Sinking'.

[4] Rutherford, *Letters*, p. 154.

[5] *Ibid.*, p. 254.

[6] *Ibid.*, p. 200.

[7] *Ibid.*, p. 185.

[8] *Ibid.*, p. 258.

[9] *Ibid.*, p. 331.

26

Thoughts on Religious Experience

Archibald Alexander

Pieter de Vries

B Y THE grace of God I was brought up in a God-fearing family. My father was an engineer and a lover of the writings of the Dutch practical writers, the Puritans, and Scottish theologians such as Thomas Boston and the Erskines (Ralph and Ebenzer). Also Luther and Kohlbrugge (the latter is less well known in the English-speaking world) were among his favourites. Actually he preferred the English and Scottish Puritans to the Dutch writers. He found them more urgent and affectionate. When he became an elder in our local independent reformed congregation, he was expected to read a sermon on those occasions when a minister was not able to officiate. My father read the sermons of Boston and the Erskine brothers, but also some of John Flavel, Thomas Watson, J. C. Ryle, and Robert Murray M'Cheyne.

By the time I was in secondary school I had started to read some of my father's books. His library was perhaps modest compared with that of a full-time pastor, but all his books were valuable. All his books were in Dutch (my father possessed Dutch translations of the English writers) with one exception: *The Select Sermons of George Whitefield.*[1] In those days I did not know anything about the Banner of Truth but that all changed in the summer of 1974. After graduating from high school, my younger brother and I visited Scotland. We stayed with a Free Presbyterian family in Inverness. On that visit I bought my first Banner book in a local evangelical bookshop: it was Thomas Watson's

[1] (London: Banner of Truth Trust, 1959).

Body of Divinity. Leafing through its pages I was impressed. The staff in the bookshop told me about a monthly magazine which was also published by the Trust. When I returned to the Netherlands and took up my theological studies, I became a subscriber to *The Banner of Truth* magazine. During my student days I ordered so many Banner books that my mother sometimes worried I was spending too much of my allowance on spiritual rather than physical food!

Archibald Alexander's Thoughts on Religious Experience

Some years later, during my first pastorate, I attended the Leicester Ministers' Conference and bought a Banner book that made a deep and lasting impression on me. It was written by a Princeton theologian I had never heard of before. Until then the only Princeton theologian I knew was Charles Hodge, the author of a large Systematic Theology. My new book was *Thoughts on Religious Experience* and it was written by Archibald Alexander. The publisher's introduction was written by W. J. Grier, and it gave me a clear insight into the greatness of this man of God. Reading the book itself convinced me that Archibald Alexander was no mean theologian and Christian.

Thoughts on Religious Experience confirmed for me that real Christianity is always experiential. In this Alexander is reflecting not only Reformed and Puritan theology, but the great Augustinian-Bernardian tradition of the early and medieval church. The experience of faith reminds us of the unity of true believers in all the ages of church history. Real Christians, regardless of what stream of Christianity they find themselves in, glorify and enjoy the triune God, the God of full salvation.

Thoughts on Religious Experience made me realize that what really matters is not that one knows the time or date of one's conversion, but that one daily shows the evidences of a new life in a humble walk with God and in a resting on Christ and his righteousness alone for salvation. What value is there in saying that one knows the day and hour one was born again, if one does not show the marks of a true Christian?

In the Dutch language there are several works which have Christian experience as their main theme, but none of them approach Alexander's *Thoughts on Religious Experience* for their breadth and depth. Not without reason was Alexander called by Dr Theodore Woolsey 'the Shakespeare of the Christian heart'. In my opinion Alexander is an even better guide in this area of Christian experience than Jonathan Edwards, who is often seen as the church's great theologian of revival and Christian experience. Alexander was very familiar with Edwards' writings and was not intimidated by the reputation of his predecessor at Princeton: 'if there be a fault in the writings of this great and good man on the subject of experimental religion, it is that they seem to represent renewed persons as at the first occupied with the contemplation of the attributes of God with delight, without ever thinking of a Mediator'.

Who was Archibald Alexander (1772–1851)?

Archibald Alexander was brought up in a Presbyterian family in Roxbridge County, not far from the city of Lexington in Virginia. His grandfather, who had emigrated from the north of Ireland to America, was converted during the Great Awakening. It seems that the religion of his parents lacked the experiential fervour of that of his grandfather. Nevertheless their children received a strict Presbyterian upbringing. Archibald, their third child, knew the Shorter Catechism by heart before he was seven years old. But his parents never spoke about their own communion with God.

One memory Alexander retained from childhood was of how critically his parents had spoken about a lay preacher whose urgent and affectionate sermon about the coming judgment and the need of a living faith had made such a deep impression on the ten-year-old boy. Alexander later often warned parents of inadvertently quenching the religious impressions and spiritual interest of their children by such graceless conversation.

Alexander entered Liberty Hall Academy at the age of ten and sat under the teaching of William Graham. Graham, although strictly Calvinistic in his views, was, according to Alexander, a somewhat peculiar man. When almost seventeen Alexander became a tutor in the family of General John Posey. The general was a nominal Christian, but in his household was a Christian woman of great spiritual maturity. Mrs Tyler often spoke with Alexander on religious subjects. She was of Baptist persuasion but sensing Alexander's reservations regarding Christian experience, she pointed him to the writings of John Flavel, a Puritan minister of Presbyterian convictions, in order that he might realize that true Christian experience is not the reserve of any one denomination.

Old Mrs Tyler often asked Alexander to read sermons not only to her but to the whole household, especially on Lord's day evenings. On one occasion, instead of continuing his readings of Flavel's *Method of Grace*, he chose another of Flavel's sermons on Revelation 3:20, which is found in *England's Present Duty* but is better known by the title 'Christ Knocking at the Door of Sinners' Hearts'. He was deeply impressed by what he read. A few days later, however, Alexander's joy disappeared and he concluded that he was mistaken to have seen this experience as true conversion.

In the year 1789 he returned home with the intention of further study. At this time a number of revivals were taking place in the western parts of Virginia, in what became known as the Second Evangelical Awakening. William Graham wanted to visit the scenes and proposed taking the young Alexander and a certain Samuel Wilson with him.

Hearing and seeing for himself deep conviction of sin and sudden conversions Alexander concluded that he himself was still unsaved and that his former hopes were without foundation. Travelling back home he came into contact with James Mitchell, a Presbyterian minister. In private conversation Alexander told him that he had not experienced conviction of sin to the same degree he had witnessed in others. Mitchell listened patiently to Alexander's concerns and reminded him that it is not necessary for all to feel conviction of sin to the same degree. The purpose of conviction is to show us our need of Christ as Saviour. From that moment Alexander entertained a joyful hope that he might yet be saved. It was not long after this that he made a public profession of faith. He was licensed to preach the gospel and was ordained to the Presbyterian ministry.

Alexander served as an itinerant preacher to several congregations for a few years. In 1796, when still only twenty-four, he became president of Hampden-Sidney College, but still continued his preaching and pastoral ministry. In 1806 he accepted a call to the Third Presbyterian Church of Philadelphia. However, the year 1811 was to be the major turning point in his career. The General Assembly of the Presbyterian Church in the United States appointed him as the first professor of the newly formed theological seminary at Princeton. He was to hold this position until his death in 1851.

Thoughts on Religious Experience contains the fruit of a long life spent in the service of the Christian gospel, part of which was during remarkable days of revival. It was first published in 1841.

Alexander's definition of religious experience

Alexander defines religious experience as the impression of divine truth on the human mind rightly apprehended. Deviations in the understanding of the truths revealed in Holy Scripture lead to deviations in experience. Hence we find that, according to Alexander, those Christian denominations that receive the system of evangelical truth only in part tend to have defective religious experience as a consequence.

Knowledge of divine truth is essential to real piety. It is difficult to state, according to Alexander, how many deficiencies in doctrinal understanding may exist alongside true piety. Here we have one evidence of the real catholic attitude of Alexander. In him we see the same spirit as found in John 'Rabbi' Duncan, the nineteenth-century Scottish theologian: 'I am first a Christian, next a Catholic, then a Calvinist, fourth a Paedobaptist, and fifth a Presbyterian, and I cannot reverse this order.'

In Alexander's opinion the reformed understanding of faith and grace is the clearest expression of biblical truth. Experience not formed by and based upon biblical truth cannot be seen as true Christian experience. Diversity in experience is related not only to the extent to which divine truth is understood and apprehended, but also to what Alexander calls the variety of the constitutions of human minds.

Alexander's book contains many important and relevant insights that will help us in our Christian living today. Perhaps more than ever strong emotional feeling (whatever its religious content) is seen by many as a fruit of the work of the Holy Spirit. Post-modern theologians lay an emphasis on the importance of authenticity and emotion at the expense of truth. Alexander rightly warns us that, although true piety always touches the emotions, strong emotions themselves say more about a person's constitution than about the biblical content of the experience.

As a preacher and pastor Alexander's aim was to inform the head and move the heart. Sermons must have solid biblical and dogmatic content, but a preacher must not stop with instruction. His aim must be to move the hearts of his hearers to trust in Christ, grow in the knowledge and love of Christ, and to be more conformed to Christ. There is a real danger of being orthodox and reformed in doctrine but not matching that with fervent piety and heartfelt love for Christ and his church. It is possible to be deficient in doctrinal understanding and yet to sincerely trust in Christ; it is also possible to have an impeccable understanding of Christian doctrine but never to experience the power of the new birth.

The reality of the new birth and the need for self-examination
Alexander's great emphasis is the new birth. The Holy Spirit, convincing us of sin and misery, enables the sinner to receive and rest upon Christ for salvation. But until that supernatural work takes place in the soul the sinner understands biblical truth as a blind man understands colours. But in God's light we see light.

Is conviction of sin by the law prior to our being reborn by the Spirit and united to Christ by a living faith, a necessary element in conversion? Alexander acknowledges that conviction of sin often precedes the new birth but argues that it is very difficult to prove from Scripture that such a preparatory work is *always* necessary.

Most believers cannot pinpoint the exact moment they were born again. The first clear and lively exercise of faith and repentance should not be seen as the origin of spiritual life. Often new life may exist in a feeble state long before. Far more important than trying to determine the moment of our new birth is to daily demonstrate the fruit of the Spirit's presence and work within us, in a heartfelt sorrow for sin and joy in God through Jesus Christ.

How important then is self-examination! Yet in distinguishing between true and counterfeit religious experience we must realize that God is the ultimate judge. In his *Thoughts on Religious Experience* Alexander skilfully, and with biblical precision, balances these two things: a resting on God's promises as the ground of one's salvation, and self-examination to see that one has a real faith, wrought by the Holy Spirit in the heart. Both emphases are necessary in faithful preaching.

Final word

Much more could be said about the importance of *Thoughts on Religious Experience*, but let me give you one last piece of advice: buy the book, and read it more than once, and you will discover that it has true and lasting value!

27

Redemption Accomplished and Applied
John Murray

Albert N. Martin

T O THE left of my computer desk there is a ledge along the wall, just wide enough to serve as a convenient bookshelf. On that ledge there are usually about twelve to fifteen books that are especially useful to me when engaged in writing projects.

These books fall into several distinct categories. There is a dictionary, a synonym finder, and several books dealing with effective writing. Then there are various versions of the Bible and a Strong's concordance. In addition to these there is a Westminster Confession of Faith and Catechisms.

One other book stands out among the others. It is a red leather hardcover volume. Within those covers is the 1961 Banner of Truth edition of Professor John Murray's classic work entitled *Redemption Accomplished and Applied.*

This book has earned its place on that ledge because of the frequency with which I consult it for my own edification and in my efforts to write things that will edify others. As the title indicates, the heart of its contents is an examination of the biblical doctrine of salvation—a salvation purposed and planned in eternity, purchased by the obedience and vicarious curse-bearing of Incarnate Deity, and applied with transforming power by the person and ministry of the Holy Spirit.

In my early thirties when my study of the Scriptures was gradually, but inexorably, leading me into an understanding of what I now know as historic Reformed and confessional soteriology, a copy of this book was placed in my hands. When I first read the book and followed the painstaking exegetical labours of Professor Murray I was persuaded that what is labelled Reformed soteriology was nothing more or less than the biblical teaching concerning various dimensions of God's gracious and grand rescue mission of sinners.

The book begins by demonstrating the biblical teaching concerning the accomplishment of redemption by the atoning sacrifice of our Lord Jesus Christ. Starting with the necessity of the atonement, the author then discusses the nature and the perfection of the atonement, culminating in an exposition of the extent of the atonement. In each of these chapters the reader is led by the hand of careful and precise exposition of Scripture to 'Behold the Lamb of God' in all the glory of his person and the perfection of his sacrificial death.

The last half of the book addresses the subject of how God applies the various benefits of the atonement to the individuals upon whom he has set his love and placed within the orbit of his saving purpose. After demonstrating from the Scriptures that there is an order to this application, the Professor leads us to consider the specific elements of this order from its inception in effectual calling to its consummation in glorification. In between these two aspects of the application of redemption, we are given a thoroughly exegetical and clearly organized presentation of such redemptive blessings as regeneration, justification, adoption, sanctification, and perseverance. The last chapter of the book, which expounds the subject of glorification, is preceded by what I regard as the crown jewel in the book. It is the chapter entitled 'Union with Christ'. Here we read Murray's words that

> Union with Christ is really the central truth of the whole doctrine of salvation not only in its application but also in its once-for-all accomplishment in the finished work of Christ. Indeed the whole process of salvation has its origin in one phase of union with Christ and salvation has in view the realization of other phases of union with Christ.[1]

[1] John Murray, *Redemption Accomplished and Applied* (Edinburgh: Banner of Truth Trust, 2009), p. 153.

Towards the end of the chapter the author further writes that

Union with Christ is the central truth of the whole doctrine of salvation. All to which the people of God have been predestined in the eternal election of God, all that has been secured and procured for them in the once-for-all accomplishment of redemption, all of which they become the actual partakers in the application of redemption, and all that by God's grace they will become in the state of consummated bliss is embraced within the compass of union and communion with Christ.[1]

While we should be grateful for the renewed emphasis on the biblical doctrine of union with Christ reflected in the number of recent books written on this theme, I doubt anything will be written in a relatively brief, concentrated, yet comprehensive way, that will rival the biblical substance, clarity, and spiritual impact of this chapter written by Murray.

Another chapter that was of particular help to me in my earlier days is the chapter on 'Faith and Repentance'. As a boy, having been reared in the context of Arminian decisionism, I had made a number of 'decisions for Christ'. However, I was truly converted just prior to my eighteenth birthday. A short time after my conversion, with the encouragement and guidance of two elderly men of God in a local gospel mission, I began to preach on a street corner and also in the mission hall which was under the direction of these two old saints. From that early beginning I always preached the reality of human sinfulness, the centrality of the cross in God's provision for sinners, and the absolute necessity for sinners to repent and believe the gospel. However, as I matured in my understanding of the word of God, I encountered the long-standing debate among theologians with respect to whether or not faith was prior to repentance, or whether repentance was prior to faith. Realizing that one's answer to this question had manifold practical implications, both for preaching and for living the Christian life, I could not dismiss the question as a theological storm in a teacup. I shall never forget the tremendous sense of relief which came to my mind and heart regarding this vexing question when I read the chapter in Murray's work in which

[1] *Ibid.*, p. 161.

he addresses this question. He refused to treat repentance and faith in separate chapters. Furthermore, he was bold enough to assert the following (all emphasis mine).

> *The question has been discussed: which is prior, faith or repentance? It is an unnecessary question and the insistence that one is prior to the other futile. There is no priority.* The faith that is unto salvation is a penitent faith and the repentance that is unto life is a believing repentance.[1]

It was in this same chapter that I came across Murray's definition and description of saving faith which, through the years, I have had occasion to quote numerous times in preaching. He states that

> the essence of saving faith is to bring the sinner lost and dead in trespasses and sins into direct personal contact with the Saviour himself, contact which is nothing less than that of *self commitment to him in all the glory of his person and perfection of his work as he is freely and fully offered in the gospel.*[2]

The biblical doctrines of regeneration, justification, adoption, and sanctification constitute the very heart of the salvation procured by the work of Christ. None can be too well established in the biblical teaching concerning these aspects of '*Redemption Applied*'. From the apostolic age until this very day Satan has always been at work to blur or distort these truths and to deflect men and women from understanding and embracing these central blessings of salvation. In treating these aspects of the application of redemption Murray excels in demonstrating what they do not mean, highlighting the various heresies concerning these things that have plagued the church throughout its history. He then establishes their proper meaning by the careful definition of these biblical words and by the use of parallel passages in which he makes Scripture the infallible interpreter of these blessings of salvation. As surely as every preacher needs to be clear in his understanding and bold and biblically grounded in his preaching of these wonderful provisions of God's salvation, it is equally vital that the rank and file of God's people possess a clear grasp upon these blessings of God's grace if they are to be stable and fruitful as the children of God. *Redemption Accomplished and Applied* is just the

[1] *Ibid.*, p. 107.
[2] *Ibid.*, p. 106.

kind of book to furnish preachers with a model of how to teach and preach these truths, and to assist serious believers to become rooted and grounded in them.

The current spate of false teaching concerning the biblical doctrine of sanctification and the Christian life constrains me to highlight the chapter dealing with this doctrine. After addressing some crucial presuppositions, Murray goes on to focus on what he describes as the 'concern of sanctification, and the means of sanctification'. In handling the subject he offers a clear biblical case to prove that in the life of everyone who comes within the orbit of God's saving work, sin is dethroned from its ruling and governing power. He writes,

> The Holy Spirit is the controlling and directing agent in every regenerate person. Hence the fundamental principle, the governing disposition, the prevailing character of every regenerate person is holiness—he is 'Spiritual' and he delights in the law of the Lord after the inward man (1 Cor. 2:14, 15; Rom. 7:22).[1]

He then proceeds to substantiate from the Scriptures that though sin no longer *reigns* in the believer, it yet *remains* and must be dealt with in the way of God's appointment and by the means God has chosen. In addressing this vital aspect of the Christian life, he demonstrates that there is a biblical synergism at work in the true believer. Unlike regeneration that is monergistic (that is, God alone is at work to bring about the new birth), in the ongoing process of sanctification the believer is consciously and deliberately active as a new man in Christ. By the enablement of the Holy Spirit the believer seeks to put sin to death (Rom. 8:13) and to cultivate an increasing measure of moral likeness to Jesus Christ (1 John 2:6). This crucial subject is handled in such a way as to leave no room for the so-called 'carnal Christian'. Also, Murray effectively slays every species of quietism, or that teaching commonly designated by the term the 'deeper life'. Furthermore, those in our day who have embraced the truncated and unbiblical notion that the exclusive method of sanctification is 'to preach the gospel to ourselves' would do well to sit down with Murray and with their Bibles, and either disprove or embrace the view of sanctification set forth in this chapter.

[1] *Ibid.*, p. 134.

In fact, I would be so bold as to suggest to pastors who read these pages to prayerfully consider supplying their church book-tables with an ample number of copies of this book; then inform the congregation that it is their plan for a number of months to preach sermons structured by the outline and pattern of Professor Murray's handling of the subjects in this masterful book. I would further urge pastors to encourage their people to purchase a copy of the book and to read it through, keeping pace with the specific chapter being considered in the sermon.

I am quite sure that many who read these pages will have read books that have greatly informed their mind and transformed their life. With that experience there is often an accompanying deep desire that one could have had the privilege of knowing the author personally. God was gracious to me in that he gave me the opportunity to know Professor Murray. I had merely met him briefly on several occasions in conjunction with various ministries at Westminster Seminary in Philadelphia, Pennsylvania. However, my first visit to the United Kingdom was undertaken in conjunction with an invitation to speak at the 1967 Leicester Ministers' Conference. Professor Murray and W. J. Grier were the 'resident patriarchs' of the conference at that time. Needless to say, having just celebrated my thirty-third birthday the thought of preaching with these two proven and highly esteemed men of God as part of my congregation was both intimidating and humbling. However, it was on that occasion that I saw Spirit-ripened humility displayed in an unforgettable way. Professor Murray and I had each been assigned to speak at three preaching sessions. However, as the conference progressed, he insisted that he step aside for his last planned lecture and permit the young American Baptist preacher to take his place! Further interactions with the Professor in subsequent ministers' conferences and a school of theology in London have left an indelible imprint upon my spirit. If it is indeed true that 'the life of a minister is the life of his ministry', then Professor Murray embodied that aphorism as few men have done.

Most likely, some of my readers had their curiosity aroused by my opening remarks concerning that special 'red leather hardcover volume', that holds an honoured place on the shelf to the left of my computer desk. Perhaps you wondered whether or not there was a special limited edition of such a volume. No—no such volume has been produced for general consumption. Permit me to tell you where my copy came from.

As I began to cultivate friends among the British preachers who attended the Leicester Ministers' Conferences in the late 1960s and throughout the 1970s, one such brother became a special friend. As we nurtured our friendship my appreciation and love for Professor Murray's book must have been quite patent to this dear brother. As a result, in November 1970 he presented me with the mysterious 'red leather hardcover volume' of *Redemption Accomplished and Applied*. Realizing what such a gift would mean to me, he took an ordinary paperback copy of the 1961 Banner of Truth edition, and placed it in the hands of an accomplished bookbinder. That precious volume has been my companion in my travels to many parts of the world since 1970. It continues to exert a powerful influence upon me as I seek to press on in my journey to the Celestial City, confident that there is indeed a glorious redemption that has been accomplished and applied for sinners such as I.

May the commendation of this book result in many others purchasing this gem, carefully and prayerfully reading and absorbing its contents and thereby attaining a deeper understanding and experience of this 'so great salvation'.

May the preachers who read these words be stirred to proclaim the truths contained in this book with the care, clarity, precision, and practical application with which Professor Murray has opened them up to us.

28

Precious Remedies Against Satan's Devices

Thomas Brooks

J. Ligon Duncan

I THINK I was in my twenties when I first read Thomas Brooks' *Precious Remedies Against Satan's Devices*.[1] My original copy (I still have it at my desk, always ready to hand) fell apart with use, wear, and marking. I had it re-glued professionally, but it fell apart again from continued usage. Brooks so helped me that I bought the six-volume set of his collected writings *The Works of Thomas Brooks*[2] as soon as possible. Only later did I learn that he was a favourite of C. H. Spurgeon (which did not surprise me). Brooks has been a pastor and a mentor to me through his writing.

Precious Remedies is one of my favourite books for at least three reasons. First, it helped me more with sermon application than any other book I had read up to that point. Like many young preachers, I found exposition the easiest part of sermon preparation and delivery, and application the most difficult. My application lacked discrimination and specificity. That is, I failed adequately to account for the different kinds of hearers that were sitting under the word and thus made generic application without sufficient particularity. Some of this was due to lack of life experience. Only living, growing, and

---

[1] Thomas Brooks, *Precious Remedies Against Satan's Devices* (Edinburgh: Banner of Truth Trust, 1968).

[2] Thomas Brooks, *The Works of Thomas Brooks*, 6 vols. (Edinburgh: banner of Truth Trust, 1980).

groaning can remedy that. But Brooks opened my eyes to the way a good pastor carefully considers the different kinds of people, and the different kinds of spiritual issues and challenges, that are present in any given congregation. That was huge for me.

In our own time, this is still a major issue in preaching, even in the reformed world. Today, in the wake of a generation-long revival of interest in the doctrines of grace, you will hear many preachers essentially give the same sermon every Sunday. It goes something like this: 'The law says "do" but the gospel says "done." The law commands you to do "X", but you can't because you are a sinner. But the gospel says Jesus has done it for you, trust him and praise God for his grace.'

Now there are dozens of things we could say about this, but I would draw your attention to two. For one thing, this kind of message makes no distinction between believers and unbelievers. It assumes that their basic spiritual condition and problem are the same. While I wholeheartedly agree that believers need the gospel just as much as unbelievers do, they need it in a different way. Brooks understands this and so makes distinctions in his preaching and writing that take into account such significant differences in his hearers and readers. Some are unconverted; some are converted but struggling with assurance; some are converted but in the grip of besetting sin; some are believers under long and hard trials; some are tempted to pride, while others are tempted to despair. Their situations are different and God's word speaks specifically to them in their particular situations.

Another way Brooks helped my application was in specificity. It is so tempting for young preachers in application on a passage dealing with, for instance, sexual purity, to say to the believers in the congregation by way of application: 'be sexually pure' or 'don't lust' or 'don't look at pornography'. The application is superficial and unspecific, and offers no help to the struggling saint (and ironically makes the approach in the paragraph above attractive to many, preachers and preached to alike). Most believers in well-taught congregations know they should be sexually pure, but they are longing for their pastor to help them with how. Brooks does so. He explains to them why they are tempted, points out a dozen different ways they can be tempted, and gives them a hundred different 'remedies' with which to battle the various temptations! This was mind-blowingly helpful to me. This is why I say that Brooks was a 'game-changer' for me in this area. And I think he could benefit numerous preachers in improving application (and frankly, variety) in our preaching.

Precious Remedies is a favourite book of mine for a second reason. It speaks to my soul. It helps show me my sin and show me the Saviour. It lays me low and then gives me gospel hope. When I first read *Precious Remedies*, I read it not looking for ideas for teaching and preaching, but for my own life, my own heart, and my own walk. The benefits it yielded to me in preaching and teaching were secondary to the benefit it had for my communion with God and life in this world.

When Brooks told me that Satan often tempts us by 'presenting the bait and hiding the hook', I immediately recognized that strategy, both in my Bible and in my experience. When he said the evil one often 'paints sin with virtue's colours', I realized he was speaking right into my own vain self-justifications. When he talked about Satan getting us to 'extenuate and lessen' our sin, I heard my own excuses echoing in his words. When he spoke of 'showing to the soul the best men's sins and hiding from the soul their virtues, their sorrows, and their repentance' as a way Satan tempts us to be careless with sin, it intuitively registered with me. When he wrote that the devil 'presents God to the soul as one made up all of mercy', I had seen that—in myself and in others.

When he addressed the adversary's tactics of 'persuading the soul that repentance is easy and that therefore we need not worry about sinning', or 'making the soul bold to venture upon the occasions of sin', or 'representing to the soul the outward mercies enjoyed by men walking in sin, and their freedom from outward miseries', or 'presenting to the soul the crosses, losses, sorrows, and sufferings that daily attend those who walk in holiness', or 'causing saints to compare themselves and their ways with those reputed to be worse than themselves', or 'polluting the souls and judgments of men with dangerous errors that lead to looseness and wickedness', or 'leading men to choose wicked company'—all these made instinctive sense. Brooks' diagnoses reveal both his knowledge of Scripture and his pervasive pastoral wisdom. He had encountered these 'devices' in his own life and ministerial experience, and thus was able to give me the benefit of his biblical counsel.

Faithful ministers cannot be made or sustained without this kind of heart-work. This is another reason I think we need Brooks today. He locks in on our sin like a laser beam and harasses our hypocrisy. Sin doesn't just rob a pastor of joy, it cripples his confidence and motivation. This is, of course, true for every believer as well, but especially so for those in ministry.

There is a third and very personal reason I resonated and still resonate with *Precious Remedies*. It has been a part of a journey in Christian friendship. Almost twenty years ago, I identified four young men in whom I saw gifts for the eldership in the congregation I was then serving. I invited them into a weekly Bible study and fellowship. That little gathering lasted through thick and thin, and eventually all of them became elders in God's church. One of the first books we read together, if not the first, was *Precious Remedies*. I think I can speak for them all in saying that it remains our favourite.

We shared crushing heartbreaks, deep bereavements, vocational trials, family struggles, church crises, cultural shifts, as well as regional and national calamities together (one of them was responsible for the massive recovery operation in the wake of the devastating Hurricane Katrina, which ravaged the whole Mississippi Gulf Coast in 2005). We talked and discussed and argued and theologized and reflected and prayed and laughed and wept and lived life together. We confessed and confronted the most intimate of sins in one another. We tenaciously held on to one another in trial and temptation. And Brooks was ever and almost always referenced and quoted.

We loved Brooks' aphorisms (and so did Spurgeon; he collected a book-full of them in the aptly titled *Smooth Stones Taken from Ancient Brooks*!).

Whatever sin the heart of man is most prone to, that the devil will help forward.

Sin is bad in the eye, worse in the tongue, worse still in the heart, but worst of all in the life.

Let the thoughts of a crucified Christ be never out of your mind.

Talk not of a good life, but let thy life speak.

Know that it is not the knowing, nor the talking, nor the reading man, but the doing man, that at last will be found the happiest man.

There are many more of them. He is the master of the pithy, memorable, didactic, edifying phrase (among a generation of past masters in that art).

But we also found Brooks hilariously funny (even when he was unintentionally so) and endearingly biased on certain matters. For instance, we often remarked with amusement on his very English take on the world. There is his twice-told unflattering tale of the malevolent Italian 'who first made his enemy deny God, and then stabbed him, and so at once murdered both body and soul'. Then there is his sermon against the Scots, preached before parliament, and based on Isaiah 10:6: 'I send it against a godless nation and commission it against the people of my fury to capture booty and to seize plunder, and to trample them down like mud in the streets.' Clearly, the Italians and Scots (not to mention the Russians!) did not rate highly with Mr Brooks! As one of Scottish descent myself, I happily forgive him.

Often, we would catch ourselves remarking on something in the services and sermons that reminded us of biblical truth that Brooks had driven into our hearts with his words, or we would text one another favourite quotes or share particularly timely or meaningful passages. Brooks became a companion to us in life and conversation, who delighted us, warned us, helped us, encouraged us, and taught us. He was a real presence in our friendship and fellowship.

Who was Thomas Brooks?

Thomas Brooks (1608–80) was an English Puritan preacher and author. Very little is known about him. He studied at Emmanuel College, Cambridge, beginning in 1625, and may have rubbed shoulders there with giants such as John Milton, Thomas Hooker, John Cotton, and Thomas Shepard. But we lose track of him until the 1640s. He very much identified with the parliamentary cause during the English Civil War, and, like John Owen and Thomas Goodwin, was congregational in his view of church polity.

Brooks was the minister at Thomas Apostle's in London, preached at least twice before the House of Commons, and later served St Margaret's, New Fish Street Hill, London (which burned down in the Great Fire of 1666). In 1662 the infamous Act of Uniformity forced him out of his church, but (like Matthew Henry's father Philip) he seems to have stayed in his parish and even preached occasionally. He later became minister of a congregation at Moorfields, near St Margaret's. He stayed in London during the Plague of 1665 and Great Fire of 1666, caring for his people (the London Puritans were renowned for this kind of brave, self-sacrificial ministerial conduct).

Brooks was twice-married, outliving his first wife, Martha Burgess (who passed away in 1676), and predeceasing his second and much younger wife, Patience Cartwright. Brooks died in 1680. He is buried in London's famous Bunhill Fields cemetery, the Valhalla of English nonconformity, which can still be visited today, just across the street from John Wesley's house.

What is Brooks hallmark? Usefulness

S. M. Houghton (who wrote the biography of the author in the Puritan Paperbacks edition of *Precious Remedies*) reckoned Brooks to be among the mighty men of Puritanism (not the mightiest but 'among the thirty' to make allusion to 2 Samuel 23 and David's last words). Alexander B. Grosart quotes Brooks' contemporary Edmund Calamy as saying that Brooks was 'a very affecting preacher and useful to many'. Grosart (the editor of the 1866 edition of Brooks' collected *Works*) goes on to say that if Richard Sibbes is, in one word, 'heavenly', then Thomas Brooks is 'useful'. Grosart's estimation of Brooks is worth reading:

> His slightest 'epistle' is 'bread of life'; his most fugitive 'sermon' a full cup of 'living water': the very foliage of his exuberant fancies 'leaves' of the tree of life: his one dominating aim to make dead hearts warm with the life of the gospel of him who is life; his supreme purpose to 'bring near' the very truth of God. Hence his directness, his urgency, his yearning, his fervour, his fulness of Bible citation, his wistfulness, his intensity, his emotion, and that fine passion of enthusiasm sprung of compassion, and his iteration and forgetfulness, and Pauline accident of choice words or melody of sentence. His desire to be useful to souls, to achieve the holy success of serving Christ, to win a sparkling crown to lay at his feet, breathes and burns from first to last. Everything is subordinated to '*usefulness*', and while he gathered around him the cultured and the titled … it was his chief rejoicing that like his Master, 'the common people' heard and read him 'gladly'.

An outline of **Precious Remedies**

There is hardly a wasted word in any of Brooks' fore-pieces to *Precious Remedies*. Do not skip them! An editor could not remove a sentence from them without loss. Here is a gem, when he explains in 'The Epistle Dedicatory' that

> Christ, the Scripture, your own hearts, and Satan's devices, are the four prime things that should be first and most studied and searched. If any cast off the study of these, they cannot be safe here, nor happy hereafter. It is my work as a Christian, but much more as I am a Watchman, to do my best to discover the fullness of Christ, the emptiness of the creature, and the snares of the great deceiver.

Centuries before the talk of 'spiritual warfare' became *au courant* in evangelical circles, the Puritans wrote searchingly, profoundly, and biblically about the reality of Satan and the extra-personal dimension of temptation in the Christian life. We struggle not simply against the world and the flesh, but also against the devil.

In his 'Word to the Reader', Brooks issues a stirring warning that gripped me the first time I ever read it, and still does so today.

> Reader, If it be not strong upon thy heart to practise what thou readest, to what end dost thou read? To increase thy own condemnation? If thy light and knowledge be not turned into practice, the more knowing man thou art, the more miserable man thou wilt be in the day of recompense; thy light and knowledge will more torment thee than all the devils in hell. Thy knowledge will be that rod that will eternally lash thee, and that scorpion that will for ever bite thee, and that worm that will everlastingly gnaw thee; therefore read, and labour to know, that thou mayest do, or else thou art undone for ever. When Demosthenes was asked, what was the first part of an orator, what the second, what the third? he answered. Action; the same may I say. If any should ask me, what is the first, the second, the third part of a Christian? I must answer. Action; as that man that reads that he may know, and that labours to know that he may do, will have two heavens—a heaven of joy, peace, and comfort on earth, and a heaven of glory and happiness after death.

Not many are the authors who warn you against reading their books if you are unprepared to implement their teaching.

In Brooks' 'Introduction', he makes an exegetical case to prove the point that 'Satan hath his several devices to deceive, entangle, and undo the souls of men.' He goes to three key passages:

(1) Ephesians 6:11: 'Put on the full armour of God, so that you will be able to stand firm against the schemes of the devil.'

(2) 2 Timothy 2:26: 'And they may come to their senses and escape from the snare of the devil, having been held captive by him to do his will.'

(3) Revelation 2:24-25: 'But I say to you, the rest who are in Thyatira, who do not hold this teaching, who have not known the deep things of Satan, as they call them—I place no other burden on you. Nevertheless what you have, hold fast until I come.'

Many more, of course, could be added:

(1) 1 Timothy 3:7: 'And he must have a good reputation with those outside the church, so that he will not fall into reproach and the snare of the devil.'

(2) Ephesians 4:27: 'And do not give the devil an opportunity.'

(3) James 4:7: 'Submit therefore to God. Resist the devil and he will flee from you.'

(4) 1 Peter 5:8: 'Be of sober spirit, be on the alert. Your adversary, the devil, prowls around like a roaring lion, seeking someone to devour.'

What is striking is the attention that Brooks, and the Puritans in general, give to this dimension of the Christian life and the long war of sanctification. They soberly remind us that our battle is not against flesh and blood.

The first main section of the book is *Satan's Devices to Draw the Soul to Sin*. In this and most of following divisions of *Precious Remedies*, Brooks gives a list of 'Devices' (ploys, strategies, schemes) of Satan, and then underneath each he gives numerous 'Remedies' (biblical cures, truths, promises, and graces with which to fight against sin). Here, he lists twelve Satanic devices and then anywhere from four to eight remedies in response to each of the devices. One particularly searching passage deals with the 'deceitful and bewitching nature of sin'. I tremble when I read it, because I have seen it and experienced it. Brooks says:

Sin gives Satan a power over us, and an advantage to accuse us and to lay claim to us, as those that wear his badge; it is of a very bewitching nature; it bewitches the soul, where it is upon the throne, that the soul cannot leave it, though it perish eternally by it. Sin so bewitches the soul, that it makes the soul call evil good, and good evil; bitter sweet and sweet bitter, light darkness and darkness light; and a soul thus bewitched with sin will stand it out to the death, at the sword's point with God; let God strike and wound, and cut to the very bone, yet the bewitched soul cares not, fears not, but will still hold on in a course of wickedness, as you may see in Pharaoh, Balaam, and Judas. Tell the bewitched soul that sin is a viper that will certainly kill when it is not killed, that sin often kills secretly, insensibly, eternally, yet the bewitched soul cannot, and will not, cease from sin.

Only God's sovereign power at work in the believer can deliver from such a dread opposition. That is why what Paul says in Philippians 2:12-13 is so important. We do not despair, because God is at work in us.

The second part is *Satan's Devices to Keep Souls from Holy Duties, to Hinder Souls in Holy Services, to Keep Them off from Religious Performances*. In this part, Brooks shows how the evil one attempts to keep us from taking full advantage of the means of grace. He works to hinder our use and even our motivation to use them. He aims to keep us away from them, so that we are more vulnerable to his assaults. He lists eight devices of Satan, and between three and eight biblical remedies for each one.

The next section is *Satan's Devices to Keep Saints in a Sad, Doubting, Questioning and Uncomfortable Condition*. Here Brooks shows how Satan works to undermine the assurance of the believer. Once again, eight devices of Satan are compiled, with between two and six gospel remedies provided.

The following section is about *Satan's Devices to Destroy and Ensnare All Sorts and Ranks of Men in the World*. Here, five devices are enumerated and the categories bear recounting.

(1) *Devices against the Great and Honourable of the Earth*. Here, he lists two devices. What are they? (i) To cause them to seek greatness, position, riches and security, to be self-seeking rather than to be God-centred. (ii) To cause them to act against Christians.

(2) *Device against the Learned and the Wise*. It will not surprise you that Brooks says that by this device the devil moves such to be proud of their own abilities and to look down on those who have lesser abilities but greater grace.

(3) *Device against the Saints*. This device is, significantly, to divide Christians and to introduce strife and disunity.

(4) *Device against Poor and Ignorant Souls*. This device is to encourage people to excuse their own ignorance of the truth, and to neglect and despise the means of the knowledge of salvation.

The *Appendix* to Brooks' little book is filled with solid gold under these headings:

I. *Touching Five More of Satan's Devices*. All of these devices are an attempt by Satan to get us to lose hope in God's grace to us.

II. *Seven Characters of False Teachers*. This section is downright prophetic! Brooks outlines the marks of false prophets:

(1) they are man-pleasers;

(2) they scorn Christ's most faithful servants;

(3) they teach their own ideas rather than the truth;

(4) they pass over the great and weighty things of the word of God and concentrate instead on minutiae;

(5) they cover their dangerous teaching with fair speech;

(6) they are more interested in winning people over to their views and opinions than promoting their sanctification as Christians; and

(7) they seek to prosper on the backs of their followers.

III. *Six Propositions Concerning Satan and His Devices*. Again, these propositions are so wise and insightful:

(1) don't blame Satan for all your temptations;

(2) nevertheless, recognize that Satan has a hand in most sin;

(3) remember, Satan has to have double permission before he does anything against us: God's and ours;

(4) no weapons but spiritual weapons will do in fighting Satan;

(5) we can learn a lot about Satan from his names in Scripture; and

(6) God will soon trample down Satan under our feet.

IV. *Conclusion: Chiefly, Ten Special Helps and Rules against Satan's Devices*. Don't miss what he calls '*Five Reasons of the Point*' that come right before these ten helps; but again, I must say, these helps are astonishingly profound, useful, wise, insightful, and encouraging. And that is the note on which Brooks' book ends. Useful encouragement.

His final applications should be savoured. The use, or the application of all these helps should make us: (1) thankful for deliverance from sin, and (2) long to be at home with the Lord. For instance, Brooks says this: 'Remember this, that deliverance from Satan's snares doth carry with it the clearest and the greatest evidence of the soul and heart of God to be towards us.' I know what that means, and feels like, from experience. And it does move me to the deepest possible gratitude.

Brooks concludes with this exhortation to a holy longing to be with the Lord. He says that these truths

> bespeak Christians to long to be at home! Oh! long to be in the bosom of Christ! long to be in the land of Canaan! for this world, this wilderness, is full of snares, and all employments are full of snares, and all enjoyments are full of snares.

If you are looking for a book to be your companion in the lifelong fight for joy and against sin, to lay out a sound, substantial, scriptural, spiritual view of sanctification, and to open your eyes to the stratagems of Satan without losing sight of the sovereign work of the Spirit, the glories of union with Christ, the purposes of the Father's love, and the manifold provisions of God's grace at work in you, then I don't have a better uninspired nomination for you than *Precious Remedies*.

29

D. Martyn Lloyd-Jones:
Vol. 1: The First Forty Years; Vol. 2: The Fight of Faith

Iain H. Murray

John MacArthur

I DON'T remember when I first read the two-volume biography of David Martyn Lloyd-Jones by Iain H. Murray. That is a bit uncommon for me, since I usually write the date inside the front cover, where I also put page numbers reminding me where to find important points accumulated through my reading. As I took the two Lloyd-Jones volumes from their familiar location among my favourite biographies, I found I had written many page numbers but no dates inside either volume.

Actually, that was a fitting omission and an unwitting testimony to the fact that this particular biography has had a profound influence on me for many years. Some books have a short non-shelf life. Not these two volumes.

Why? Because I had never encountered another pastor whose biblical convictions and philosophy of ministry rang so true with me. Through Iain Murray's record of his life, Martyn Lloyd-Jones continues even now to teach me, encourage me, challenge my thinking, and provide a model of the kind of courage, conviction, and faithfulness I aspire to.

When my formal seminary training ended in the summer of 1964, I began to apply the tools I had been given to develop a biblical ecclesiology, starting with a strong view of Scripture. Seminary reinforced the core values I had already learned from my father's ministry—an unwavering commitment to the inspiration, inerrancy, infallibility, authority, and sufficiency of the Bible. I understood that those convictions were the necessary foundation, but not the totality, of a biblical philosophy of ministry. I knew that every aspect of my service to the Lord needed to be rooted and grounded in Scripture.

When I began reading Iain Murray's biography of Dr Lloyd-Jones, it was as if I finally had found a mentor who fully understood my passion and had already marked out a trail I could follow. I had been reading Scripture and commentaries along with theological works. I was beginning to see a cohesive working understanding of the church under the headship of the Lord Jesus Christ. At the same time I was looking for a model—someone whose follower I could willingly become; someone who saw in Scripture what I was seeing and had faithfully lived out the truth in actual service. I had many teachers, professors, even examples who left indelible marks on my heart. But no one seemed to pull it all together and model it in a life where I could see the complex of these matters all interacting in faithfulness and effectiveness—until I came to know 'the Doctor' through Iain Murray.

What originally drew my interest to Martyn Lloyd-Jones was the immense benefit I received in the late 1970s from reading his *Studies in the Sermon on the Mount.* I did so slowly, though, as I prepared fifty-nine Sunday morning sermons from Matthew 5-7. His work showed me a highly useful pattern of theological exposition. Along with some other Reformed commentaries on Matthew, he helped me shed the last vestiges of some tired and unsupportable interpretations of our Lord's most famous discourse.

So when the first volume of Murray's biography was published in 1982 (within a year of Lloyd-Jones' being taken to heaven), I acquired an early copy and began reading, hoping to get to know this man better. It was a timely discovery, because those were the maturing years of my ministry at Grace Community Church. Though I had never heard the Doctor's voice, he became influential in my life. And Murray's biography, with its careful analysis of doctrinal, ecclesiological, and practical ministry issues, was precisely what I would have hoped for. No pastor I had ever encountered so closely paralleled my own thinking about the church, the gospel, doctrine, conflict, cooperation, and especially preaching. It seemed that the Holy Spirit by the word of God (apart from institutions and denominations) had pressed home to the minds of Martyn Lloyd-Jones and Iain Murray many of the same convictions that were foundational to me.

Iain Murray is a brilliant biographer. He makes his subjects come alive in a vivid way, but it will be clear to any reader that Murray's real interest (and mine likewise) is the theological texture underlying the mind and ministry of the person he is writing about. Indeed, the real value of Murray's *Lloyd-Jones* volumes is not merely (or even mainly) the biographical features, but the theological elements set in the context of a faithful life empowered by the Holy Spirit.

When volume 2 was released in 1990, I was pleased to see that it was more than twice the size of its predecessor—862 pages, compared with the 412 pages of volume 1. I read it as eagerly as I had the first, and gained an even deeper appreciation for the courage, wisdom, and biblical convictions that energized the ministry of this great preacher.

In preparation for writing this review I went back to my lists inside the two volumes' front covers and followed them back through all the underlined portions in the books. I noticed that the main principles that resonated with me could easily be arranged into a few categories. I decided to take that approach in this thankful tribute. Below are several lists (without much comment), noting the key ideas I wrote down as I read these two volumes.

Although this is no substitute for a careful reading of the biography, I hope it can serve as a helpful summary of the Doctor's distinctive ministry principles, which I trust will benefit and encourage other pastors. I don't know of any resource more sound, clear, convicting, insightful, and eye opening than the insights I've gleaned from Murray's biography of Lloyd-Jones. I think you will see why this two-volume biography stands as one of the most singularly helpful works I have ever read.

For the sake of flow and readability I will not connect all these features back to quotations and page numbers in the biography. Neither will I quote explicitly from the text, since the reader should read the two volumes and discover them there for himself. But I will try to give a fair representation or paraphrase in each case.

This is a simple scroll of the categories into which I have grouped key principles and convictions that resonate with me from Iain Murray's record of Lloyd-Jones' life. They are all things I have found instructive, illuminating, informative, or otherwise insightful. Many of them affirmed what I already believed but might have struggled to articulate. (Iain Murray is masterful at clarifying difficult or complex thoughts in a few succinct words.) My lists are ordered in such a way that they generally follow the flow of the books.

I trust this will be useful, not only as an abstract on Martyn Lloyd-Jones' ministry philosophy, but even more so as a challenge and an encouragement to my fellow preachers. We should all strive to order our approach to the preaching ministry soberly, methodically, carefully, and (above all) biblically, as we see exemplified in Dr Martyn Lloyd-Jones. Iain Murray is clearly like-minded as well, since these are principles he purposely highlights—not as passing comments, but as the major convictions that drove the ministry philosophy of the man he assisted for three years, from 1955 to 1959.

Personal

Murray notes these personal characteristics:

Martyn Lloyd-Jones could give no date for his conversion. Of course he was keenly aware of his own sinfulness and spiritual poverty, and his once-indifferent heart had truly been awakened unto saving faith and sincere love for Christ as Lord and Saviour. But grace had moved on him progressively, over a period of time, and there was no dramatic moment that he could confidently point to and say *that* was when he passed from death unto life. (My own testimony is similar.)

He rejected emotionalism and sentimentality in preaching in favour of carefully reasoned biblical arguments.

His keen, logical, observant mind was his greatest asset. The same powers of observation and deduction that made him a great diagnostician as a medical doctor made him a disciplined, perceptive exegete.

Nevertheless, he understood that holiness, not skill, was what made a pastor worthy of respect.

He was always searching for clarity and was able to cut through muddled thinking.

Though he left a highly successful medical career and laboured for years in relatively obscure places of ministry, he never made reference to ministry as a personal sacrifice. 'I gave up nothing', he said.

Personal references in his preaching were rare. (I should note that my father had always cautioned me to beware of any preacher who is the hero of his own stories. The fact that the Doctor rarely even made any reference to himself was a welcome virtue.)

He understood that prayer is primarily fellowship with God.

He knew the value of time. Few people succeeded in occupying his time unnecessarily.

He was lonely. He said, 'I am the loneliest man in the room.'

Because he stood so firmly for what he believed in, Lloyd-Jones was always winning friends and making enemies. He lived in the familiar middle where all strong preachers with firm convictions belong—gaining and losing influence at the same time.

People who did not share his strong convictions accused him of being divisive, and that charge hurt his reputation in the wider evangelical world.

Yet the Holy Spirit clearly empowered him; it was eminent grace more than natural gifts that made him what he was.

Scripture

Murray also highlights some of Lloyd-Jones' convictions about Scripture:

We do not 'discover' truth through philosophy or human reason; it is revealed. Still, all truth is rational, not irrational, and one can reason about it after receiving it.

Formal theological training is not necessary; thinking deeply about Scripture is.

Spirit-blessed ministry requires absolute dependence on the authority of Scripture.

The Bible is the sole source of infallible truth and the final judge of all religious experience.

The preacher is at his strongest and most persuasive when he can show clearly that the principles he is enunciating possess biblical authority.

The credibility of Christianity does not hinge on a flexible approach to Scripture, but precisely the opposite.

Churches lose their spiritual power when they undermine the authority of Scripture.

Theology

As noted, Iain Murray likes to keep doctrinal issues clearly in focus. Lloyd-Jones likewise held strong convictions about the supreme importance of sound doctrine. He was devoted to theological convictions that left him deaf to the pragmatic argument of wider influence. This also closed his mind to any degrading of Scripture:

Erroneous doctrine severely weakens the church. For example, the illegitimate restoration of the gift of charismatic prophecy lessened the need for scholarship. Supposed 'guidance' from 'new knowledge' militated against accurate interpretation.

The Quietist idea of the Deeper Life popularized by the Keswick movement is not a pathway to true holiness. The notion that effort and intellect are detrimental, and that Christians just need to 'let go and let God' actually undermines sanctification.

The popular idea that Christianity depends on personal experience rather than truth-claims and propositions is hostile to a biblical understanding of faith.

Contrary to the popular notion, it is not uncharitable to contend for theological principles. To pit truth against love is to misunderstand the true nature of Christianity.

The central doctrine and theological high point of all preaching is the sovereignty and glory of God.

Failure to understand doctrine causes failure in practice.

A defective doctrine of sin cripples the church. To regard sin lightly is practically the pure essence of unbelief.

Christians are defeated because they are controlled by subjective feelings rather than a clear understanding of the truth.

Conversion is to be judged valid or not based on whether one's life is truly made new.

The most decisive influence for holiness comes from rebirth itself. It is an error to separate justification from sanctification in a way that makes sanctification optional.

Errors and misrepresentations of the gospel *must* be confronted and answered with the truth. This is not optional.

The whole plan of salvation demonstrates divine sovereignty (from which all true doctrine derives) and points to divine glory (where all true doctrine realizes its end).

Submission to the lordship of Christ is the essential evidence that a person's faith is genuine.

Confusing psychology with spiritual life is dangerous, because there is a fundamental difference. Psychology says man's primary need is to know (and love) self; Scripture says humanity was created to know (and love) God.

Evangelism

Because the church exists on earth for gospel impact, evangelism was Martyn Lloyd-Jones' first love. He always preached evangelistic sermons in the Sunday evening services. He held these convictions about evangelism:

Seeking 'decisions' for Christ by sinners is backward—as if someone dead in trespasses and sins ever could or would choose Christ.

True repentance cries out to the Lord for rescue. The sinner sees it as *the Lord's* decision to save him: 'God be merciful to me, a sinner.'

Consciousness of a man's sin causes him to seek God; sinners will not be made to see their spiritual need or be attracted to authentic faith by church stunts.

Calls for immediate public profession of faith and all attempts to count converts at the end of an evangelistic meeting are pure folly. Such tactics also encourage shallow, false conversions.

A decision to come forward is no proof of conversion. Unregenerate people can be convinced to walk forward, giving the impression of spiritual results beyond the reality.

Sinners must be made to feel they are under the condemnation of God. This is the preacher's duty.

Gospel work is the regular, ongoing work of the local church—not sporadic efforts and campaigns. Mass events lack the corporate testimony of the church.

No place should be given for emotional manipulation. Aiming for an emotional response is the surest way to produce counterfeit Christians.

The preacher must be careful lest by mere appeal to self-interest he induces a useless and deceptive decision.

The test of true salvation is not a decision, but a life utterly transformed.

Evangelism must aim to produce conviction of sin in the hearer. The unbeliever must not simply be told he is a sinner; he must be shown to be one.

The staple of preaching is law work. Preaching must display the peril of man's guilt and helplessness.

Redemption does not hinge on a human choice. God's grace does not wait for a sinner to decide; God acts by his own sovereign will.

The new birth is not subject to human control, timing, or operation. It is a work of God's sovereign Spirit.

Church

Lloyd-Jones saw the church biblically, not through the lens of any denomination, institution, or tradition.

He was strongly averse to every strategy for marketing the church or hawking the gospel to the world.

He never equated the church with his own country.

He understood that the church is a gathering of the elect.

He viewed the corporate meetings of the church primarily as a place where people would come to hear a sermon from Scripture.

He rarely had visiting preachers in his pulpit. He was 'as regular as Big Ben and almost as fixed'.

He saw the pastoral prayer as the highest point of corporate worship, and the pastor's duty was to lead the flock to that pinnacle. Lloyd-Jones prayed without using any singular first-person pronouns, and his pastoral prayers were about fifteen minutes long.

He believed worship hymns should be focused on objective truth about God.

His calling was to shepherd one congregation, and he believed all pastors should have that perspective. Although his influence ultimately extended far beyond London, he remained devoted to his own flock as the first and highest priority of his calling.

Cooperation

Lloyd-Jones' biblical convictions put clear limits on his willingness to cooperate with other ministers. His firm resistance to ecumenical compromise went boldly against the grain of popular evangelicalism.

He was cautious about any public identification with ministries not doctrinally compatible with his own.

He was wary of the popular push for ecumenical unity.

It was asserted that the church needs to repent of her disunity; he suggested that before she repents of her disunity, she must repent of her apostasy.

He understood that certain key truths are absolutely essential to Christianity (including the deity and full humanity of the Lord Jesus, the principle of substitutionary atonement, the authority of Scripture, and other similarly vital doctrines), and he refused to embrace as fellow Christians those who questioned or rejected those doctrines.

He declined to cooperate in any form of evangelism or religious activity with those who would not affirm the Bible as the true and authoritative word of God. Indeed, he knew he had a biblical duty to oppose them.

He despised non-doctrinal religion based on mere sentiment and experience.

He also found it difficult to associate or cooperate with shallow, light-hearted preachers.

He immediately saw that the neo-evangelical dream was folly. (Neo-evangelicalism was an attempt to maintain the evangelical *credo* while repudiating any kind of separatism. The movement was driven by a craving for widespread acceptance and academic stature.) Lloyd-Jones correctly discerned that this was an illegitimate form of ecumenical patronage and that it would draw the evangelical movement away from its moorings.

Conflict

Lloyd-Jones took strong and righteous stands that occasionally led to conflict.

Because he held strong biblical convictions and opposed the spirit of his age on so many different fronts, he received criticism from all sides.

He saw the Roman Catholic Church as the ultimate, comprehensively anti-biblical system.

When conflict arose in the wake of his defence of historic

evangelical and Reformed principles (especially his refusal to seek ecumenical union), popular opinion seemed to blame Lloyd-Jones, rather than the innovators or the apostates, for causing division.

He was accused of being proud due to his willingness to take unpopular positions.

He opposed every trend to secularize the church—especially the rising popularity of psychological and pragmatic methodologies.

He saw great danger in modern evangelicals' yearning for worldly acceptance. He understood that it is folly to seek acceptance and influence with the world or (worse yet) with religious leaders who reject biblical authority.

He therefore opposed 'cooperative evangelism', a strategy championed by the Billy Graham organization, whereby church leaders known to be hostile to evangelical principles were nevertheless actively recruited for partnership and public participation in Graham's evangelistic crusades.

He emphatically rejected Billy Graham's famous claim that 'The one badge of Christian discipleship is not orthodoxy, but love.'

When the Graham organization proposed a congress on evangelism and asked ML-J to be chair, the latter proposed a pact: '[If Graham would] stop having liberals and Roman Catholics on the platform and drop the invitation system (altar calls), I would whole-heartedly support him and chair the congress.' After a three-hour conversation, Graham declined those conditions. Despite the criticism it brought him, Lloyd-Jones held firm to his conviction that such conflict was righteous.

Preaching

The preaching of ML-J is his paramount legacy (whether read or heard). He set a standard to be attained by only a few.

He understood and embraced the fact that faithfully preaching a biblical message would make the church intolerable and uncomfortable to all except believers.

He believed preaching designed to comfort the unconverted is not blessed by the Holy Spirit, because the preacher's task is to proclaim a message that will heal the spiritually sick, not offer soothing drugs that merely mask the problem.

He knew that no preacher can effect conversion through style or gimmickry; the Holy Spirit alone awakens the spiritually dead, employing the truth of God's word.

He stressed the necessity of doctrinal content in preaching. His goal was always to set out the principles or doctrines in whatever text he was preaching.

He said there should be a note of authority and a tone of earnest intensity in all preaching.

He was dismissive of arguments from experience, because they could be matched by anyone. Proper preaching is not a subjective sharing of personal experience, but the authoritative proclamation of objective revelation from Scripture (including the threats of the law, the promises of the gospel, historical facts, biblical doctrines, and propositional truth-claims).

His sermon-preparation time was an all-consuming necessity with which nothing should interfere.

He was harshly critical of preaching that did not start with the Bible. After all, he said, the preacher's one business is to bring the word of God to the people.

In his view, preaching should be closely reasoned discourse with the aim of proving the truth.

He listed three prerequisites of good preaching: truth, clarity and passion.

He had no interest in sermon titles.

The central themes in all his preaching were the sovereignty of God (the source of all theology) and the glory of God (the end of all theology).

His sermons were notable for their length. By the time most Anglican clergy were concluding their homilies, Lloyd-Jones was just emerging from his introduction.

He was devoted to extensive, sequential, theological exposition through extended passages of Scripture. For example, he spent eight years in Ephesians (1954–62), preaching thirty-eight sermons on the first chapter alone.

Though he followed the text closely and carefully, he believed word studies and running commentary are not enough to qualify as biblical exposition; the preacher must carefully set forth principles of doctrine.

He said the text must be opened by deduction, argument and appeal—all with divine authority.

He stressed that repetition is essential to good preaching.

He further pointed out that merely stating truth is not enough; one must walk around in it.

He famously said, 'What is preaching? Logic on fire! Preaching is theology coming through a man who is on fire.'

Any unfinished sermons carried over to the next Sunday.

Though he preached sequentially through whole books, he did not map out his course in advance. He could not look weeks ahead and schedule a specific text. His series on the Sermon on the Mount ran to sixty sermons, though he never planned that number.

He believed the best counselling came from God's word through the pulpit. That helps hundreds at once. In that same vein, he suggested that the church needs more preachers, not more counsellors.

Lloyd-Jones' distinctive approach to Scripture brought a dramatic, much-needed change in preaching in an era when evangelical preaching was becoming steadily more frivolous and superficial.

While still a practising physician, he preached to the Welsh Congress on the decline of preaching as a cause of national disintegration. He said preaching in Wales had become professional, psychological, and political.

He believed the trouble with contemporary preaching was not that the preacher knew too little about modern man and his problems, but that he knew too little about Scripture and the Holy Spirit's power.

❧

That incomplete and cryptic list of insights and convictions is representative of the features that Murray records as the very fabric of D. Martyn Lloyd-Jones' philosophy of ministry. As a consequence, his preaching was used mightily by the Holy Spirit for the salvation of countless sinners and the edification of multitudes of saints.

All this and more explains the Doctor's immense abiding influence. The world is still benefiting from sermons transcribed and made into books. Because recordings of the sermons are now freely available on the Internet, millions likely will hear him until the Lord returns.

What makes his ministry so enduring is the power and clarity with which he taught the truth of Scripture.

It was thought by some that the Doctor needed to be freed from his pastoral commitment in order to play a fuller, more international role in the kingdom. He never believed that, because he was convinced that preaching to one congregation was the primary duty of his calling.

Time has proved him right about that. His week-by-week preaching at Westminster Chapel was precisely what ultimately guaranteed that his ministry would have the widest impact and longest-lasting influence across the world.

Conclusion

John Stott said of Lloyd-Jones at his death: 'The most powerful and persuasive voice in Britain for some thirty years is now silent.' The Doctor had always been silent for me because I never heard him preach through all those years of reading him and books about him.

But in Murray's brilliant account of Lloyd-Jones' life, his voice became audible, clear, and convincing in a unique way. Murray suggests Lloyd-Jones will be best remembered for his books, even though the writing ministry was always secondary to him. 'He was a preacher', writes Murray with a sense of loss, I think. But by the providence of God many of his sermons were recorded and are now easy to obtain online. Anyone with the means to download can literally hear that voice. During his life hundreds, sometimes thousands, heard him regularly. His books have been read by hundreds of thousands. Now he has the potential to preach to millions.

The Doctor's preaching is as timely as Scripture. He being dead, his inimitable logic, clarity, authority, and power still speak. The Holy Spirit is still using those sermons to convert sinners and edify saints. Martyn Lloyd-Jones is and always will be 'the preacher'.

Iain Murray records one more detail that reflects the amazing humility of Martyn Lloyd-Jones. He said when he was interviewing the Doctor in the early stages of research for the biography, Lloyd-Jones sounded more like an onlooker commenting on someone else's life than a man reliving his own.

May the humble preacher continue to be exalted.

30

The Life and Letters of Benjamin Morgan Palmer

Thomas Cary Johnson

John R. de Witt

WHAT shall I say about the debt I owe the Banner of Truth Trust, and in particular Iain Murray? It has been my privilege to know both of the men who established the Trust: D. J. W. 'Jack' Cullum and Iain H. Murray, and to count them friends. I remember as though it were yesterday my first acquaintance with the Trust. It was while I was a student at Western Theological Seminary in Holland, Michigan that I first caught sight of Banner publications. As it happened, during my senior year Banner books began to appear on the shelves of the seminary bookshop. They were handsomely produced and offered at a price even divinity students could afford to pay. I purchased what was available at the time, little thinking that over the course of many years the Trust would so profoundly influence my thinking and enrich my work as a preacher of the gospel/servant of the word of God. It is an occasion for thanksgiving that I have an opportunity to express now what Iain Murray has meant to me both personally and through the treasury of transforming books with which he has gifted the Christian church.

Three truly significant biographies of eminent nineteenth century Southern Presbyterians have been reprinted by the Trust: *The Life and Letters of James Henley Thornwell*, by Benjamin Morgan Palmer; *The Life and Letters of Robert Lewis Dabney*, by Thomas Cary Johnson; and *The Life and Letters of Benjamin Morgan Palmer*, also by Dr Johnson. Each of these books has profoundly affected me. I have found them a reproach in relation to my own deficiencies as a minister of the gospel and at the same time a great encouragement. Dr D. Martyn Lloyd-Jones once described Thornwell as 'possibly the greatest theologian the Southern Presbyterian Church has ever produced' and adds that 'he was also a great preacher and a most eloquent man'.[1] Dabney's *Lectures in Systematic Theology*, the three volumes of his *Discussions,* and his *Evangelical Eloquence*, all published by the Trust, leave us in no doubt as to his stature as a theologian and spokesman for biblical truth.

I want now to commend *The Life and Letters of Benjamin Morgan Palmer* to a new generation of Christian readers; or rather, I mean to call attention to a great Christian preacher and pastor whose long ministry is splendidly chronicled in this fine biography. In my view Palmer's life stands out still as a landmark in the religious history of the United States. It is not too much to say that I have found this biography engaging, convicting, and a powerful stimulus in my own life's work as a Christian minister. It is no exaggeration to say one can hardly read this remarkable volume without being humbled and driven to one's knees before the cross.[2]

A few introductory words are surely necessary here. Dr Palmer was born in Charleston, South Carolina on 25 January 1818. At age fourteen he enrolled at Amherst College in Massachusetts, where he became acquainted with Henry Ward Beecher. The two were drawn together by common interests and a love for chess, 'a game in which it is said that Mr Palmer excelled Mr Beecher'.[3] Upon returning to South Carolina he taught in village schools, uncertain as to his future course and still a stranger to the grace of God. His conversion occurred at age seventeen, through the agency of a relative, I. S. K. Axson, then minister of the famous Midway Church in Liberty County, Georgia. Axson spent a night in the Palmer home and seized the opportunity to speak of eternal things to young Ben. "'My cousin", he said, "you are growing up fast to manhood; is it not a good time to give yourself to the Saviour, when you are soon to choose the course in life which

[1] *Preachers and Preaching*, p. 98.
[2] Several volumes published by the Trust which describe this remarkable Christian minister are *Southern Presbyterian Leaders 1683-1911; Preachers with Power: Four Stalwarts of the South*, by Douglas F. Kelly; and *Selected Writings of Benjamin Morgan Palmer*, edited by C. N. Willborn.
[3] *Life and Letters*, by Thomas Cary Johnson, p. 48.

you shall pursue?" "Subdued by his gentleness", I replied: "Cousin Stockton, I am doubtless regarded by all around me as thoughtless and flippant, because I turn the edge of every appeal into a jest, but I am free to confess to you that for eighteen months I have lived in the bosom of as fierce a storm as ever swept over a human soul." But when this gentle Nathanael said to me, "Close it up, my cousin, close it up, and be at peace with God", before reaching the door of his chamber, I took the solemn vow that I would make the salvation of my soul the supreme business of my life, even if it should not be attained until the last hour of a life as long as that of Methuselah. It was long before peace came; for the sea is slow to subside after it has been tossed by a tempest. Six weary months, full of darkness and disappointment, elapsed before the prison door was opened and the captive was free, and the temptation was strong to abandon all in despair but for the solemnity of the form in which the vow was taken. When the peace came, it came to stay. ..."[1] He made profession of faith on 10 July 1836 and was admitted to the membership of the Stony Creek Presbyterian Church, of which congregation his father was the pastor.

Subsequently he attended the University of Georgia from which he was graduated with first honours in 1838 and then entered Columbia Theological Seminary as a divinity student. After short service as a supply preacher in Anderson, South Carolina he and his bride, Mary Augusta McConnell, moved to Savannah where he became pastor of the First Presbyterian Church, ordained to that office on 6 March 1842. The next year he accepted a call to be minister of the First Presbyterian Church in Columbia, South Carolina, preaching his first sermon on 29 January 1843, and continuing in that work until December 1855, when he joined the faculty of the seminary as professor of ecclesiastical history and polity. Mrs Palmer's comment is worth noting. To those who pressed him to leave the pastorate and become a teacher she said: 'You will soon lose both pastor and professor. Your new made professor must be a pastor; you have, in taking him out of this church, made it inevitable that he shall soon accept a call to another church.'[2]

[1] *Ibid.*, p. 56.
[2] *Ibid.*, p. 149.

The summons came from the First Presbyterian Church of New Orleans where he began his service in December of 1856. It was then that he embarked upon the great work of his life and there he remained for almost forty-six years, until his death on 25 May 1902.

My aim in the space allotted to me is to underscore several of the qualities which made Palmer such a beloved, powerful, and effective minister of the gospel.

Palmer as pastor

In each of the congregations Dr Palmer served he was an assiduous and disciplined visitor, but it was particularly in New Orleans that his pastoral care became legendary. On the occasion of his twenty-fifth anniversary as minister of the New Orleans congregation, so his aged father reported, 'it happily occurred to him to investigate his church records, in order to get at the fruits or results of the labours of a quarter of a century', something he had never before attempted. Seventeen hundred individuals had been received into membership, on the average sixty-one or sixty-two each year. 'The number of baptisms, together with that of marriages, deaths, funerals, *etc.*, he could not accurately articulate.' More to the point, he showed his father the list of families he visited each year, in some cases twice or more, 'and the number amounted to three hundred and forty, so that on his visiting days, which were usually the first four days after the Sabbath, he had to pay from three to ten daily calls in order to meet the demands', in addition to which were the many private visits in his study.[1] On the latter point, a recent publication of the Trust, *Selected Writings of Benjamin Morgan Palmer*, gives deeply affecting specimens of those 'private visits'.

During the nineteenth century outbreaks of the Yellow Fever afflicted New Orleans, the cause of which was not understood at the time. Many fled the city for safer ground. Not so Dr Palmer. As it happened he was away from his charge in the summer of 1878 when yet another epidemic occurred. Upon hearing of what was taking place he immediately returned to his post.

According to his own account, each day he paid from thirty to fifty visits, 'praying at the bedside of the sick, comforting the bereaved, and

[1] *Ibid.*, pp. 432-3.

burying the dead; and that, too, without intermitting the worship of the Sabbath or even the prayer meeting in the week.'[1] And this he did without regard for the church connection of the sufferers. Wherever there was fear and sorrow he offered the hope and consolation of the gospel. Such selfless devotion in the course of time made him the 'first citizen' of New Orleans.

In other instances, too, he was attentive to the needs of those outside the bounds of his own congregation. After his death Palmer's daughter received a letter from Varina Davis, wife of Jefferson Davis, who had been president of the Confederacy, in which she wrote of Dr Palmer's care for her husband.

> About a year before my husband died he became very restless and announced his intention to go to New Orleans. We had several guests in the house and I suggested his waiting until Monday, but he said decidedly, 'I want to go today.' It was Saturday. He came back on Monday evening very calm and cheerful. In a day or two he said, 'I went to commune with Dr Palmer, and it has done me a world of good.' I asked him if Dr Palmer would accept an Episcopalian at his communion table. He answered, 'Dr Palmer would never break a bruised reed.' Something had disquieted him and he went to Dr Palmer for comfort. ... I think he was the only man with a great reputation and large following of whom I never heard an evil word; and a proud privilege is yours to be his child.[2]

Palmer as correspondent

I cannot tarry here, but it seems to me essential, if I am to be in any measure adequate in depicting the great man in view, to say something about his incomparable gifts as a correspondent. The biography is justly called *The Life and Letters of Benjamin Morgan Palmer*. It is replete with deeply moving expressions of joy and sorrow, advice and admonition, carefully written to a great number of people in various conditions. He possessed an unusual ability to express sympathy and to offer wise counsel. No doubt the gentle kindness which he exhibited in his correspondence, and in all his pastoral dealings,

[1] *Ibid.*, p. 431.
[2] *Ibid.*, p. 432.

flowed at least in part from his own personal suffering. The Palmers lost five of their six children at an early age. The eldest, their only son, died when little more than an infant. His *The Broken Home; or, Lessons in Sorrow* is an affecting and profoundly spiritual account of these losses and that of Mrs Palmer herself. Such letters as he wrote hardly have counterparts now. Most of us are content to send a few words through the internet. To read Palmer's letters is to be given an example of how powerful the written word can be, and how much valued by those to whom it is addressed.

Palmer as public figure

Palmer is remembered for his famous 'Thanksgiving Sermon', delivered on 29 November 1860 to a vast audience in his own church. In that address he advocated withdrawal from the Federal Union and defended the institution of slavery. It was speedily sent abroad in printed form and proved a key factor in moving Louisiana to secession. We remember that Palmer was very much a man of his own time in the American South. It is surely the part of wisdom, however, to read the sermon before passing judgment upon it.[1]

Of much greater interest to us now is his role in defeating the Louisiana lottery. The lottery company, a malevolent enterprise whose tentacles reached across the United States, had been chartered in 1868 during 'Reconstruction,' and sustained itself through bribery and corruption. Opposition became intense in the summer of 1891 when the Louisiana Anti-Lottery League was formed. On 25 June ten thousand people crowded into the Grand Opera House in New Orleans for a public meeting of protest against this evil institution. The chairman, Col. William Preston Johnston, son of General Albert Sidney Johnston, introduced Dr Palmer, the principal speaker, as 'a man who by his talents, his eloquence, and his virtues, well deserves the title of the first citizen of New Orleans'.

Palmer spoke without notes, his biographer reports, 'but of an open sore that had provoked his indignation for a score of years. ... When he declared that the partisans of the lottery, who had corrupted legislative, judicial, and public morals, might drive him and his fellow citizens to the brink of the precipice, but that they

[1] *Ibid.*, pp. 205-19.

would there turn and 'destroy them by actual revolution,' the house cheered the bold declaration in the most enthusiastic manner. Men and women, almost the entire audience, 'stood on their chairs, shouting and gesticulating,' says Dr William O. Rogers, 'in a frenzy of applause and concurrence that expended itself only in successive waves of excitement'.[1]

The observations of a Jewish Rabbi are worthy of being quoted:

> I have heard the foremost American public speakers, in the pulpit, or on the rostrum. Beecher commanded a more lurid rhetoric than Palmer. For a combination of logical argument and noble and brilliant rhetoric, neither he nor any other has equalled Palmer when *he* was at his best. I heard him that night in the Grand Opera House. Always except on this occasion, when listening to an address, even a great one, I have been able to say to myself,——, how far do you agree with the speaker? What do you reject? How far will you go with him? Where will you stop? But I give you my word, sir, that night Dr Palmer did not permit me to think for myself, nor to feel for myself, but picked me up and carried me whithersoever he would. It did not seem to me that it was Palmer that was speaking. He spoke as one inspired. It seemed to me that God Almighty was speaking through Palmer. He had filled him with His Spirit and Message as He filled the Hebrew prophets of old.'[2]

The next morning this Rabbi encountered a wealthy man who had invested heavily in the lottery. After the usual courtesies an extraordinary conversation took place. The Rabbi said:

> Mr B. you had better draw out of the lottery. It is doomed.'
> 'Why do you think so, Rabbi?' said Mr B.
> 'Dr Palmer has spoken', said the Rabbi.
> 'Ha! the speech of one parson cannot kill this lottery', said Mr B.
> 'I repeat', said the Rabbi, 'your lottery is doomed and you had better draw out.'
> 'Pshaw! The speech of this parson cannot kill the lottery. We have the *money.*'
> 'Once more, I say, Mr B.', said the Rabbi, 'your lottery is doomed,

[1] *Ibid.*, pp. 561-2.
[2] *Ibid.*, p. 562.

your holdings will soon be worthless as chaff. Not one parson has spoken! Ten thousand persons have spoken! Every man, woman and child that heard that address last night is to-day a missionary against your lottery and its doom is as certain and as inexorable as death.'[1]

Palmer as preacher

It was as a preacher that Dr Palmer particularly excelled. The pulpit was truly his throne, and the heralding of the gospel his joy and his delight. Specimens of his pulpit work are to be found in the biography, and in the two volumes of his sermons, bound as one and issued by Sprinkle Publications. The following account of a service in the First Presbyterian Church of New Orleans is perhaps the best way of illustrating his wonderful power.

> Of considerable interest is an account of a Sunday morning service in the First Presbyterian Church of New Orleans, written by the Rev. William Frost Bishop on February 11, 1885.
>
> Sunday morning, upon entering the Church, I found it crowded to the very door. Approaching the sexton or usher, I said, 'Please give me a good seat: I am a stranger here.'
>
> To this he replied: 'No seats are left, except the chairs in front of the pulpit, and they are for gentlemen accompanied by ladies. You had better go into the gallery.'
>
> Finding all seats in the gallery occupied, I walked boldly forward and seated myself on the steps in the left gallery and within sixty feet of the speaker.
>
> Dr Palmer was reading an account of our Lord's passion, as given in John's Gospel at the eighteenth chapter.
>
> There was a peculiar tenderness in his voice, and I was early persuaded that the preacher had been in the sick room a great deal during the past week, or else in the house of affliction.
>
> In the prayer which followed the reading, he prayed very beautifully, and touchingly for one of his flock, 'smitten with a disease from which there was no earthly escape'.
>
> He offered special petitions that she might be reconciled to the Divine will and made ready for the change. Nor did he forget the little

[1] *Ibid.*, pp. 562-3.

children, who should lose by this providence a mother's care. There was something deeply touching in his allusion to these little ones.

While the collection was being taken up, I looked around the audience. There were over one thousand five hundred persons present.

Dr Palmer announced the following as his text: 'The cup which my Father gave me, shall I not drink it?' John 18:11. He wore a vest cut very low, exposing a great deal of white linen, and the coat was left unbuttoned. His enunciation was distinct and his delivery deliberate. The calmness of manner continued till the chariot wheels took fire toward the close of the sermon, which lasted an hour and ten minutes.

The great preacher began his sermon in the simplest manner possible, describing the closing conflict of our Lord's life, with occasional flashes of interpretation which showed that he had studied the context carefully and also that a storm of eloquence was gathering.

About the close of his introduction, a passing band of music so filled the house with its din and noise that the speaker's voice was scarcely audible. This lasted for a minute or more, but Dr Palmer did not seem to notice it. The audience, too, behaved remarkably well.

The subject was treated first in reference to Christ, the motives which lay back of his submission, such as the cup coming from the Father and none else—its being a cup and therefore a *limited* measure of suffering—its being a token of a covenant relation—the suffering being the vestibule of the glory which should follow. These and like considerations were presented with great power. He also unfolded for us the pregnant comment of Dean Alford, that 'the cup here spoken of had allusion, no doubt, to the cup of the Lord's Supper.' The old economy, with the paschal lamb, died in the act of giving life to the new dispensation of the Christian Sacrament.

The second application of the subject was to the sufferings of believers. The great preacher had not proceeded far with this theme when I perceived that he was moving upon what a certain poet has termed 'the unknown seas of feeling' in my heart. I tried to show myself a man and keep my handkerchief in my pocket—but it was no use. The man who sat next to me was rough and unlettered—a man of the world. He found it convenient, just at this time, to brush his rough hand over his eyes, in order to see better. I looked down upon the one thousand who sat beneath me, and they reminded me 'of the mulberry trees' when the wind is shaking them. The men were shielding their faces with their palm leaf fans, while their wives made public use of the handkerchief. It was the most *effective* eloquence I had ever known. A pew in the centre of the Church arrested my attention. At either end were the parents, now melted unto the eloquent and powerful description of the sufferings of the human heart. Between them were three sweet children, with nicely dressed hair and broad, white collars, turned down over their nicely-fitting jackets. One was writing upon the fan which he held in his lap; another was toying with a bit of string, while the third was softly slumbering, with its head in its mother's lap. How suggestive and how touching! How it carried me back to the sunny days of childhood! I have no doubt that those little ones thought the sermon long and uninteresting, but their parents were feeding upon the manna of the Gospel and gaining strength for the battle of life.

I have no words to tell you of the soaring thoughts which marked the close of Dr Palmer's sermon, in which a comparison was instituted between philosophy and religion. There was the unction of Spurgeon with the eloquence of Beecher.

Walking away with the preacher and his family from the Church, I ventured to ask why the speaker had chosen the theme of suffering for such an audience of strangers and men of the world. The reply was, 'I have reached the conviction that the best way to reach the unregenerate is to show him what Christianity is able to do for the believer.'[1]

It will, I think, serve to whet the appetites of new readers if I cite yet another illustration of our subject as preacher. The account given here is from Miss Mary Caldwell of Charleston, South Carolina.

In the fall of 1866, he [Dr Palmer] went to New York to perform the marriage ceremony for a former beloved parishioner and spiritual child, Miss Anna Jennings. The Sunday after reaching New York, he, together with his travelling companion, went over to Brooklyn to hear Dr Scott, who had been his predecessor in the First Presbyterian Church in New Orleans. Dr Scott recognized Dr Palmer immediately on his entering the church; he betrayed surprise and something akin

[1] *Ibid.*, pp. 524-5.

to chagrin at seeing him there. Turning his eyes from the pew in which Dr Palmer sat, he was careful not to look that way any more. Nor did he greet Dr Palmer after the sermon. In a day or two, Dr Scott wrote him a note saying that *he* would have been glad to have him in his pulpit but had been prevented by the sense he had of his people's impatience with him for his course during the war. The next Sunday they went to Dr Van Dyke's church. Dr Van Dyke had arranged for Dr Palmer to preach for him. He was absent himself. Dr Palmer began without an introduction. He preached on the Comforter, 'I will send you another Comforter', *etc.* He began in his apparently simple way with sentences short, clear, and crisp. The people were electrified and held as under a spell. That evening the house was crowded. People had gone home from the morning service talking of the modest-looking little gentleman with such command of the teachings of Scripture and such wonderful eloquence in setting the truth forth, whose name nevertheless they could not tell. The sermon in the evening was of equal eloquence. An old veteran of the Northern army inquired who the wonderful preacher was. He finally learned that he was the Rev. B. M. Palmer, of New Orleans, La. 'The arch rebel of that name!' he exclaimed. "He preaches like an archangel!"[1]

The final paragraph in Thomas Cary Johnson's biography provides a fitting summary of a radiant Christian life.

Taken all in all, he [Palmer] was a very great man; he has often been put into a small group with which the great Head of the Church blessed the Southern Presbyterian Communion. Thornwell, Dabney, Palmer, and Hoge have often been named together. Dr Palmer was not the least of these. In some particulars, some of them surpassed him. For example, in the sheer power of thought, Thornwell and Dabney did. But when we consider his ethical and religious character, his freedom from petty vanities, his Christ-like humility, his transparent simplicity, honesty and honour, his broad and intense love for his fellow men, regardless of race or condition, his noble devotion to God; when we consider his great powers and achievements as a preacher, as a pastor, as a theologian, as a defender of the faith once delivered to the saints; as a philosopher, as a statesman, as a patriot, as an orator

[1] *Ibid.*, p. 295.

of Demosthenic power; when we remark the energy, the harmony, the ease, the balance and splendour of all his mental, emotional and practical working, we unhesitatingly rank him as the peer of the great uninspired preachers and defenders of the faith of the ages, and one of the greatest of men, fit companion to other greatest leaders in the world's march into Christian civilization, whether statesmen or scientists, or philosophers, or leaders of the hosts of Jehovah.[1]

[1] *Ibid.*, p. 676.

31

The Glory of Christ

John Owen

—————

Sinclair B. Ferguson

T HE seventeenth-century mini-biographer Anthony Wood famously described John Owen, when Vice Chancellor of the University of Oxford, in these sneering words:

> While he did undergo the said office, he, instead of being a grave example to the university, scorned all formality, undervalued his office by going in quirpo[1] like a young scholar, with powdred hair, snakebone bandstrings (or bandstrings with large tassels), lawn band, and a large set of ribbons pointed, at his knees, and Spanish leather boots, with large lawn tops, and his hat mostly cock'd.[2]

Doubtless the portrayal was overdone. The author's complaint was, essentially, that Owen should have looked more like a distinguished cleric. Instead Wood was describing a Puritan, some might even say *the* Puritan *par excellence*, at least as far as Christian theologians are concerned. And why should one's attire not reflect the freedom, reality, colour and even joy of Christian doctrine?

---

[1] From the Spanish *cuerpo* (body. Cf. the Latin *corpus*). The suggestion here is that Owen walked around without a cloak or outer garment, so that the shape of his body was visible. Perhaps the author used the somewhat recondite expression because it stretched to the notion of being naked—suggesting in Owen an intolerable flaunting of etiquette and thus being a deeply insulting comment to make about him.

[2] Anthony Wood, *Athenæ Oxonienses: An exact history of all the writers and bishops who have had their education in the University of Oxford, to which are added the fasti, or annals, of the said university* (London: 1691-92), vol. 2, p. 556.

John Owen

John Owen was born in 1616 the son of a Church of England minister, graduated from the University of Oxford, and served two congregations as an Anglican minister. In 1649, still only thirty-three, he was appointed to preach to the British Parliament the day after the execution of Charles I. A one-time confidante of Oliver Cromwell, he fell out of favour with the Lord Protector when it seemed likely that the latter would be offered the throne. Forced out of the Church of England in 1662, he continued to exercise an influential public role in both church and state. He was a prolific author: Anthony Wood required more space to list his published works than to describe his life. He died in 1683, leaving behind already published and posthumously published writings that now fill twenty-four volumes of approximately six hundred pages each.

By any measure Owen was the greatest Puritan theologian; in the esteem of some, probably the greatest English theologian since the Reformation.

But perhaps the most remarkable fact about Owen is this: today more Christians possess and read his works than ever before, whether in small paperback editions or hefty six-hundred-page multi-treatise volumes. If you read or 'listen' carefully between the lines, and sometimes actually on the lines, of many authors or preachers today who are serious 'thought-leaders' of younger generations of ministers, you will probably find the influence of John Owen. It is safe to say that he goes down deeper, stays down longer, and comes up with greater spiritual riches than can be found in the vast bulk of contemporary Christian literature. Speaking only for myself, whenever I return to something written by Owen I wonder if I am wasting my time reading lesser works.

So if you want to develop strong roots in Christian thinking and living, then climb Mount Owen and breathe in its rich and healthy atmosphere—and if you are a preacher, or teacher, or pastoral counsellor, or for that matter simply finding ways to serve the Lord in his church and world, Owen will help you.

But confronted by twenty-four substantial volumes, where do you start? Actually as with most great authors it isn't too difficult to suggest: 'Try this one' or 'Try that one, and see how you get on.'

The Glory of Christ

In John Owen's case it isn't such a bad idea to begin at the end.

The day Owen died a friend visited him to tell him that his last book was now going through the press. Sure enough it was published in 1684 with the title (it was an era when titles often substituted for contents pages): *Meditations and Discourses on the Glory of Christ in his Person, Office, and Grace: with The Differences between faith and sight; applied unto the use of them that believe.* It is usually referred to simply as *The Glory of Christ.*

The title says it all. The book's theme is Jesus Christ. He is, says Owen, 'the principal object of our faith, love, delight, and admiration'.[1] This, the first sentence of Owen's preface, is already enough to give one pause. His second sentence is a lament that we understand and experience so little of it.

There is food for thought here.

Think about yourself first. What do you think about when you do not have much on your mind? Do you know enough about Christ to find your mind almost unconsciously admiring his actions and character and love for you? Or do you 'dry up' after a minute or two?

Then think about the preaching and teaching you hear (or provide). Is its best energy, its most insightful exposition of Scripture, its rich variety, its emotional atmosphere, full of Jesus Christ—or, despite everything, does it focus only on our own lives—perhaps even subtly, albeit seriously focused horizontally, on sin, repentance, and even mortification? Owen has much to teach us about all three—he wrote about them at length—but never apart from his central focus on who Jesus Christ is and what he has done and is doing for his people and the world.

Owen wants to change our focus. He wanted to see it changed in himself, and then in the Christians he served. So his book on *The Glory of Christ* is the refined echo of personal meditations on Scripture, which he preached probably in private homes. Three hundred and thirty years later *The Glory of Christ* still retains its freshness and power. That is the chief reason to read the book yourself.

Here, to encourage you to begin, is what Owen does.

[1] John Owen, *Works of John Owen*, vol. 1 (London: Banner of Truth Trust, 1965), p. 275.

YOU MUST READ

Foundations

Owen's starting place is John 17:24—Jesus' prayer that his people
will see him in the glory the Father has given him. This is his 'High
Priestly Prayer' and in many ways his 'Last will and testament'. In
this prayer (contrast Gethsemane) his words are not 'If it is possible
… Nevertheless not my will but yours …'. Rather, as the eternal Son
of God, Jesus is coming to the Father who has promised him the
nations for his inheritance and saying: 'Father … you promised.'

What is the Saviour's desire? He wants me to see him in his glory.
That is everything. And it will be enough. Because for Owen (sitting
at the feet of the apostles) this is: (i) the Christian's highest privilege;
(ii) the means by which we are transformed into Christ's likeness,
as Paul notes in 2 Corinthians 3:18; and (iii) the Christian's ultimate
destiny, as John notes in 1 John 3:1-2: when we see Christ as he is we
will be forever made like him. This—beholding and becoming like
Christ—gives us comfort now as we view him by faith and promises
us perfect joy then when we view him by sight.

Owen then more fully expounds and explains the glory of Christ
by means of a penetrating analysis of biblical teaching.

Christ—God's representative

Glory is seen in Christ because he is God's representative to his people.
Sin has rendered the human race blind to and ignorant of the glory of
God.[1] Only in Christ is God's glory restored and revealed. Thus, for
example, only in him do we see the wisdom of God clearly expressed
and the love of God convincingly displayed. True, people tell us they
believe that God is love (it is the one axiom that unites everyone
from liberal theologians, through Unitarians, to those whose letters
appear in the correspondence columns of the newspapers). But Owen
acutely observes,

> The most of the natural notions of men about it [God's love] are
> corrupt, and the best of them weak and imperfect. Generally, the
> thoughts of men about it are, that he is of a facile and easy nature, one
> that they may make bold withal in all their occasions, as the Psalmist
> declares, Ps. L. 21.[2]

[1] Rom. 3:23.
[2] *Works*, vol. 1, p. 301.

250

Owen's words are as relevant to the twenty-first century as they were to the seventeenth. His point is well taken. What people 'believe in' is not a God of love at all, but a superior being made largely in their own image, who tolerates them doing and being anything they want to be, including being wholly indifferent to him.

Would you know who God really is, and what it means to admire and experience the overwhelming reality of his love and glory? Then you must fix your gaze diligently on Christ as he is described in the Scriptures. Alas, 'the most of those who at this day are called Christians, are strangers unto this duty'.[1] Can that be true? Then beware, Owen warns us, for 'Slothful and lazy souls never obtain one view of this glory.'[2]

Christ's Person

Christ's glory is also seen in his Person, presented to us in three ways in Scripture. First, by specific and direct descriptions; second, by means of prophecies; and third, by means of the typology of Old Testament worship and liturgy. We therefore turn to Scripture like the man in Jesus' parable,[3] seeking spiritual pearls of all kinds. But when we find Christ in Scripture we know we have discovered the pearl of great price.

If this is so then meditation on Scripture is essential. Only by such means will thoughts about the Christ we find there become habitual, accompanied as they should be by '*admiration, adoration, and thanksgiving*'.[4]

Condescension

Christ's glory is then seen in the way in which he became, and remains, the Mediator between the thrice-holy God and sinful man. He took our flesh in condescension and love. There is an infinite distance between God and man—yet the Son came among us; there is an infinite self-sufficiency in God, and yet God's Son humbled himself by taking our nature—not by *laying aside* the divine nature but by *taking* our human nature:

[1] *Ibid.*, p. 303.
[2] *Ibid.*, p. 306.
[3] *Matt.* 13:45-46.
[4] *Works*, vol. 1, p. 320.

Had we the tongue of men and angels, we were not able in any just measure to express the glory of this condescension; for it is the most ineffable effect of the divine wisdom of the Father and of the love of the Son,—the highest evidence of the care of God toward mankind.[1]

Love

Not only do we see here the wisdom of God in the incarnation, but also his amazing love. It is utterly free and undeserving. Nothing either foreseen in us, or accomplished by us, constrains it.

This is a counter-intuitive thought for sinners. We love because love's object draws forth that love. By contrast God's love is manifested in Christ to sinners, weak and helpless, not constrained by our virtue. Further, Christ is the way God the Father manifests his love for us, not the cause of it. Indeed,

In this love he is glorious; for it is such as no creatures, angels or men, could have the least conceptions of, before its manifestation by its effects; and after its manifestation, it is in this world absolutely incomprehensible.[2]

It is not merely by mastering this biblical revelation, but by its mastering us through our loving meditation on it, that the sheer incomprehensibility of God's love for us in Christ is seen by us as glorious and we are overwhelmed by it, 'lost in wonder, love, and praise'. With this in mind Owen traces out Christ's work for us through its various stages: his obedience to God's law; the fact that this was for us, not for himself; that it was universal (without the least exception) and perfect (without the least defect). He was obedient in a context of opposition and difficulty, not of comparative comfort (the First Adam lost the battle against Satan in a garden, blessed, and standing in front of a tree; the Last Adam conquered him in the wilderness of Calvary, and hanging by nails from a tree).

Exaltation

Christ's mediatorial ministry does not finish at the cross, or even in the resurrection and ascension. It continues in his present exaltation

[1] *Ibid.*, p. 330.
[2] *Ibid.*, p. 338.

in glory. There his humanity is

> *filled with all the divine graces and perfections* whereof a limited, created
> nature is capable. It is not deified, it is not made a god;—it doth not
> in heaven coalesce into one nature with the divine by a composition of
> them;—it hath not any essential property of the Deity communicated
> unto it, so as subjectively to reside in it;—it is not made omniscient,
> omnipresent, omnipotent; but it is exalted in a fullness of all
> divine perfection ineffably above the glory of angels and men. It is
> incomprehensibly nearer God than they all—hath communications
> from God, in glorious light, love, and power, ineffably above them all;
> but it is still a creature.[1]

Such eloquent outbursts of Christ-centred and exalting admiration
and adoration, in the high rhetoric of someone familiar with what he
describes, may leave us staggering a little in Owen's footsteps. But
strain to follow the logic and the language and Owen becomes like
a father lifting a child onto his shoulders, enabling us to see what he
sees. For we must be lifted up, Owen insists, because

> They who endeavour not to see the glory of Christ in this world, as
> hath been often said, shall never behold him in glory hereafter unto
> their satisfaction; nor do they desire to do so, only they suppose it a
> part of that relief which they would have when they are gone out of
> this world.[2]

I am reminded of a programme I once heard on BBC Radio in
which a variety of well-known people were asked how they envisaged
heaven. But as the programme continued a consistent pattern
developed in their answers. It was maintained throughout the half
hour: *not one person mentioned the presence of Christ in heaven!* This
is Owen's point: think little or not at all of Christ's glory *now* and at
best we regard the Lamb on the throne as a necessary inconvenience
to be, if possible, tolerated.

But this is a religious illusion, not saving faith. The genuine
Christian believer is someone increasingly gripped by Christ and
the great exchange he has made with his people: "'O blessed change!

[1] *Ibid.*, p. 345.
[2] *Ibid.*, pp. 346-47.

sweet permutation!" as Justin Martyr speaks', notes Owen.[1] In the sight of both men and angels Christ is glorious because in him heaven's justice and heaven's love have met ('the one in punishing … the other in pardoning').[2]

An appreciation of these gospel truths prompts in us a deep longing to live apprehending this and to die into fully and everlastingly enjoying it.

Implications?

But does this make any practical difference to my life (and to the impact of my preaching or teaching if that is my calling)? Or is this simply deep theology? We have surely become a generation detached from apostolic Christianity if there is any seriousness in our asking that question. Was not Philippians 2:5-11, among the profoundest Christological statements in the New Testament, written in order to deal with the practical issues of pride and potential disunity in the church? Does not the Saviour's prayer in John 17, overheard by the apostles, deal with the deep things of God in a context in which the disciples desperately needed practical comfort and hope? In reality, claims Owen, the deeper the theology, the stronger the foundations for practical Christian living:

> *This is that glory of Christ whereof one view by faith*
> *   will scatter all the fears,*
> *   answer all the objections,*
> *   and give relief against all the despondencies of poor tempted souls;*
> *   and an anchor it will be unto all believers,*
> *   which they may cast within the veil,*
> *   to hold them firm and steadfast in all trials, and temptations in life*
> *   and death.*[3]

The wonder is this: all that is treasured up in Christ, communicated to him by the Father, is in turn brought to us by the Spirit. He takes what belongs to Christ and reveals it to us.[4] Indeed the One who

---

[1] *Ibid.*, p. 358.

[2] *Ibid.*, p. 359.

[3] *Ibid.*, p. 359; the quasi-poetic setting is mine. Owen is not, after all, obscure, abstruse, or prosaic.

[4] John 16:14-15.

was given to the Son by the Father is now through the Son given to believers so that as 'in his incarnation he took our nature into personal union with his own; so herein he takes our persons into a mystical union with himself. Hereby he becomes ours, and we are his.'[1]

Consummation

Ultimately this glory we already see in Christ will be fully and finally manifested in '*the recapitulation of all things in him*, after they had been scattered and disordered by sin'.[2] The fulfilment of this hope[3] will display the glory of Christ in ways most Christians have never imagined. For example, Owen directs us to the fact that the 'union between the two families of God—human and angelic—was disturbed, broken, dissolved by the entrance of sin'.[4] Now, where sin abounded grace has super-abounded. For in Christ something greater than the separate restoration of these two families has been accomplished. Now the angelic and the human families are gathered *into one* in their common head to whom belongs all authority in both heaven and earth.

No wonder Owen comments,

> Who can declare this glory of Christ? who can speak of these things as he ought? I am so far from designing to set forth the whole of it, that I am deeply sensible how little a portion I can comprehend of the least part of it. Nor can I attain unto any satisfaction in these Meditations, but what issues in an humble adoration.[5]

And so Owen closes his study with an extended discussion of the difference between beholding the glory of Christ in this world by faith and in the world to come by sight.[6]

Surely this brief summary whets the appetite for more. And Owen has more to give us, for after his death two further chapters, written in his own hand, were discovered among his papers: another forty

---

[1] *Works*, vol. 1, p. 365.
[2] *Ibid.*, p. 367.
[3] See Eph. 1:8-10.
[4] *Works*, vol. 1, p. 370.
[5] *Ibid.*, p. 374.
[6] *Ibid.*, pp. 374-415.

plus pages[1] of application, first to those who are 'strangers to Christ', and then for those who are anxious to know how they may recover from spiritual decay.

Even a cursory reading of *The Glory of Christ* leaves one asking 'Do I own another book quite like this—for richness of exposition, for profundity of meditation, and for fulness of application?'

Owen is reminiscent of such Fathers of the church as Irenaeus, Athanasius, and others. Their passionate love for Christ demanded that they should describe their Saviour in a manner that was as detailed as possible and as biblical as their understanding allowed. It was not philosophical interests, or academic reputations they sought. They would no more have countenanced our slack and indifferent approach to describing their Lord and Saviour fully than they would have tolerated indifference in their own children in describing the mother who gave them birth. To lack this devotion, to be disinterested in true description of the Lord Jesus would have been for Owen, as for the Fathers, an unnatural and monstrous breach of trust.

Owen—worth reading

When the young John Owen wrote his 'To the Reader' prefacing what has become his most famous work, *Salus Electorum, Sanguis Jesu; or The Death of Death in the Death of Christ*, he commented:

> If thou intendest to go farther, I would entreat thee to stay here a little. If thou art, as many in this pretending age, *a sign or title gazer*, and comest into books as Cato into the theatre, to go out again—thou hast had thy entertainment; farewell![2]

True, Owen realized his works would never appeal to the superficial reader in search of a quick fix, to the person who thinks that the Christian faith is lived largely if not exclusively at the emotional level, or who naively imbibes the mantra that doctrine divides while experience unites. If we are like that then Owen bids us goodnight. But he farewells us as people destined to know little about Christ (and who will tend to see him as serving our own ends rather than

[1] *Ibid.*, pp. 419-61.

[2] *Works*, vol. 10, p. 149. Owen wrote this when he was no more than thirty years old, and perhaps the sharpness of his words needs to be set within the context of his youthful idealism! Cato was a second century B.C. Roman consul.

God's glory), as people who have slight thoughts of heaven and eternal glory and therefore live ephemeral lives here on earth.

The same would be true, by implication, of pastors and teachers. Not to want to know Christ better, not to pursue a sense of his glory approximating to the understanding Owen displays, not to want to be like Paul and say 'Him we proclaim, striving with all the energy he mightily inspires in us' (Col. 1:28-29)—surely this would be inexcusable in a preacher of the gospel?

But if we want to know Christ, and to make him known, clothed in the wonder of the gospel and the effulgence of his exalted glory, Owen is our man. We can sit at his feet and learn, or better, be lifted up on his shoulders and begin to see what he saw. This is what *The Glory of Christ* does for us.

We began at the end of Owen's life. But not quite. The friend who called on Owen on the morning of August 24, 1683 was William Payne, a minister in Saffron Walden. 'Doctor', he said for his encouragement, 'your book on the *Glory of Christ* is in the process of publication.' Owen gave the reply which constitutes his last recorded words:

> I am glad to hear that that performance is put to the press; but, O, brother Payne, the long looked-for day is come at last, in which I shall see that glory in another manner than I have ever done yet, or was capable of doing in this world!

Until then, however, his *Glory of Christ* remains one of the fullest glimpses of that glory you will ever read.[1]

---

[1] On a personal note, without the vision of Iain and Jean Murray it is altogether possible that, like many others, I would have read few if any of the words and works of Owen. With all the other contributors to this volume I express my gratitude to them for their friendship and for the service they have rendered Christ and his church.

32

The Forgotten Spurgeon

Iain H. Murray

Ian S. Barter

IN THE early summer of 1961 my wife Gillian and I had just celebrated our first year of marriage. We were living in an old cottage in the pretty Surrey village of Cranleigh, and on a warm sunny Saturday we set out to explore more of the woods and villages surrounding our home. As we drove through Albury village, a notice-board behind the hedge along the road caught our eyes, and we pulled up to read it. It announced that the 'Abinger[1] Convention' would be holding meetings in a tent in that same field each evening the following week, and that the meetings were open to all. The precise wording I have long since forgotten, but something in the notice caught our attention. We had both been brought up among Plymouth Brethren, but a few months earlier had severed our connection with them and were without any church or denominational affiliation of any kind. We decided to attend. On the following Monday evening we arrived, were surprised to find how many were present, joined in the hymn-singing, listened with interest and pleasure to the preaching, and were charmed by the warm welcome we received. We returned on Tuesday and again each evening until the end of the week.[2]

---

[1] Abinger lies further east along the road to Dorking. We discovered later that the convention had been established a few years earlier by Fred Pride at Abinger, where he and his wife lived.

[2] Alas! All my notes have long since disappeared during our many house moves since then, and I can no longer remember the names of the preachers that evening. Some of the speakers during subsequent years were: Martyn Lloyd-Jones, John

At the convention meetings we learned that in addition to the annual tent meetings, the organising committee held monthly meetings in Peaslake, a small village a few miles from our home, on Friday evenings during the winter. Several months later the memory of the summer meetings encouraged us to attend one of the winter occasions, and towards the end of the year we found ourselves once a month in Peaslake village hall where a considerable congregation drawn from the neighbouring villages gathered. On one of those evenings in that winter of 1961, the speaker was Iain H. Murray. I knew nothing about him, nor had I heard of the Banner of Truth Trust, several of whose books were included in the display on the book table at the back of the hall. In his preaching Iain referred to the Puritans. His words caught my interest, and I made it my business to speak to him at the end of the service. Our conversation was necessarily brief, but sufficient to leave me determined to find out more about those remarkable men and women who had stood so courageously for the gospel during the extraordinary changes and upheavals of the seventeenth century. I took home a copy of the current *Banner of Truth* magazine, the forerunner of many more. In fact, I believe I have read every issue since.

The following spring I received my copy of the March 1962 edition of the *Banner* magazine. As I looked through it my attention was instantly caught by the title of one of the articles. It read simply 'The Forgotten Spurgeon'. *Forgotten Spurgeon?* Even to me the name Spurgeon was well known. Surely as the most famous preacher of the Victorian age, the name of Spurgeon was far from forgotten. I wondered what the author, Iain Murray, had to say to justify that arresting title. As I began to read, I little imagined the effect this book was to have on me.

I was not far into the series of articles that were to become the book before I discovered what the author had in mind. It was not the popular preacher of his middle period, preaching to vast congregations sermons that were distributed in immense numbers around the world, who was forgotten. Rather it was what Spurgeon preached and the battles for the gospel in which he was involved that were forgotten. 'The Spurgeon of the sermons was a forgotten man' and 'some of the

Caiger, Paul Tucker, Iain Murray, Eric Alexander, and Leslie Land.

most important aspects of his ministry have been forgotten'.[1] In *The Forgotten Spurgeon* the author justifies and illustrates this judgment by concentrating on 'three major controversies of his ministry'.

The first of these was 'Spurgeon's early witness against a diluted evangelicalism and the controversy which ensued'.[2] The discussion of this controversy was the greatest help to me, and I return to it below.

The second controversy to involve Spurgeon arose out of his concern regarding the growth in influence of the Tractarians, and of an Anglo-Catholicism in the Church of England that had as its object, Spurgeon feared, reunion with Rome. 'Against this background of a resurgent "Catholicism" in the Establishment … Spurgeon's preaching on church issues entered upon a new phase …'[3] On 5 June 1864 Spurgeon delivered his sermon on 'Baptismal Regeneration' based on Mark 16:15-16. The controversy it aroused was widespread. Soon as many as 350,000 copies of the sermon were in print, together with 'a multitude of articles, pamphlets and sermons in reply … many by evangelicals in the Establishment'.[4]

The third great controversy which cast a shadow over Spurgeon's last years was 'The Down-Grade'. From the middle of the nineteenth century 'higher criticism' was developing increasingly greater influence in Nonconformity. Having become established in Presbyterianism, by the 1880s the new school was dominant in Congregationalism. Spurgeon had grounds for hoping that the Baptists would stand against the trend, and in 1887 in the August issue of his magazine, *The Sword and the Trowel*, 'he drew attention to the consequences already attendant upon the new teaching'. All his efforts were in vain, and when at the Baptist Union meeting in October 1887 the 'Down-Grade question was entirely avoided … Spurgeon withdrew from the Union'.[5]

The discussion of each of these controversies is important, both for the light it sheds on the spiritual state of Great Britain in the nineteenth century, and as a help to understanding today's conditions.

[1] Iain H. Murray, *The Forgotten Spurgeon* (Edinburgh: Banner of Truth, 2009, retypeset ed.), p. 4.
[2] *Ibid.*, p. 5.
[3] *Ibid.*, p. 133.
[4] *Ibid.*, p. 135.
[5] *Ibid.*, p. 152.

But it was the first part of the book that particularly gripped me, opened my mind to understanding what the Scriptures declared the gospel to be, and brought me to a view of biblical truth that has remained with me to this day.

In the first part of *The Forgotten Spurgeon*, the author emphasises that the prevailing doctrinal belief among the Protestant churches in December 1853, when Spurgeon was called to the pulpit of New Park Chapel in London, was Arminianism, '… and it was chiefly because Spurgeon stood against this that his arrival in London was looked upon with such disfavour by the religious world'.[1] Thus it was his determined opposition to Arminianism that drew Spurgeon into his first great controversy. For Spurgeon it was the doctrines of grace (or 'Calvinism' under another name) that alone were faithful to the biblical revelation. Spurgeon as an unashamed Calvinist found himself under attack from the first, and it was his battle with Arminianism and, to a lesser extent Hyper-Calvinism, that dominated his first years in London.

In this section of the book, the author explains the leading aspects of the three theological evangelical systems most in evidence at the time: Calvinism, Hyper-Calvinism and Arminianism. The author explains clearly that only Calvinism (or the system known as the doctrines of grace, as he prefers to call it) can properly be denominated scriptural. And he convincingly shows, and this is the principal argument of this section of the book, that from his earliest days as a preacher Spurgeon's conviction that Calvinism was only another name for scriptural truth permeated all his preaching, and led him constantly to explain and refute the unbiblical doctrines of Arminianism on the one hand and Hyper-Calvinism on the other.

Hyper-Calvinism is dealt with comparatively briefly. Spurgeon regarded it as having 'comparatively small and scattered influence within the Baptist denomination'. Arminianism on the other hand was influential throughout Nonconformity, as well as within the Church of England. 'Spurgeon's exchanges with Hyper-Calvinism were only skirmishes compared to the battle which he had to fight on quite a different and much wider front.'[2] The principal subject

[1] *Ibid.*, pp. 55-6.
[2] *Ibid.*, p. 56.

accordingly in the first main section of the book is Spurgeon's constant battle with Arminianism.

The author makes an important point that preachers today would do well to heed. 'In his early days Spurgeon tended to use "Arminian" as a descriptive label to be applied to individuals; this practice ... he later abandoned as far as possible and for a revival of the use in this sense there is nothing at all to be said.'[1] Furthermore, the word is so little used today that its use can hinder understanding. For my part it was a considerable surprise to discover in 1962 that Arminianism was still alive, and still being preached from evangelical pulpits. I had read about it at school in connection with the Synod of Dort and later on in the seventeenth century with Archbishop Laud and his supporters in the Church of England, but was quite unaware that it had survived into the nineteenth century and been embraced by Nonconformity.

As I continued to read *The Forgotten Spurgeon*, I suffered an even greater surprise for it appeared that all unknowingly I too was an Arminian! I neither believed in Arminianism as a formally stated system, nor opposed it. I simply did not know what it was. I had become an Arminian without knowing it, and without having any notion that I was one. And the preachers to whom I listened would have been perplexed to find themselves described as Arminians. I imagined that I was an ordinary evangelical believer, and many like me who heard a preacher speaking against Arminianism would simply have assumed that he was condemning doctrines that had long since faded into history.

In two important chapters in *The Forgotten Spurgeon* Iain Murray explains that Spurgeon opposed Arminianism on two principal grounds. He opposed it because it is against Scripture,[2] and also because it is 'a departure from the purity of New Testament evangelism'.[3] These chapters lucidly demonstrate that Arminianism, far from being one strand of biblical teaching, is in fact opposed to Scripture. I believe this exposition of Arminianism and Calvinism and their differences is as much needed today as it was when the

[1] *Ibid.*, p. 7.

[2] *Ibid.*, p. 73 'Arminianism against Scripture'; and p. 105 'Arminianism and Evangelism'.

[3] *Ibid.*, p. 112.

book was written. As I read the chapter headed 'Arminianism against Scripture' one statement struck me with terrific force:

> For Spurgeon the error of believing that Christ died equally for all men led to a further removal from the Bible in misleading Gospel hearers on the nature of saving faith: ... 'I have heard it often asserted', he declared in one sermon, 'that if you believe that Jesus Christ died for you, you will be saved. My dear hearer, do not be deluded by such an idea. You may believe that Jesus Christ died for you, and may believe what is not true ... Do not say, "I believe that Jesus Christ died for me", and because of that feel that you are saved. I pray you to remember that the genuine faith that saves the soul has for its main element—trust—absolute rest of the soul—on the Lord Jesus Christ to save me ... and relying ... wholly and alone on him, I am saved.'[1]

The idea that it was a delusion to imagine that if I believed that Jesus Christ died for me I would be saved simply amazed me, but then as I considered the point it became an enormous relief. The subconscious Arminianism (subconscious because neither the preacher nor his hearers knew it was Arminianism or indeed what Arminianism was) of the kind of preaching to which I had for many years been subject had long been a great trial to me. For years I had listened to sermons in which I was exhorted to believe that Jesus Christ had died for me personally, and that if I did believe it I would be saved. But to believe that Jesus had died for me personally—that caused me endless trouble. It seemed that what was being proposed was this: 'Jesus died for you. Believe it and you will be saved. If you don't believe it you won't be saved.' But, I said to myself, 'If he had died for me, then I was saved anyway. How should my believing a fact make any difference to the fact?' It seemed that everything depended on what *I* believed. And indeed it was often put like that. 'God has done everything he can, and now it's up to you.' But how could I know that Jesus Christ had died for me in particular? And if I could not know for certain, then how could I believe that he had?

The Forgotten Spurgeon blew all that to pieces, and put a rock under my feet.

---

[1] *Ibid.*, pp. 82-3.

Epilogue: The Books from Three Perspectives

(1) A View from Latin America

William Barkley

I HAVE known the work of the Banner of Truth since its very earliest days. It was my privilege to know both of the co-founders of the new publishing house set up in 1957, and even, in that year, to live in the same large residence in North London with one of them. Personal contact with that highly esteemed brother has continued through these last fifty-eight years! There has been considerable contact since then with all of the succeeding managers and staff of the Trust, and I have always been on the receiving end of much generosity and co-operation in all business transactions. Quick visits to The Grey House in Edinburgh[1] on a few occasions hold very pleasant memories for me. What a change from 78b Chiltern Street, London![2] As I reflect on all of these precious years I ask myself the question: Does anyone owe more to the Banner of Truth Trust than I do?

There is no doubt that the Banner of Truth Trust has been God's instrument to make an indelible mark on the lives of many people throughout the world. While those from every walk of life, professionals and non-professionals, bear that mark, this has been especially so regarding those called by the Lord to serve him in the proclamation of his word. Various good publishing houses have come into existence during the past sixty years but has any other had the same impact as the Banner of Truth? One is tempted to ask: Is there a God-honouring ministry in the United Kingdom today whose minister or leaders have not been influenced by Banner books? Alas,

1 The main office of the Trust since 1973.
2 The office of the Trust from 1958–73.

the rich heritage that has been unearthed by the Trust was largely unknown back in the mid-1950s. What meagre measure we fed on in the theological colleges of London during the early years of that decade! How grateful we should all be for the labours of those who have 'dug deep' to make these treasures available to us!

Personally, I have been enriched and helped by the wide range of challenging titles—not to mention the thought-provoking and edifying articles in the monthly *Banner of Truth* magazine (of which I possess an almost complete set—now well over 600 issues!).

To choose for comment a few titles that have been of particular help is not an easy task. Each new book has had its own contribution to the larger project, and some have ministered to the specific needs of the hour—none were published just to bring another title to the market! Yet, without hesitation I mention *The Autobiography of John G. Paton*. It is the most challenging missionary autobiography I have ever read (and I have read quite a number!).

Born in 1824, in a lowly three-roomed thatched house in Dumfries, Scotland, John G. Paton had to leave school at the age of twelve in order to help sustain his family. A short time later he was converted, and from the earliest days of his Christian experience he felt the call of God to missionary service. After ten years of zealous witness in the great industrial city of Glasgow, the way began to open for him to answer the call for missionary workers in the South Pacific. It was an irresistible call, and regardless of the consequences, he set his face like a flint towards that far-distant region, although his friends tried to dissuade him by telling him he would be eaten by cannibals! He married Mary Ann Robson in 1858, and soon thereafter departed for his field of service. The record of his farewell to his godly father, who had cradled him in the gospel from childhood, is one of the most touching descriptions I have ever read. Who can ever forget reading of that dear man's head popping up above the ditch as he watched (hopefully unseen) his precious son disappear from view as he started out on the journey to his new field of labour many thousands of miles away? The emotions of that hour must have been so hard to express.

The South Sea Islands (New Hebrides), known today as Vanuatu, were home to dangerous, warring, cannibalistic tribes that often threatened Paton's life and demanded his departure. Sadly, on the island of Tanna, the health of his dearly beloved wife quickly declined and he buried first her and then their first-born son only three weeks later, about a year after their arrival. Paton was crushed. 'Had it not been for Jesus, I would have gone mad and died beside that lonely grave.' But he remained faithful to God's call. Though often carried out under threat to his personal safety, John Paton's prodigious mission work, on various islands of that archipelago, were richly blessed. He left behind two orphanages, various schools, a church, and a school for training native evangelists. Because of his obedience to God's call some of the fiercest men on earth heard the gospel of God's sovereign grace and power. Eternity alone will reveal the full blessed results. Those who have never read this wonderful autobiography have missed out on the very best missionary literature!

Could any other title show more clearly the necessity, nature and results of true biblical conversion than Joseph Alleine's *A Sure Guide to Heaven*? The bankruptcy of the sinner without the saving grace of Christ is a most derelict picture. Often in boyhood and adolescence I had to listen to a very man-centred message, which gave the impression that God had done all he could do to save the lost and it was now up to the sinner as to where he would spend eternity. But with Joseph Alleine there is no frenzied appeal to 'make a decision for Christ' to be sure of going to heaven; rather, there is a clarion call to repent from sin and to earnestly seek the God of mercy and forgiveness. Apart from Christ and his cross there is no certainty of salvation. What follows in the life of the saved sinner, when mercy is obtained, is a hunger and thirst for God, for his word, and for holiness of life. A mere 'decision' can never produce such effects. It is alarming that so many people have been deluded into thinking they are right with God because they have 'raised their hand' or 'gone forward' or 'signed a card' to indicate they have 'accepted Christ'! But where is the emphasis on the holy law of God, on conviction of sin, on hell, and on repentance?

I love Alleine for the way he sets out the clear, biblical message. I have never heard a modern evangelist plead with sinners the way Joseph Alleine does in this book: 'The furnace of eternal vengeance is heated for you!' 'O man, what do you think about being a bundle of firewood in hell forever?' 'Can thine heart endure, or can thine hands be strong, in the day I shall deal with thee?' (*Ezek.* 22:14). Yet it has pleased God to use this book to the salvation of many souls and even to bring revival. It could rightly be said of the author: 'The gospel of Jesus Christ never burned more fervently in any other English heart.'

The Life of Martyn Lloyd-Jones 1899-1981, by Iain H. Murray, will surely establish itself as one of the most informative and precious publications of the Banner of Truth Trust. What a debt we owe to the author! To trace the hand of God through the Doctor's eighty-two years is a most profitable and stimulating exercise. From the very beginning it is evident that God was preparing his servant for something 'big'. Unhappy school years and severe economic family trials were a necessary part of the preparation for difficult days ahead. As he matured during his medical career and was able to diagnose the real problems of the world and the church, it seems that he resolutely moved to the same position as the great Augustine had done many years earlier: 'to myself a heart of steel, to others a heart of love, to God a heart aflame'. From that vantage point, he gave himself unstintingly to restore long-lost truths to preaching, regardless of who accompanied him or not. Programmes, fund-raising events, and gimmicks had no place in his conception of what the church should do. His anointed preaching and wise counsel, not confined to Westminster Chapel, helped many—perhaps sometimes even those who disagreed with him. The results speak for themselves. This new edition of the Doctor's life can only enrich, enlighten, edify, and challenge all who take its contents seriously. God's faithful servant bore the onslaught of harsh and malicious critics as he withstood the manoeuvrings of the ecumenical movement and the weakness (cowardice?) of those who should have stood with him. How tragic that good Christian men should be seduced by numbers and petty denominational ties, rather than stand firmly on the clear teaching of the word of God: 'Wherefore come out from among them and be ye separate, saith the Lord, and touch not the unclean thing; and I will receive you' (2 Cor. 6:17). Dr Lloyd-Jones remained faithful to the end and died triumphantly, resting in the confidence that God will accomplish all his good purposes in and through *his* church.

Knowing Dr Lloyd-Jones personally was a special privilege. Two unforgettable incidents, which say much about his humility and his greatness, remain vividly in my memory. As I left the hospital where my new-found friend in our first year at London Bible College was a patient (1951), the Doctor came to visit him. In spite of all the demands on his time he had the welfare of an unknown young Jamaican at heart! Many years later, at a conference in North Wales I met God's servant in the book room and asked if the last message he was due to preach was going to be recorded, because I had to return to London for an engagement the next day. 'I hope not', was the immediate reply. When I expressed my disappointment, he spontaneously took me by the arm, drew me to a small room nearby, and gave me the gist of the message for the following evening. '"Take heed unto thyself and unto the doctrine …" (*1 Tim.* 4:16). Notice the order in the exhortation!' Can the reader imagine how I felt as I left that little room, having, of course, assured him that my lips were sealed until after the conference?

I also had the opportunity of hearing Dr Lloyd-Jones preach many times. I have read most of his expository works and have had the great privilege of directing a small publishing house that has put much of the Doctor's literary legacy at the disposal of the Portuguese-speaking world. It might be safe to say that through these feeble efforts the books of the Banner of Truth Trust (and those of Dr Martyn Lloyd-Jones in particular) are well known wherever the Portuguese language is spoken. Today, Lloyd-Jones is one of the most sought-after authors among God's faithful servants in Brazil. Perhaps the words that have often been heard in a certain downtown office are at last beginning to bear fruit! 'It is not the reading of many books that makes a man holy and happy, but the reading of a few, could he but know that he has the best.'

Of course, Banner of Truth and the Doctor's books have gone to many other countries where Portuguese is spoken. Even my own homeland of Ireland has benefited, for there are many Brazilians living in Dublin!

Banner of Truth books have been a blessing to the world. The Trust's careful selection of the great authors and stalwarts of the Reformed faith, the solid doctrinal content, and the quality production of Banner books, have been like seeds that have blossomed in the life of countless young men and budding theologians, which has no doubt greatly contributed to the revival of Reformed theology that has taken place since the 1950s. How wonderful it was to see such a tremendous blessing coming to the church of Christ in Brazil, a country which for so many years was a wilderness when it came to Reformed literature, belief and practice! To have such quality books available to men and women in their native Portuguese language was like the miracle Ezekiel witnessed in the valley of dry bones. If some books that have ben especially helpful to us were to be singled out (although all have been important), among them would be the translation of Iain Murray's *The Forgotten Spurgeon*, Martyn Lloyd-Jones' *Romans* series, and the biography of *George Whitefield* by Arnold Dallimore. The circulation of these books, coupled with other reformed efforts and the promotion of reformed conferences throughout Brazil, soon produced a reformation in preaching which now echoes the glorious teachings of those servants of God, which had been brought to us by means of Banner books. As a result, we now harmoniously sing the same tune of God's sovereign grace, 'grace notes' which are heard whenever the glorious gospel of Jesus Christ is truly proclaimed.

I would like to conclude this chapter with words of appreciation for the ministry of the Banner of Truth Trust from two of my Brazilian brothers.

Solano Portela

I was once in an evangelical publisher's office in Brazil when a seminary student came up to the manager and, instead of asking him what was the 'price' of a certain book, he asked what was the 'value' of it. (The book in question was one of the good titles from the Banner of Truth Trust). The manager replied that the 'value' of that book was very high, but if he wanted to buy it he could do so for a reasonable 'price'!

As a young seminary student I was introduced to Banner books by two older students who often talked about revival and prayed earnestly for it. There is now a very good range of Banner of Truth titles available in Portuguese: commentaries, biographies, sermons, and books on special subjects, such as spiritual depression, guidance, marriage, divorce, the afterlife, *etc.*). Today Portuguese speakers have access to the sermon series of Dr Martyn Lloyd-Jones, the biographies of George Whitefield and C. H. Spurgeon, and Robert Murray M'Cheyne's sermons. These are precious materials for which we are thankful, but we need many more of them!

Yes, we are so thankful to God for Banner of Truth books. They have introduced many Brazilians to the very best of historic Christianity's gospel-centred literature. It is our prayer that God will visit Brazil with a true spiritual awakening.

Alberto Gonçalves

Thank God for the Banner of Truth Trust and in particular for Dr Lloyd-Jones' published sermons. May this great literature ministry continue to be produced for many years to come. We will uphold in prayer all who have a part in it.

(2) A View from the Philippines

Brian Ellis

THE first Banner book I ever owned is still on my bookshelf: Berkhof's *Systematic Theology*. I had worked the summer of 1962 on a children's mission, and 'Auntie Pat', one of the team, knew that in the autumn I would be going to the Bible Training Institute in Glasgow to begin missionary training. So she kindly sent me the copy of Berkhof. I cannot remember much now about its early use but over many years I have dipped into it to study various areas of doctrine, particularly when preaching on a doctrinal text of Scripture. As I began to write this chapter I took the book off my shelves and noticed the markers in the pages. The first is on 'Man as the Image of God—The Reformed Conception', the next on 'The Elements of Repentance', and a third on 'The Institution of the Lord's Supper'.

However, perhaps I had better say a little more about myself and my situation back then. In the early to mid-1960s I was an exponent of the '1-2-3-pray-this-prayer-and-you-will-be-saved' method of evangelism. That was the evangelism I had been exposed to and the only one I really knew. I practised it and tried to lead people to Christ. To my shame I did that for a good number of years in my early twenties. However, it was this very methodology that made me begin to think more seriously about what I was doing. I began to ask questions: Is this 'decisionist' formula the right way to present the gospel? Am I just trying to get people to say 'the prayer' so that I can assure them, on the basis of John 1:12, that if they have truly asked Jesus to come into their heart then he will have come in? To tell them they are now children of God because of what they have done?

During one of the term breaks, when I was hitch-hiking home to my parents' house in Norfolk, I made a diversion to visit one of my former school friends who lived in Leicester. He was married and had a family. I stayed the night at his house and witnessed to him. I followed the evangelistic formula and led him through the steps of the sinner's prayer. But as time passed I was puzzled that to see that he never showed any real signs of true conversion.

Back in Glasgow I attended a large Methodist church. One Sunday evening an after-service youth fellowship meeting took place at which one of my fellow Bible-school students preached an evangelistic message and made 'an appeal'. A young man in his late teens went forward in response to the appeal and I began to counsel him. We knelt down beside two chairs and I led him through the well-worn pattern—the usual Scripture verses before encouraging him to say 'the sinner's prayer' and to ask Jesus into his heart. I then assured him that he was now a Christian and that his sins had been forgiven and taken away by Christ. He was now a new creature in Christ and was on his way to heaven.

The next Sunday evening the young man did not come to church. I wondered why. Had something happened to him? The following Sunday he was nowhere to be seen, so I decided to visit him. I knew his address and climbed the stairs up one of the Glasgow 'closes', an old tenement building with four or five floors of apartments accessed by a central stairwell. I knocked the door and his older sister answered. I asked for her brother but she said he was not there. However, over her shoulder I caught a glimpse of her brother diving out of view and hiding behind a sofa! Clearly he wanted nothing to do with me, the gospel, or the church. And yet *he had prayed the prayer!* I had assured him from John 1:12 that he was now a child of God. I had done everything I was supposed to do. But something was very wrong.

On another occasion while at the Bible Training Institute a week-long mission was organized in one of the Presbyterian churches in the Gorbals district of Glasgow. At that time the Gorbals was one of the worst slums in the city. I was assigned to be one of two student preachers at the mission. One of the church elders became very unhappy when we did not have an 'altar call' at the end of the evangelistic services. By this time I was already questioning the practice. Instead of following the usual pattern we issued an invitation to anyone who wanted more information about the way of salvation to attend an after-meeting in a basement room of the church. The unhappy elder complained that we should not have done that. 'If you don't have an appeal, an altar call, then you will lose the atmosphere.' That got me thinking even more: What was 'the atmosphere' that was necessary for a person to be converted? Is the work of conversion dependent upon some kind of technique, upon the manipulation of emotions of men and women? Were we not to look to the Holy Spirit to do his supernatural work in the human soul?

For a while I struggled to know God's will for my future life of service. Should I go into the Methodist ministry along with two close friends of mine at the BTI? As I struggled to know what course to take I gradually came to believe that the Lord was directing me overseas and that I should apply to the Overseas Missionary Fellowship for missionary service in the Far East. As I had not been a member of an evangelical church, the OMF assigned me to serve for a year in a Methodist church in Plumstead Common, south-east London. This church had a godly pastor who was also a regular attender at the Westminster Fellowship in London, a fraternal led by Dr Martyn Lloyd-Jones. He was the right man to help me come to clearer views of the work of God in the soul of man. Looking back I fondly remember Don preaching at a special week-night series of meetings in another church. He took as his theme 'Human Nature in its Fourfold State'. His messages were inspired by a book of the same title written some two hundred years ago by the Scottish minister

Thomas Boston. Don Davies' sermons were very searching and helped me greatly in my understanding of what was wrong with the 'gospel' I had been preaching.

While at Plumstead I joined the young people for a day trip to the seaside. On the way home I sat next to a young man in his late teens and began to witness to him. This time I did not ask him to pray 'the sinner's prayer'. He seemed to be under conviction so I told him to get alone with God and to plead with him for mercy in Christ's name, asking forgiveness for his sins. I spoke to him a week later and to my great delight he was now full of joy. He told me that he had spent the whole night wandering around Plumstead Common crying out to God to have mercy on him and to forgive him his sins. He said that he now knew he was forgiven for Christ's sake and that the Lord Jesus was his Saviour.

In March 1966 I sailed to the Far East and in August arrived in the Philippines where I began my missionary service under the auspices of the OMF. Dennis Lane, the Overseas Director of the Mission, once told me that the Philippines was the most Arminian country in the Far East. From my own experience I can understand why he should have said that. Every day we used to listen to the news on a Christian radio station. In the middle of the programme there was invariably a short presentation of the gospel. On one occasion the presenter stated that 'God has done all he can to save you; he can do no more. It's now up to you!' I also remember meeting a missionary who had just returned from Manila where she had attended a conference on evangelism. The main conference speaker taught that if you can get someone to pray 'in the name of the Lord Jesus' then they must be converted. I think he must have based his teaching on the words of 1 Corinthians 12:3: 'no man can say that Jesus is the Lord, but by the Holy Ghost.' Be that as it may, but since about 70% of the population of the Philippines claim affiliation to the Roman Catholic Church, few Filipinos would have any difficulty praying in the name of the Lord Jesus!

My first year in the Philippines was taken up with language study. Without a working knowledge of the language there was little I could do and so I had quite a bit of time on my hands. I was still struggling with some big questions: What is the gospel? How should one present it? What have I been doing wrong as a gospel preacher?

My dear friend and mentor Don Davies had pointed me in the direction of Banner books. I wrote to the Banner of Truth Trust to purchase some books in early 1967. I wanted a copy of Spurgeon's *Sermons* as I was keen to discover how that great soul-winner presented the gospel. I also thought Iain Murray's recently published booklet *The Invitation System* would be useful to me because it provided a critique of the evangelistic methods so popular at the time. But I received another book I had not ordered, John Owen's treatment of the nature and extent of the atonement in his famous treatise *The Death of Death in the Death of Christ*. I did not need to pay for these books as they were kindly sent to me free of charge, through the ministry of the Banner of Truth Book Fund.

I do not recall being very affected at the time by the introductory essay to the *Death of Death* written by Dr J. I. Packer. In fact I cannot even be sure whether I read all of it at the time. However, I have certainly read it often since! But what I did find most helpful was Owen's treatise and in particular his examination of the Scripture texts dealing with the extent of the atonement. Owen is not easy to read but he more than repays the effort. I devoured the book!

After Owen, I read Iain Murray's *The Invitation System*. In it the author examines the 'system' much used in popular evangelism at the time, most notably by Dr Billy Graham. What helped me most was the second part of the booklet where the author discusses doctrine. He said something which I do not think I had ever heard before, or perhaps it had simply never registered with me. Murray argued that regeneration *precedes* conversion. Regeneration *precedes* faith in Christ. A person believes in Christ because of the work of the Holy Spirit in the miracle of the new birth—the glorious sovereignty of God. Around this time I was also studying Paul's Epistle to the Ephesians: suddenly it all made sense! Chapter 1 came alive: election, redemption—all according to the riches of God's grace—'to the praise of the glory of his grace, wherein he hath made us accepted in the beloved, in whom we have redemption through his blood, the forgiveness of sins, according to the riches of his grace' (Eph. 1:6-7).

I was married in 1968 and the Banner of Truth Trust played another important role in the life of the newly-wed couple. My wife and I were no longer Methodists, and we needed to find a church in the United Kingdom we could join as members. I wrote to the

Trust for guidance. Since we were now Baptists the Banner put us in contact with Mr Erroll Hulse, one-time manager of the Trust's work. He in turn put us in contact with Gordon Hawkins who had worked part-time for the Banner, delivering parcels of books all over London. Gordon was the pastor of Wattisham Baptist Chapel, Suffolk. We joined Wattisham and it has been our spiritual home in the U.K. for forty-three years!

I am not sure when I obtained my first copy of A. W. Pink's *The Sovereignty of God*. This book, I believe, has been one of the Trust's most important publications, along with Walter Chantry's book *Today's Gospel: Authentic or Synthetic?*, which I also received as a gift from the Banner's Book Fund. When it arrived I began to read it one night. I have never been a fast reader but I read it through in just one sitting! I simply could not put it down. It is a marvellous book and I have over the years given away hundreds of copies of it. The two books I always give to new Christian workers, especially new staff members of our Christian Compassion Ministries Foundation, are *The Sovereignty of God* and *Today's Gospel*. Such books open up the Scriptures and clearly set forth the Bible's teaching on God's sovereignty and the doctrines of grace.

Another book I must mention and of which we have given away hundreds of copies is Professor John Murray's excellent book *Redemption Accomplished and Applied*. I always regret that I never met or heard John Murray preach. I first attended the Banner of Truth Ministers' Conference at Leicester in 1972, but Professor Murray was unable to attend that year due to illness. Many of his articles in his four-volume *Collected Writings* are assigned reading in our Grace Ministerial Academy.

Another title that has made a deep and lasting impact on me has been J. C. Ryle's *Expository Thoughts on the Gospels*. On one occasion, back in the late 1980s, an evangelical denomination in the Philippines ordered seventy sets of *Expository Thoughts* from us which were to be given free of charge to the pastors of their churches. I can't begin to imagine the help and encouragement Ryle's work will have had on those preachers of the gospel of the grace of God! We are so thankful for the Trust's literature and for the work of the Book Fund.

The Philippines today may no longer be the 'most Arminian country in the Far East'. Many Christian groups are moving away from decisionism to a more scriptural gospel. However, other challenges face Filipino Christians: charismatic extremes, a health-and-wealth gospel, and a multiplicity of cults, some imported and others home-grown. Moreover, the Philippines is a country still blighted by the spiritual darkness of Rome. But as with the Reformers of sixteenth-century Europe so with us in twenty-first century Asia: only the gospel of the grace of God, preached in the power of the Spirit, will dispel the darkness.

(3) A View from the Grey House, Edinburgh

John Rawlinson

THE Land Rover pulled over to the side of the track that led down home from the hilltop quarry, and came to a halt. The elderly man, who had been driving, put a hand into his jacket pocket and pulled out a small greaseproof-wrapped package and a penknife. Opening the package he sliced off a piece of Stilton cheese and, turning to the young boy seated alongside him, said, 'Would you like some of this?'

The boy turned up his nose and declined, waiting for what he knew would come next. The man ate the cheese, wiped the penknife clean, wrapped up the cheese and put the package and knife back into his pocket. Then he pulled out of the other pocket a small blue box of extra-strong mints. This time the offer was gratefully accepted and the young boy sat looking out over the beautiful Lancashire valley while sucking on the mint.

It was occasions like this, family visits to my grandparents, which lay behind my lifelong love of Land Rovers. My granddad had one and I loved going in it with him. But little did I realize at the time that many years later I would start on a career as an engineer working for Land Rover Ltd!

Granddad died in 1968. I remember it well for the news came when we were on holiday at a Banner of Truth family conference.

و٠ه

The wing-backed armchair in the minister's study was like a cocoon of peace and safety for the young boy who curled up there. The room was quiet as the boy's father studied for Sunday's sermon. Just the sound of an occasional turn of the page of his Bible or a book, or of a pen writing on paper as notes were made. But there on the bookshelves in front of the young boy were some volumes, part of a set of books. They had numbers on the spine and at the bottom of the spine was a green box with the picture of a man inside. The boy was fascinated; there was one more volume there this week than last. Last week, as he had sat in the chair taking some time out in the peace of his dad's study, he had counted 1, 2, 3, 5, 7, 9, 11, 14, and 15. This week there was a 12 as well.

There was an author's name on the spine of those books too: 'That bit's my name', thought the little boy—'John'.

The Works of John Owen read the whole of the wording on the spine, and the logo at the bottom was that of the Banner of Truth Trust; the man in the box, of course, was George Whitefield. It was the mid-1960s and the Banner of Truth was then in the process of reprinting the sixteen volumes of the *Works of John Owen* (1965–68). The boy's father was adding volumes to his collection as they were made available.

At the time, it never occurred to me, the little boy, that after a career as a professional engineer, I would find myself working as General Manager of the organization whose logo appeared on those books.

From those early days of life, the Banner of Truth Trust, whether I was conscious of it or not, was a constant influence in my life. My father, Leslie Rawlinson, was a minister of the gospel and Banner books were an important part of his library, a significant part of his regular reading and study. He also did some editorial work for the Trust long before I ever really understood what the Banner of Truth Trust was. Looking back now, I can see just how influential those Banner books were on his ministry, and consequently on the churches he served, and on our family life.

I am not the only one whose life was influenced in this way. Over the years I have met many others whose lives were similarly influenced for good through the impact that books published by the Banner of Truth Trust had made on the lives of their parents. As in my case, the full realization of this impact was not understood until much later, when they were old enough to read and understand things for themselves. I have also met many people who have told me of the influence the Banner of Truth has had on their pastor and church.

My interest in Banner books started when I was about 13 years of age. I went with my dad to a preaching meeting one Saturday in a village just outside our town. There was a bookstall at the meeting and from it I bought the first volume of Spurgeon's autobiography, my very first Banner book. It won't be a surprise to learn that my second Banner book was purchased a year later from the same bookstall—volume 2 of the autobiography!

∽

In this book many contributors have testified to the way in which God has been pleased to use one or more Banner titles to influence their lives. Thinking has been changed; ministries have been shaped and guided; congregations have been taught biblical doctrines with greater clarity and have been persuaded to embrace the 'truth as it is in Jesus'. But over the years there has been more to the Banner of Truth Trust than the publication of books. Yes, the books have been key, and the books have been the backbone of the Trust's work on which other things have depended; however, a book such as this would not be complete without at least a brief mention of other aspects of the Trust's work.

Ministers' conferences

Back in 1962 a ministers' conference was started in England. This conference continues today and is often simply referred to as the 'Leicester Conference'. Countless men have attended the conference over its fifty-plus years, finding it a place of fellowship and encouragement where their souls are fed. The four days together at Leicester provide a precious respite for ministers. Here they can take time out and be ministered to and have their spiritual 'batteries' recharged and energized for their ongoing work in God's church. Nowadays I have the privilege of attending the conference as one of the organizing staff, and I would like to think that the men go home with the same kind of excitement and energy with which my father used to return after his time at Leicester. I have fond memories of sitting at the dining table and hearing reports about the conference. He enthusiastically told us about what had been preached and gave us summaries of the historical addresses that had been given; we learned about some of the interesting people from other parts of the country (and world) he had met for the first time; and, of course, supplied the latest news about old friends he had met again and with whom he had renewed fellowship. We were also told about the remarkable singing (all men of course), and the earnest times of prayer. And the food, which was good, wholesome, and plentiful—this was all part and parcel of the Banner of Truth conference experience!

Similar ministers' conferences have been held in the U.S.A. since 1978 and bi-annually in Australia since 1979. For many years now there has also been a Borders conference organized by the Trust, which takes place annually, usually in the north-west of England, and which caters for men and women who live in the north of England and the south of Scotland.

Youth conference

The year 1971 saw the start of what was to become another annual event, the Banner of Truth Youth Conference. The first one that I went to was in 1979, but on that occasion it was just to drop off my sister; I could not be persuaded to stay. But the next year, I must have lost my shyness for I attended the first of several youth conferences. Iain Murray has written: 'Of all the conferences, the Youth Conferences were among the most encouraging ... there were conversions as well as young people finding wives and husbands.' Certainly, that conference in 1980 was a significant milestone in my own life. I remember sitting listening, my attention riveted, as Achille Blaize preached on the subject of 'What is a Christian?' Then there was a conversation with Iain Murray over breakfast and on leaving Cloverly Hall that year I had been given that blessed gift from God—the gift of assurance. Having been raised in a Christian home, converted I believe in my mid-teens, I had struggled with the whole question of assurance. But now I knew for certain that I was a Christian.

The youth conference continues to be an encouragement today (I still get to go as an organizer despite being just a little bit too old to qualify as a 'youth'!). I meet young people at the conference today whose parents I had met back in the 'olden days'. It really is true to say that a whole generation of young people have been influenced by the Banner youth conference. I know that I am not the only one who can testify to having good friends in many parts of Britain whose friendship was first forged at Banner of Truth youth conferences.

The Trust provides a fairly full range of our books for the youth conference and it is interesting to see the books that young people buy. Titles such as *Discovering God's Will*, *Call the Sabbath a Delight*, and *Grow in Grace* have always been popular, and of course there's always a few who sneak to quietly purchase the little, but very helpful booklet *Whom Shall I Marry?* Books such as *God and Cosmos* and *The Divine Challenge* are picked up by those more scientifically minded young people, and quite a number of Puritan Paperbacks are also bought, the John Owen abridgements being particularly popular. I remember buying a copy of *Sketches from Church History* in my younger days, and leaving it with missionaries in Africa for them to read, while I was on a short-term visit; such a book is one of the perennial favourites at the youth conference. But the breadth and depth of what the young people buy is such an encouragement, perhaps a challenge too—to those of us older Christians—to maintain good reading habits.

The Banner of Truth magazine

How, then, did the work of the Banner of Truth begin?[1] It all started in Oxford in September 1955 with the publication of a little plain magazine entitled *The Banner of Truth*. When it was published, there were no definite plans or funds to produce a second edition. It could so easily have been a 'flash in the pan', a 'one-off'. But in the providence of God a second magazine appeared a few months later, and a few years later *The Banner of Truth* became a monthly magazine to which readers could subscribe. The magazine is still

[1] For readers not familiar with the history of the Banner of Truth, a short history is available on the website, www.banneroftruth.org

being produced today and at the time of writing has reached Issue 617 (Feb. 2015).[1]

For many people the magazine has been their introduction to the work of the Trust. In the early magazines especially, readers were exposed, sometimes for the first time, to the names and writings of the great authors of reformed Christianity. This whetted the appetite and created a desire for more. So when the Trust was established in 1957 and the first Banner of Truth titles began to roll off the presses, there was a small number of eager readers waiting to snap up the new releases. Today the magazine continues to introduce authors and books to subscribers. Over the years it has also been a proving ground for writers and not a few Banner books have come from articles that first appeared as serials in the magazine. Perhaps two of the most notable examples of this are *The Forgotten Spurgeon* and *Jonathan Edwards: A New Biography*, both written by Iain Murray. More recently, Walt Chantry's exposition of Habakkuk and his life of David both started life as magazine articles before being reworked into new books. The magazine has been invaluable for introducing new generations to forgotten heroes of the faith; opening readers' eyes to periods of little-known church history; showing readers the way in which God had sovereignly worked through powerful movements of his Spirit in times of revival; opening and feeding readers' minds with the old but vital truths of Scripture; and providing encouragement and heroic examples of Christian living and suffering to many. The magazine has been a key part of the ministry of the Trust for sixty years.

The digital age and social media

We now live in a digital age, and much of what may have been published in the magazine in days gone by is now freely made available through our website. Here one will find a large and ever-growing catalogue of short articles. The Banner of Truth also has a presence on social media such as Facebook and Twitter. Regular contact with people who are interested in keeping up with our news is done through email. The world of digital communication changes rapidly and we recognize the challenge of keeping up with it in order

[1] All the back issues of the magazine are being prepared digitally and we hope to make them available soon in electronic format.

to stay in touch with our readers and supporters. Maybe it is hard for us to imagine right now, but perhaps in years to come someone will read the above words and wonder what on earth Facebook was![1]

The Banner of Truth book fund

Another important part of the work of the Trust is the Book Fund. In the early 1960s, inspired by the example of Mrs Susannah Spurgeon's Book Fund, the Banner Book Fund was set up and has been supplying Banner titles at highly subsidised prices and even free of charge to pastors, missionaries, theological colleges, and needy Christians all over the world.[2] A significant work has also been done through the Book Fund with prisoners in jails around the world.

The finances for the fund come from donations made to the Trust from people and churches with a concern for getting good books to people who otherwise could not afford them, or into strategic places that will encourage Christians in their life and ministry. Moreover, as a non-profit organization, the Banner of Truth Trust does not have shareholders who rely on the profits from the organization's business; the surpluses generated from the selling of books are used to fund the ongoing work of the Book Fund. Such surpluses vary from year to year and so the Trust is very grateful to donors who give sacrificially to enable this important work to continue. The Lord has been gracious and faithful to us in this aspect of the work, and we are encouraged to report that whenever a request has been made to the Book Fund, or a need identified for books to be supplied through the fund, there has never been a time when lack of funds prevented books from being sent out.[3]

We could tell many stories of how books supplied through the Book Fund have brought encouragement to people and changed lives. We know of whole churches being transformed through books

[1] If you would like to join our mailing lists, you can do so from our website. You can also follow us on Facebook and Twitter—see the links on our website.

[2] A fuller account of the Book Fund can be read on the Banner of Truth website, www.banneroftruth.org

[3] For readers who may like to donate to the ongoing work of the Banner of Truth Book Fund, this can be done by sending gifts to the U.K. or U.S.A. offices and identifying them as donations for the Book Fund, or by going to the website and following the 'Support Banner' links in the 'About' section.

supplied to the pastors. It is also thrilling to be able to send books to areas of the world where it would be very difficult for missionaries to enter or for other Christian work to take place.

Many of us have large numbers of Christian books, and it is probably true to say that we do not place as high a value on them as we ought (and we may even complain about the price we have to pay for them too!). But spare a thought for our fellow Christians with whom the Trust deals through the Book Fund. For them to get hold of even just one Banner book is a matter of great joy and rejoicing, and they treasure that book as if it were gold! To a poor pastor in a remote part of the world, receiving a gift of a box of Banner books is a huge encouragement and help to their ministry. Members of staff at the Trust who deal with Book Fund matters consider it a huge privilege to be able to serve the cause of Christ around the world in this way.

Translation of Banner books into other languages

When I think of the wealth of literature we have on our shelves (or on our e-reader), it reminds me that we are very privileged, and that there are many people around the world who do not have this kind of access to good literature largely because it is not available in their own language. Over the years, and continuing to this day, the Banner of Truth has worked with many overseas publishers to contract with them for the rights to translate and publish our books in many different languages. In cases where there has been a financial difficulty, we have counted it a joy to help fund some of this work, in some instances paying for the translations, and in others for a print run to get the translated book out to people.

In addition to this, for many years the Trust has been involved in translating and publishing Banner books into Spanish. There is now a very good range of Spanish titles available. More recently, we have started to translate and publish books in Chinese. These books are being published legally in mainland China. It is a slow process to translate and publish in any language but there are additional hurdles to negotiate in getting books legally available in China. However, despite the slow progress it has been encouraging to see our books being sold in China.

Two important Bible verses

I would love to tell you more about the various aspects of the work of the Banner of Truth. For many of us who work with the Trust, what we do is far more than just a job, and it is easy for us to talk passionately for hours about our work. But there are word limits to these chapters and I have probably exceeded mine! So let me conclude by quoting two verses of Scripture. The first, which gave rise to our name, is Psalm 60:4:

> You have given a banner to those who fear you, that it may be displayed because of the truth.

This text conveys at least two vitally important truths for our work. Firstly, this *banner* that is being displayed is given by God to his people, *to those who fear you*. This reminds us that we need to examine ourselves regularly to ensure that we have that right filial fear of the Lord God and that our attitude to our work springs from a sincere desire to glorify him and not ourselves.

But secondly, it reminds us that we have *the truth*, the truth of God's word, the truth that is the only effectual weapon in our combat with Satan, the father of lies. Keeping that truth to ourselves is not an option; it needs to be *displayed*. That is our mission here at the Banner of Truth Trust—to spread abroad the truth of God's word.

As we look back over the past sixty years we thank God and give him all the glory for the way in which he has blessed and prospered this work. And that reminds us of the second Scripture verse, Psalm 127:1:

> Unless the Lord build the house, those who build it labour in vain. Unless the Lord watches over the city, the watchman stays awake in vain.

How we feel the powerful truth of these words! So as we look to the future, we turn our eyes to God alone and pray, 'O Lord, strengthen, bless, and protect the work of the Banner of Truth Trust! For without you we labour in vain.'

Soli Deo Gloria, to God alone be the glory!

Jean and Iain Murray

Iain Murray has been an example and an inspiration to an enormous number of Christians, young and old, throughout the world in his work as founding editor of the Banner of Truth Trust, through his numerous books, and by his godly life. This volume is, in some small way, a recognition of the debt owed to a man who has brought to our attention not only the writings of contemporary preachers but also of great Christians of the past who have long since gone to glory. His strong advocacy of all aspects of the piety found in Puritan and Reformed literature has well served the church of our Lord Jesus Christ: it has enriched the ministry of many pastors and deepened the spiritual lives of countless church members. In paying tribute to Iain, I would be remiss not to commend the loving and faithful support of his wife, Jean, and their children.

Irfon Hughes

List of Contributors

William Barkley, Missionary, Brazil

Peter Barnes, Minister, Revesby Presbyterian Church, Sydney

Ian S. Barter, Formerly Chairman of the Trustees of the Banner of Truth Trust and Bursar of King's College, Cambridge

Joel R. Beeke, Minister and Professor, Heritage Netherlands Reformed Church, Grand Rapids, Michigan

Alistair Begg, Senior Pastor, Parkside Church, Cleveland, Ohio

Jerry Bridges, Author

Iain D. Campbell, Minister, Point Free Church of Scotland, Isle of Lewis

Walter J. Chantry, Minister and Author

Faith Cook, Christian Biographer

Mark Dever, Senior Pastor, Capitol Hill Baptist Church, Washington D.C.

Pieter de Vries, Minister and Professor of the Hersteld Hervormde Kerk, Netherlands

John R. de Witt, Former Senior Minister of First Presbyterian Church, Columbia, South Carolina

Edward Donnelly, Minister and Professor of the Reformed Presbyterian Church of Ireland

J. Ligon Duncan, Chancellor, Reformed Theological Seminary

Brian Ellis, Missionary, Philippines

Sinclair B. Ferguson, Professor of Systematic Theology, Redeemer Seminary, Dallas, Texas

Ian Hamilton, Minister, Cambridge Presbyterian Church

Sharon James, Author

Mark G. Johnston, Minister, Bethel Presbyterian Church, Cardiff

Hywel Jones, Professor Emeritus of Practical Theology, Westminster Theological Seminary, California

John MacArthur, Pastor/Teacher, Grace Community Church, Los Angeles, California

Albert N. Martin, Minister and Author

R. Albert Mohler, President of The Southern Baptist Theological Seminary, Louisville, Kentucky

John J. Murray, Minister of the Free Church of Scotland (Continuing)

Stuart Olyott, Minister and Author

Cor L. Onderdelinden, Minister of the Old Reformed Congregation 'Bevervoorde', Rijssen, Netherlands

John Rawlinson, General Manager, Banner of Truth Trust

Thomas E. Richwine, Businessman, Carlisle, Pennsylvania

Maurice Roberts, Minister of the Free Church of Scotland (Continuing)

R. C. Sproul, Founder and Chairman of Ligonier Ministries, Orlando, Florida

Andrew Swanson, Missionary, Cyprus

Derek W. H. Thomas, Senior Minister, First Presbyterian Church, Columbia, South Carolina

Geoffrey Thomas, Pastor, Alfred Place Baptist Church, Aberystwyth,

Keith Underhill, Missionary, Nairobi, Kenya

Jonathan Watson, Editorial Director, Banner of Truth Trust